W9-AMP-732

When Moses came down from Sinai
the first time, he brought with him
a set of tablets.
The second commandment was:
Thou shall have no other gods before Me.
Upon finding his people worshiping a
Golden Calf, he smashed the tablets—
only to be given a second set.

One set of broken tablets is enough.

Time Dollars say: Reject the Golden Calf.
We have each other.

Co-Production says: Amen.

No More Throw-Away People

The Co-Production Imperative

Edgar S. Cahn

Creator of Time Dollars and Time Banking

SECOND EDITION

Essential Books

Published by:
Essential Books
P.O. Box 19405
Washington DC 20036

Distributed in the UK by:
Jon Carpenter Publishing
Alder House, Market Street
Charlbury, Oxfordshire OX7 3PH
Phone 01608 811969

First Edition

Cahn, Edgar S.
No More Throw-Away People: The Co-Production Imperative

Printed in the United States

ISBN Number: 1-893520-02-1
Library of Congress Control Number: 00-132295
CIP

Page Design	Clay Marshall, Rock Creek Publishing Group, 8004 A Norfolk Avenue, Bethesda, MD 20814
Cover Design	Clay Marshall based on original art by Judybeth Greene
Illustrations	Fair Shares, Gloucester, United Kingdom

If you have any questions or comments concerning this book or for permission to copy excerpts, please write:

Edgar S. Cahn
Time Dollar Institute
5500 39th St. N.W.
Washington, D.C. 20015
E-mail: contact@timedollar.org
Web: www.timedollar.org

Dedication

To Chris — my Beloved, my Partner, my Friend—
And to my family, and my many, many families
who have supported me
on this lifelong quest.

TABLE OF CONTENTS

Acknowledgments

This book distills a journey that now extends over twenty years. It is impossible to acknowledge all those who have played critical roles over that long time span. I must beg the forgiveness of who are mentioned below for the incomplete and partial acknowledgment of their contribution as well the many whose contribution I may have omitted but who know who they are and will forever remain among the remembered unremembered.

To the Annie Casey Foundation whose commitment to rebuilding the village has made this inquiry possible and whose belief in family and children has yielded so many of the illustrations that enrich and corroborate the Co-Production thesis and to Janice Nittoli, wise friend and counselor who "got it" from the outset, who was willing to gamble on a new idea, and who undertook, as an act of faith, to co-produce the survival of this inquiry.

To Chris, my new wife and partner, who has turned a lonely pilgrimage into a labor of love and joy, who lived with countless rewrites, major, minor, and total; who supported the vision, provided the emotional and intellectual touchstone, gave me both good news and bad news with gentle, unrelenting candor. Her intellect helped clarify, integrate, structure and refine the concepts and the message. "The best is yet to be."

To Susan Kanaan who as editor was willing to tell me the truth. Just when I thought I had reached the end of the road, her honesty prompted three re-writes; she has been champion and spokesperson for future readers who could not have survived the journey to which she was subjected through multiple chaotic manuscripts.

To the Mesa Refuge and Peter Barnes who provided the nurturing environment, the respite and the opportunity to digest and distill much of the raw material that found its way into this manuscript

To my mother, Lenore Zola Cahn, whose last gift to me was an insistence that I take the time at the Mesa Refuge to make headway on the manuscript, knowing that by insisting on my going, she was giving me a special kind of gift of those last weeks of her life.

To Florine Camper who never stopped believing that this mattered and who reached out to my new partner as only family can to provide love, support and acceptance, unburdened by guilt or obligation

To my sons, Jonathan for the intellectual jousting, Reuben, the quiet steadfast faith, encouragement and support and to Marna and Dominique for their understanding and tolerance of my relentless fixation with this endeavor.

To the foundations which have provided critical support for this endeavor along the way:

- the Robert Wood Johnson Foundation for its willingness to invest in an untested idea on a massive scale.
- the Retirement Research Foundation for its support of key initiatives and Marilyn Hennessey who has had the patience of a saint because of her belief that the elderly are truly an asset and the repository of vast human capital waiting to be tapped.
- the Rockefeller Family Fund for backing a vision.
- the Ford Foundation for the investment made to get the word out through this book.
- the Rockefeller Foundation for its willingness to invest in Co-Production initiatives that did not fit neatly into any of its program categories
- the Cafritz Foundation which has steadfastly supported the Youth Court in Washington DC and to Ann Allen of the foundation for her unwavering support and encouragement.
- the Naomi and Nehemiah Cohen Foundation and Daniel Solomon for jumping in, time and again, to provide critical, flexible support coupled with important insights on structure and content.
- the National Institute of Justice and Jeremy Travis for the initial investment that made the Youth Court possible.
- the Surdna Foundation, McConnell Clark Foundation, Open Society Institute for critical repeated support of the Youth Court.
- the Dammann Family Fund for key investments, year after year, in capacity building critical to the production of a how-to-do-it kit and later, for an essential investment in making possible the entry of Time Dollars into the age of the Internet.

To Richard Rockefeller whose refusal to give up has finally yielded, under the inspired fellowship of Auta Main, an extraordinary triumph.

To Kent Gordon who has endowed the entire movement with powerful, user-friendly Time Keeper software that has transformed Time Money from an idea to a feasible reality, now available free to communities around the world.

To Ana Miyares, the international banker turned Time Dollar banker who has time and again made the seemingly impossible possible, too frequently by offering herself up as a living human sacrifice.

To Stephen Plumer who has functioned as counselor, kibitzer, nay-sayer and yea-sayer year after year throughout this enterprise.

To Albert Rosenberg who has been with me on this journey, forever, and whose feedback and encouragement have become part of the life force that flows through me.

To Ralph Nader whose public persona masks a private person of incredible humility, and generosity of spirit and whose attack mode masks a vibrant, compassionate commitment to build true community.

To John Richard who in his own quiet, self-effacing way keeps making good things happen on an extraordinary range of fronts at an outrageous and unceasing pace.

To the many heroes and heroines recognized and unrecognized who have somehow kept the faith regardless but especially to now legendary figures: Mashi Blech, Auta Main, Betty Marver.

To Ann Richardson, special friend, parser, and invisible but ever present muse.

To those laboring against all odds to keep the dream alive here at the Time Dollar Institute—Leonard Dixon, John Dortch, Rita Epps, Mary Jean Espulgar-Rowe, Nancy Johnson, Alice Matthews, Alquinston Ross, Denise Settle, Lisa Simms, Delores Swinson, Melisande Watson and Michael Williams.

To Calvin Pearce and the Chicago team whose efforts have produced such a shining example of Co-Production and to those working within the system who made it possible—Paul Vallas, Philip Jackson and Yvonne Jones.

To Elisabeth Solomon, secret agent for the disenfranchised and toiler at all levels and all hours.

To my English compatriots and comrades in arms who have made more headway in three years than I made in twenty: David Boyle, Martin Simon, Sarah Burns, Joy Rogers, and the New Economics Foundation leadership.

To Jonathan Rowe, collaborator and co-author of the first Time Dollar book, who has provided constant support, advocacy and intellectual sparring throughout our long friendship.

To Masako Kubota who has singlehandedly brought the "winds of change" to Japan and whose ceaseless championing of Time Dollars has spread it through fifty communities.

To Jill Kinney, fierce iconoclast and believer in families, in people and in the awesome untapped capacity of the uncredentialed.

To Alyce Gullattee who very simply has kept me going, whose loving faith has been ceaseless and who has helped me to understand that I must first heal myself if I would be about healing the world.

Special thanks to Rosalyn Higgins, life-long friend and counselor, now Judge at the International Court of Justice at the Hague for making my sojourn possible at the London School of Economics and for the needed mentoring in economics gained through LSE's International Center for Economics and Related Disciplines.

To Tony Watkins for the consummate artistry and commitment he brings to capturing Co-Production on video for wider consumption and Rev. Fred Williams whose computer wizardry has been so helpful.

To Magda Theodate simply for being there and helping out in so many ways at odd hours day in and day out.

My dear allies and extended family at the Antioch/D.C./U.D.C. David A. Clarke School of Law and most recently Dean Shelley Broderick for her willingness to embrace Time Dollars openly and bring their study within the hallowed walls of academia.

The list would not be complete without loving remembrance of my late wife, Jean, who would not let me come visit in the hospital during her last days without producing two new pages for the predecessor book, *Time Dollars*. Her fierce determination that the work go forward helped sustain me on this journey.

Additional Acknowledgements

As this second edition goes to press, it becomes even more impossible to acknowledge all those who have played critical roles in the past five years. As the movement takes form, new compatriots emerge. You know who you are - rebuilding community, changing professional practice, re-igniting mission and expanding vision in amazing ways. Please forgive this deliberate omission. We need to create a place to record and capture the spirit of those contributions.

One person does deserve to be singled out because his personal energy, engagement and contribution have set developments in motion that impact all of us. Two years ago, a young philanthropist, Mark McDonough, discovered Time Dollars and Time Banking. His review led him to the considered conclusion that a strategic intervention could enable Time Banking to move to hypergrowth. Acting on that conviction, he undertook the development of Internet-based software designed to radically reduce threshold entry barriers, and simultaneously invested in an organizing process to create a formal Time Dollar network that was already underway. Mark's generosity combined with his focus has in turn unleashed energy among the pioneers who produced the TIME-TO-TRUST MANIFESTO and who sought to create a national membership organization serving all Time Bank organizations. With these efforts now coming to fruition, it seems appropriate to make this one exception to an otherwise even-handedly anonymous expression of appreciation and affection.

Preface
to Second Edition

When the Time Dollar journey began, I felt useless and very much alone – confined to an intensive care coronary unit. The discreet silence and the lack of eye contact from doctors, nurses, and those few family members who were permitted to see me told me more clearly than words that my chances of surviving were slim.

Twenty-four and a half years later, I wake up each morning with the thought "I'm still here," grateful that I have been given one more day to try to make a difference, hopeful that by doing something of use for someone else, I can earn one more day. But I am no longer alone – and that for me is the real miracle.

By my side is my new partner, Chris. Despite my best attempts to warn her off (including an explanation that I was like New York City – an interesting place to visit, but not a place you'd want to live), she has taken on the formal role of Co-Director of the Time Dollar Institute, as well as that of wife, co-conspirator and soul mate. With the help of a small but diverse band of equally crazy allies, she has worked to turn a scattered array of isolated Time Dollar programs into a family, a network, an organization, and more. Their energy takes on visible form in the flow of e-mails, the non-stop dialog within multiple e-groups, the increasingly stuffed calendar taped up on the wall, and the packets of mail that now require the use of several rubber bands. When I try to capture the sense of momentum, the phrase that comes to mind is "not quite yet, but almost." I am watching a movement coming into existence.

Earlier this year, when the Schumacher Society invited me to address the plenary session of a conference on complementary currencies, I accepted on condition that the two of us would share the podium. They happily obliged, but it was Chris who asked, "Why the two of us? Why do you want me to speak?" When it came time to speak, Chris shared with audience the five words that answered her question. Those five words were "No More One Man's Vision."

It is no longer ONE man's vision because there are literally thousands, tens of thousands (and now some multiple of that), engaged in Time Banking. It is no longer a MAN'S vision because Time Banking embodies a response to Marilyn Waring's famous books, "If Women Counted: A New Feminist Economics" and its sequel, "Counting for Nothing: What Men Value and What Women are Worth." Finally, Time Banking is no longer just a VISION—it is a reality. We now know that every day, somewhere on the globe, untold thousands of people are actually earning time credits helping other human beings and, in different ways, advancing social justice.

When Chris finished sharing that key message, it became very clear the extent to which I am no longer alone. I have a genuine partner. And I have a vast, global extended family. And that family is growing.

These days, not a week goes by without some new validation that we are on the right track. So far, people seem able to master the complex mathematics of Time Banking: 1=1. One hour helping someone equals one Time Dollar or one Time Credit. That's it. More and more people understand there is something basically wrong with a society where an elderly person can be despondent because, in their words, "I have nothing left to give but love." How can love be "nothing?"

Meanwhile, the stories multiply:

- A 92 year-old member of a social HMO in Brooklyn, New York earns Time Dollars by bringing a joke or cartoon into her health care provider's office and sharing it, one by one, with staff.

- A teenager charged with truancy fulfills her sentence of community service imposed by a teenage jury by tutoring first and second graders. And magically, the learning is happening on both ends and in new ways for both tutor and tutee.

- A homeless, jobless man with special skills engraving glass refuses to volunteer to imprint the organization's logo on its display windows but says with enthusiasm, "I'll do it for Time Dollars."

- The inmates at Gloucester Remand Prison earn time credits by refurbishing bicycles that are shipped out to developing countries, and the prisoner's families then use those credits to buy the support they need from people in their local community.

- A wedding in Brixton, South London; a child birth in Portland, Maine; and a funeral in the Gorbals, Glasgow, all paid for with time credits.

- A mother of a child who has repeatedly tried to commit suicide emerges as the leader of other parents of children with severe emotional disturbances when she reports how her child seems to have a special gift with young infants. Together, these parents are developing ways of asking the helping agency to make creative use of their children's skills and talents.
- A mother of a mentally retarded child being mainstreamed into school is simultaneously trying to get off Temporary Assistance for Needy Families (TANF) by working. She uses her Time Dollars to make sure her child gets to school on time when she has to leave for work.
- A teenager, living alone with his depressed mother, saved up enough time credits so that when he went away to college, she would be able to buy the range of local support she needed.
- An 85 year-old woman earns Time Dollars doing the work of Jiffy-Lube – changing the oil in members' cars and trucks.
- An elderly woman in Rushey Green, England lived for a year in the dark because her curtains were too heavy for her to draw before a fellow time bank member came and fitted her with lighter curtains.
- An African immigrant, new to the community, has gained immediate access to the help, support and the talents of strangers who welcomed him in a way that prompts him to remark, "This is like coming home."

In a world where everything seems to be about money – where advertisers use their enormous talents to convince us that all we need is newly whitened teeth or hair that flows in a certain way or insurance protection that supplies a guardian angel – Time Bank members find that there just may be another way to know you are valued, trusted, and even loved.

NO MORE THROW AWAY PEOPLE is a battle cry summoning us to re-examine what money means and what money is doing to our species. It is needed now more than ever.

We automatically equate money with the currency that governments issue. What we have created is another kind of money – Time Dollars or Time Credits – that deliberately challenges the way money dominates our lives and the monopoly it has over our well being.

We need that choice because money is how we are accustomed to measuring value. We know that market price is determined by supply and demand, so prices are high when an item is scarce and low when an item is commonplace and available. We disregard or take for granted, however, the implications of this simple logic.

When we look at what price does, we see that it effectively devalues everything that defines us as human beings. It devalues all those capacities that are not scarce; yet those capacities, the ones we all share, are what enable our species to survive. If something is worthless because it has no market value, look at all the universal capacities we are devaluing:

- caring for each other
- coming to each other's rescue
- rearing infants
- protecting the frail and vulnerable
- standing up for what is right
- opposing what is wrong
- coming together to reach agreement
- acting as guardians of whatever we feel is precious and want to pass on to our children and their children.

If we buy into the notion that these capacities are worthless, then is it any wonder that our survival on this planet is in danger? This is why we need Time Banking to express and protect the values that are critical to shaping the kind of world we wish to leave our children.

When we first introduced Time Banking, it was slow going – much slower in the United States than in England where over 140 Time Banks have sprung up in only five years, reaching and engaging participants regarded as hardest to reach. There the impact has reached the highest levels of government. The National Health Service has commissioned research on ways in which Time Banking could energize their Patient Involvement Agenda. An Institute for Community Currencies has been established in Wales. An entire network of mental health agencies across South East London has incorporated Time Banking in its practice. A major housing development corporation has instituted Time Banking to create a sense of community and ownership throughout the 12,000 units it manages. But recently, even in the United States, we are noting a broader acceptance that keeps accelerating, and more and more, new developments provoke the question: "Have you reached THE TIPPING POINT?"

We now know that, in addition to the United States and the United Kingdom, Time Banks have appeared in Israel, Spain, Portugal, Italy, Curacao, Slovakia, South Korea and China. In Japan, although there are only a handful of Time Banks using the Time Dollar name, a great many more places use the hour as the measure of value and adhere to the principles and values of Time Banking.

Global forces are driving the Time Bank movement. Economic insecurity, replacement of labor by technology, an aging society, shortcomings of public systems, budget deficits, and neighborhood deterioration have all underscored the necessity of rebuilding family, community and civil society. Because of Time Banking's track record of tapping unused and underutilized human capacity to meet critical needs, there has been a surge in the demand for help with launching Time Banks. This demand has been reinforced by increased appreciation of the work ethic as a fundamental value of our society.

Time Banking doesn't fit into any single political category ,but it fits them all. It transcends political boundaries because the core values are universal. Time Banking is not a government program, but government agencies fund it and, in some places, are active partners and sponsors. It promotes very conservative values: family, the work ethic, volunteering, altruism. It also empowers disenfranchised groups and bridges divides of race, gender, neighborhood, age. Time Banking has demonstrated effectiveness as a part of the response to every major challenge facing our society – economic insecurity, the breakdown of government systems, fragile families, budget deficits, neighborhood deterioration.

The demand for Time Bank materials – videos, training, coaching, and consultation – has been increasing. Now there are signs that we need to anticipate a major shift in scale. We have been getting ready, building new capacity because we know that uncontrolled expansion could endanger the integrity that is a central aspect and asset of Time Banking.

The Time Bank family has been building a new collective capacity that can cope with a quantum shift in scale. In 2003, widely scattered Time Dollar and Time Banking programs gathered to begin formally organizing. The first gathering in Bethany Beach, Delaware produced a powerful Manifesto that articulated Core Values and a vision of what is within our reach. Much of that work can be summed up in two slogans:

TRUST IS THE BOTTOM LINE
and
WE HAVE WHAT WE NEED IF WE USE WHAT WE HAVE.

Since then, there have been major developments. A new name, Time Banks, is now officially replacing Time Dollars – a shift that signals a global vision not tied to any single country. The website has been redesigned. New web-based software is under development and licenses will be issued by Time Banks USA. A new How-to-Manual, published by the Annie E. Casey Foundation, has been prepared by the Time Dollar Institute, and is available at www.timedollar.org. We have created a highly intensive, interactive two-day training that draws upon the participatory methods of the Institute for Cultural Affairs and the Intercultural Development Research Association.

In addition, a national organization of Time Bank programs has been taking shape and will shortly be given formal status under the Time Banks USA umbrella. A regional hub structure for Time Banks USA has evolved naturally from the prototype of the Portland Time Dollar program, which has grown step-by-step and organically into the Maine Time Dollar

Network, and now the New England Time Bank Network. This hub now supplies services, coaching, training, staffing and fund-raising services for member organizations. It is the forerunner of a nationwide network of hubs.

For the past year and a half, a collaborative process has been developing a new business plan for the emerging network. Central to the expansion strategy is a focus on creating new generations of Neighbor-to-Neighbor Time Bank programs that utilize the new training and technical assistance to embed the core values and the user-friendly, web-based Time Banking software to reduce bookkeeping headaches and facilitate exchanges. As this edition goes to press, the Time Dollar Institute will become Time Banks USA with two relatively autonomous divisions. One will be a Research, Development, Evaluation and Training Division, housed within the existing Time Dollar Institute, which will continue to push the cutting edge of Time Bank applications. The other will be the national membership network and organization, based at the Portland office of the New England Time Bank Network, which will draw upon the experience in linking, nurturing and supporting the diverse array of Neighbor-to-Neighbor Time Banks that are proliferating nationwide.

Three other major developments complete this update.

1. More and more agencies are realizing the mission-related value of Time Banks. In the past, many non-profit organizations with specialized missions regarded Time Banks as irrelevant; that is now changing. Initiatives in numerous fields have demonstrated how Time Banks produce the informal support systems, the extended family, the peer support, and the client engagement that has been a critical missing element for many social service programs. Social programs are often criticized for creating dependencies and, as a result, there has been a new-found receptivity to Time Banking because the reciprocity that is built in transforms the client from consumer to contributor and co-producer of the desired outcome. This new appreciation of Time Banking (discussed at greater length in the postscript) has generated important new agency-sponsored Time Bank initiatives in Indianapolis, Miami, Houston, El Paso, Seattle, Oakland, Boston, Hartford, Nashua and Albany.

2. Colleges and graduate schools have begun to take note of the way that Time Banking and Co-Production change the role of staff and professionals from dispensers of scarce services into catalysts who empower and enlist clients. The School of Social Welfare at the State University of New York (Albany) is now incorporating

Co-Production into its graduate work for social workers and is accepting Time Dollars as part payment of tuition. The same thing has begun to happen on an undergraduate level at Cambridge College, which is now developing a community-building concentration for mid-career human service professionals that will include a course on Time Dollars and Co-Production. There are signs that others will follow suit because knowledge about Co-Production and Time Banking seems likely to give their graduates a competitive edge in securing placements.

3. The Third International Time Banking Congress in Toronto, Canada is the first formal joint undertaking of Time Banks UK and Time Banks USA. It foreshadows other international developments that are already beginning to emerge.

Before long, we anticipate a new challenge. We are overdue to ask ourselves an obvious question: what implications might Time Banking have for less developed countries and for offsetting the unacceptable but growing global disparity in standard of living, education, and opportunity that now threatens our survival as a species?

It will be our collective privilege to work with our Brothers and Sisters around the world to answer that question, knowing that we do not yet have the answers – but that the core values that underlie Time Banking affirm our common humanity and hold the key to our planet's future.

Edgar Cahn
August 4, 2004
Washington, DC

Introduction

In 1980, something happened. Money for social programs dried up. So I asked myself what seemed a very simple question. If we can't have more of the old kind of money, can we create a different kind of money to address these problems? In retrospect, it is clear that my chief asset was ignorance. I didn't know it could not be done. So I went ahead to figure out how it might be done.

As you will see, finding an answer came at no small cost. But once found, it seemed almost laughably simple. Let one hour of time helping someone else equal *one credit.* A credit earned by giving service could then be used to buy an hour of someone else's time. Later on, I would give these service credits a fancier name: Time Dollars. But *one* = *one* seemed a safe place to start. I was right. I was also dead wrong.

The economists quickly pounced on me, demanding to know what my kind of money could do that real money could not do much better. My provisional answer was almost tautological: If you change the characteristics of money, you change the dynamics that flow from those characteristics—and in doing so, you redefine the range of the possible.

The proof came as Time Dollar programs sprouted all across the United States. As they did so, it became clear that the dynamics built into Time Dollars operated particularly powerfully and effectively where they were most needed: in rebuilding a second economy, an invisible economy—the world of family and community where transactions take place that economists do not measure, where work takes place that the market does not value, and where vast assets exist for which the market has no use or that the private sector has already chosen to exploit, deplete, or contaminate in pursuit of profit. That world is known as the non-market economy.

As experiments with Time Dollars proceeded, three things happened.

> First, new applications of Time Dollars in different spheres proliferated. There seemed to be almost no sector of human activity where new human resources mobilized and galvanized by Time Dollars could not make a valuable contribution.
>
> Second, too many Time Dollar programs died—even when they succeeded—once the demonstration funding expired. It takes money to compensate a coordinator, cover the operating costs, maintain records, and pay for phones, offices, paper, refreshments, and events.
>
> Third, those programs that did not die persisted and flourished because, when the initial funding dried up, the costs were picked up by the host organization.

When a cadre of Time Dollar pioneers looked at why some programs died while others survived, a more fundamental principle emerged. Wherever an institution recognized that the labor contributed by the ultimate consumer was central to its mission, it would endeavor to pick up the core operating costs entailed in a Time Dollar program. Conversely, where it viewed Time Dollars as a cute volunteer add-on, it typically abandoned the program once the initial funding had ended.

That pattern triggered a follow-up inquiry. We asked non-profits, grantees, and government agencies in different sectors: How important was this labor contributed by those whom they sought to serve? Whether it was teachers trying to get students to learn, health care professionals trying to enable the elderly to remain self-sufficient, drug specialists trying to keep a detoxed juvenile clean or neighborhood organizations trying to build community, the answer came back: That participation, that involvement was indispensable to getting real results, to maximizing effectiveness, to realizing the mission. At that point we said: If that is so, why are you merely calling it participation? Why aren't you calling it work? Why aren't you regarding the producers of that work as co-workers and co-producers? And why are you not building that Co-Production into your core operating system?

That inquiry evolved into a more fundamental exploration: What was this phenomenon that we called Co-Production? What were its essential elements? What core values did it exemplify that made it essential? Were these values universals that could generate consensus? Could they be regarded as essential? In what contexts did this phenomenon appear? Would understanding this enable us to make a compelling case to funding sources for sustained financial support?

We learned a lot. First, the need for Co-Production appeared so consistently as to become a kind of universal, even if we were hazy about what it was.

Then we noted consistently that in the absence of Co-Production in some form, bad things happened. Agencies were less effective; accountability died; those most at risk got hit the hardest. Public confidence in efforts to address social problems waned. Dedicated professionals suffered burn-out, became cynical, focused on finding ways to blame their clients, and were reduced to semi-automated case processors.

In other contexts, Co-Production supplied the rationale and the leverage needed to secure support from those institutions and agencies that received the dollars to deal with the problems. Core funding was the *quid pro quo* for mobilizing the resources and discharging the functions that the market economy could not or would not discharge. We came to realize that Time Dollars are only a tool. It is Co-Production that is fundamental. Co-Production redefines the nexus between the two worlds, market and non-market. Co-Production defines the terms on which the two economies need to relate in order to produce a world that rewards decency and caring as automatically as it now rewards aggression, competitiveness and acquisition.

This book introduces the reader to Co-Production from three different perspectives. Part One tells a story. It charts a journey of discovery. Knowing what led to the discovery of Co-Production will help you understand what it is. Part Two applies economic reasoning and is more conceptual and theoretical. Part Three takes Co-Production apart piece-by-piece and examines what it means in the real world. It looks at each core value of Co-Production close-up in actual operation. Examples illustrate specific lessons and principles.

When they come to Part Two, some friends have told me they have a block when it comes to economics. I have two answers:

> Answer One: Skip Part Two. Go to Part Three because no matter how you "get" Co-Production, once you get it, you get it. It's a different way of looking at the world.
>
> Answer Two: If you understand that raising children is work and that pollution is bad, you already know all the economics you need. You won't see a single algebraic formula.

Not withstanding any aversion or block, Part II merits scrutiny for one basic reason. We have to fight for the things we care about in a new way. Flying the banner of social justice does not win the critical battles with the number crunchers. We lose. We get exiled to the realm of values and morality by those claiming to be hard-nosed economic realists. Warm and fuzzy doesn't do it. On all ends of the political spectrum, we hear one and only one response: get a job. We are confronted by assertions that the solution to all social problems is in the market and in market economics.

We need numbers. We need hard evidence. Time Dollars supply a critical tool to surface a previously invisible or discounted reality. Using that tool, Co-Production enables us to take the economists' own concepts to make the case for social justice. The economist, Alfred Pigou, defined economics as "That part of social welfare that can be brought directly or indirectly into relation with the measuring rod of money." Time Dollars enable us to ask: "What reality emerges if one changes the measuring rod?" What do we see?

We see a caring, selfless dimension to human nature. We see a previously invisible economy functioning alongside the market economy. We see Co-Production.

Time Dollars make that visible because a Time Dollar exchange is never just a private exchange between individuals. Time Dollars link people in a social network; each act of caring triggers a reciprocal act so that every transaction has social capital built in. It elevates and revitalizes this second economy.

Co-Production represents the discovery that this second economy is not second-class. It is the economy that undergirds all economics. Economics comes from the Greek word, *oikonomia*. Originally, economics really meant "management of the household." Somehow, that has been overlooked and forgotten. Co-Production resurrects *oikonomia* to a status second to none.

This journey of discovery is not over, perhaps never will be over. If you are prepared to invest your time to share this journey, I am prepared to make these promises.

As an individual:

- You will know why money does not define the limits of possibility.
- You will know ways to empower people to convert their own time into purchasing power by helping others, and you will be able to access specific how-to-do-it materials to set into motion powerful forces for change.
- You will no longer have to turn your eyes away from suffering or need or injustice, because you will know of a way to respond that can make a real difference without feeling victimized, used, or exploited.

As a community leader or spokesperson, grassroots organizer, or a community based association:

- You will have tools available to go beyond protest and confrontation in mobilizing your constituency.
- You will be able to document the vast asset base that exists among persons who are written off, dismissed, or labeled *at-risk* and you will be able to validate the contribution they make as a form of

work that earns and merits compensation.

- You will be able to transform the beneficiaries and recipients of services; they will cease to be mere supplicants for help and will become instead paying customers and co-producers of resilient families, revitalized neighborhoods, and a just society.

As a practicing professional with specialized knowledge or a decision-maker charged with addressing social problems:

- You will be able to see how pervasively we sabotage our own best efforts by failing to enlist those whom we are trying to help as co-producers of the very results we seek to achieve.
- You will learn about new ways to convert the beneficiaries of social programs into co-producers of outcomes that are different from and superior to any results those programs now yield.
- You will have an answer to the indictment, whether from outside or from the quiet voice within, that charges you with perpetuating dependency and advancing self-interest behind a false mask of caring and concern.

And whatever the role or persona you elect or for which you are ordained, you will be known, in the words of the prophets, as

One who rebuilds the ancient ruins,
who lays the foundations for ages to come;
You shall be called '"Repairer of the breach,
Restorer of streets to dwell in."

For you shall have helped elevate the human family to a trustee species honoring our obligation to hold the future in trust for our descendants and the planet in trust for whatever higher destiny to which it may be called.

Finally, you will understand why No More Throw-Away People is the Co-Production Imperative.

I.

Discovering Co-Production

Chapter 1

The Road to Co-Production— Time Dollars

The long journey to Co-Production began in a coronary care unit.

It was March 1, 1980. The chances of my making it to my 45th birthday didn't look very good. I had 22 days to go. There I was in Intensive Care, lying in a hospital bed, recovering from a major heart attack. With the enzyme tests indicating that about 60 percent of my heart had been blown away, they were not giving me very good odds. An IV tube went into my wrist. There were different lines. One was to pump medicine in if they needed to get it into my system directly and immediately. The other led to a plastic bag dangling from a pole, with fluid and nourishment to keep me going. A monitor suspended on the wall displayed serrated horizontal lines. At least the lines were moving. There were no violent jagged peaks or alarm lights going off. That was supposed to be me—but somehow I couldn't relate to it.

Just hours earlier, I had been fighting what I had thought was the fight of my life. I had been trying to save Antioch Law School, the school that my wife, Jean, and I had created nine years before. It was a unique law school, one-of-a-kind. We had put everything on the line to create it. The mission—to create a new breed of lawyers, trained and committed to fight for justice. Just as doctors are trained on actual patients in a teaching hospital, we believed that lawyers should learn about justice by fighting for it. So we had created a new kind of law school that had its very own teaching law firm. The school's law firm represented literally thousands of poor people every year.

But this law school, the dream that my wife and I had brought to reality, was about to be taken over. The parent university that had agreed to host and nurture our law school under its wing was struggling financially. The law school was holding its own, and the university was raiding the school's financial resources to bail itself out of its own financial troubles. Sooner or later, that would mean certain death for the Antioch School of Law. And I was fighting to prevent that from happening.

I didn't know that that struggle would almost cost me my life, my home, my family and my children's future.

Until late that afternoon, every waking hour had been spent preparing the legal papers, marshaling the allies, talking to TV and radio stations, calling alumni, meeting with funding sources—anything I could do to save a dream that had swiftly earned national and international recognition as a citadel of justice.

Now, I was fighting for my own life but it was hard for me to grasp that, hard for me to let go of an all-consuming struggle. I don't like to lose. I'm not used to losing. I was still in denial—not fully understanding how grim my own prospects were. I remember, in the darkened room, sending a five-word message back to my allies: *Masada shall not fall again*. It had not yet dawned on me that I had to start fighting for my own life.

No one told me how bad it was, but the doctor had already told my wife and two sons that he had never seen a patient survive with that amount of damage. It took time for me to absorb that I had really had a heart attack. Step-by-step, I understood. I had to make a choice: I could either spend what time I had left on this planet continuing to fight yesterday's battles or I could start trying to build a new future, to dream different dreams. I could keep fighting to hold on to the past and probably have another heart attack, or I could let go of the struggle I was in. Slowly, the realization dawned that even this was not really a choice. The fight for the law school had to be given up.

It was a hard truth to accept. It felt like the defeat of everything I had worked for and dreamed of. My life had been spent in the struggle for equal justice, working first for Bobby Kennedy at the Justice Department, then for Sargent Shriver in the War on Poverty—and then launching a watchdog on government to fight hunger and to challenge the colonialism of the Bureau of Indian Affairs. That's what I thought I was here to do: fight for others. I used to joke about my own commitment, explaining that if you were born a Jew, you thought the job of Messiah was still open and that it was your obligation to apply. So all I was doing was preparing my resume.

Now, it was all over. I just didn't know it and no one was going to tell me. All of a sudden, those to-do lists in my DayTimer didn't matter. The phone messages I hadn't answered didn't matter. Even the bills could wait. No one was going to run a guilt trip on me for not getting back to them.

Once out of the Intensive Care Unit, the most important thing you have to do is fill out the breakfast, lunch and dinner menu. The most important decisions you have to make involve cream of wheat, toast, and juice. They let you read the newspapers. I was reading about double digits: double-digit inflation, double-digit unemployment, companies laying off thousands, welfare rolls swelling, teenagers without jobs, growing numbers of seniors going into nursing homes, factory hands in Detroit and coal miners in West Virginia out of work.

I was surrounded by smiling faces and helping hands: nurses, doctors, orderlies, medical technicians, physical therapists, candy-striper volunteers, friends and family. My wish was their command. I didn't even have to snap my fingers or ring a bell. I had a retinue of caretakers and help beyond anything I had ever experienced and certainly, beyond anything I could ever again afford in my private life.

I remember asking myself: Why isn't this a good deal? Why can't you think of this as some kind of luxury hotel, a cruise, a tropical resort? Why aren't you enjoying all this service, all these folks helping you? It was, and wasn't, a serious question. But the answer hit hard on multiple levels. What I grasped was one of those big truths—a moment of insight that would stick with me, that would shape my future.

I didn't like feeling useless. My idea of who I was—the "me" that I valued—was someone who could be special for others, who could do something they needed. And here I was, a passive recipient of everyone else's help.

That was when it struck me: All of those people I had read about in the newspapers were being declared useless, too. And it occurred to me, I'll bet they don't like it any more than I do. And in that moment, I realized that a new fight had begun. It was the fight over being declared useless.

This fight would tax both gut and intellect. It would take me to the rarified halls of academia and to the killing streets. It would take me into the paneled board rooms of decision-makers and sit me at the table with the heads of social service agencies. It would oblige me to challenge the assumptions of profession after profession that has staked out ownership of the problem as a way to commandeer the resources dedicated to finding a solution.

For the first time in my life, I was feeling useless. I didn't like it. There was nothing I could do. Or was there? The question wouldn't go away. It never has. It became a very personal fight. I refused to be one more throw-away person. And I knew that the fight was not just about me. It never had been.

One = One: Economic Heresy

The problem looked pretty straightforward. There were people here and problems there. How could we put them together? We used to use money—but Ronald Reagan had declared that there would be no more money for those kinds of social programs intended to benefit, salvage, or utilize Throw-Away people. So my next question seemed logical. If we can't have more of that kind of money, why can't we create a new kind of money to put people and problems together?

The solution, when I hit upon it, seemed obvious. Why not bank time spent helping others—something like a blood bank? Help somebody. Earn a Time Dollar. Bank it. One hour = One Time Dollar. Use the banked Time Dollars to "purchase" help from another member: a ride to a doctor, help in preparing a meal, taking care of a pet when one went to the hospital. Like any savings account, Time Dollars could be banked for a rainy day, or donated to someone who needed immediate help.

Two things would be needed: a computerized system to keep track of what people could do for one another, and a person to act as a co-ordinator, matching person with person, need with capacity. Compared to the cost of traditional social welfare programs, hiring a co-ordinator and buying a computer would be nothing.

This new exchange system would enable individuals and entire communities to become more self-sufficient, to insulate themselves from the vagaries of politics and to tap the capacity of individuals who were in effect being relegated to the scrap heap and dismissed as freeloaders. Economists might say: Demand can only be met if it is made "effective demand" backed by dollars. But another currency could honor real need as effective demand—without dollars.

Give an hour; get an hour. One hour = one service credit or one Time Dollar. 1 = 1 = 1 did not seem like rocket science. There wasn't any obvious flaw I could spot.

The reactions to my proposal should have warned me that this was not going to be as simple as it seemed. The folks I had worked with in the War on Poverty gave the idea mixed reviews. Sargent Shriver was enthusiastic. He promised he would send it around to a few friends to get their reactions. What he relayed was not good news. Lester Thurow commented that there was little point to this approach. I was just creating a barter currency, and barter was inherently inefficient and inferior to money. And to the extent I was trying to address poverty by expanding the money supply, the Federal Reserve could wipe that out in the blink of an eye. One colleague warned me about undermining the gains made by unions. Lawyers predicted that the IRS would treat Time Dollars as taxable income.

Two other economists sought to caution me: There was this little problem called *price*. I was setting price at one hour = one Time Dollar. Frank Fisher—a nationally renowned economist at MIT and a close friend-warned me that any attempt to mess with market pricing would lead to the kind of distortion of market forces that had crippled Russia's economy. Robert Lekachman had hit the bestseller list with his assault on Ronald Reagan, titled, *Greed Is Not Enough*. He was more encouraging but counseled me that price was a fundamental issue that feminists had taken on when they wrestled with the way in which the market devalued the work done by women. He hoped that I could figure out a way around the problem of comparative worth that was tying up that movement in knots.

Alvin Toffler gave me encouragement, saying that he had a friend, a young maverick Congressman from Georgia, named Newt Gingrich, who might be interested. I never took him up on the offer—and he would remind me of that in later years. Frank Riessman, creator of the paraprofessional movement and editor of the journal, *Social Policy*, thought Time Dollars was a great idea and offered to publish a piece about it.

The Elderly—A Window of Opportunity

The greatest encouragement came from Florida International University's Center on Aging. Florida was wrestling with the emergence of a large, aging population. As nursing homes became a growth industry, the cost implications were horrific. They were looking for alternatives. The obvious alternative was for the state to do everything within its power to keep the elderly out of nursing homes—including providing care in the community and respite for families trying to take care of frail, aging parents.

All of a sudden, my idea had found a niche market. In 1985 Missouri and Florida passed the first "service credit" legislation authorizing the creation of "service credit" programs. Congresswoman Carrie Meek (then a state senator) carried the legislation in Florida that I had helped draft. Meanwhile (wholly independent of my efforts), similar legislation was enacted in Missouri—and the State even guaranteed the credits, promising that people who earned credits helping keep individuals out of nursing homes could count on the State to provide similar services for them when they needed it.

From Missouri came an unexpected bonus. The State applied for a tax ruling on those credits, and from the bowels of the regional IRS office, someone who must have been a closet gerontologist wrote the first tax ruling on service credits. It pronounced that they had "no tax implications" and were not barter. One of the reasons given was that since the State of Missouri was doing the bookkeeping, this was hardly a form of tax evasion. This was coupled with an observation that people would not volunteer if they were taxed for doing so. There was a flurry of legislative activity. For a moment, it looked like the idea would take off. But then came the problem of implementation. No one wanted to spend money on implementation. And legislation without funding for implementation doesn't go very far.

Florida was different. The state appropriated $50,000 to test the idea, thanks to the valiant efforts of State Senators Carrie Meek and Jack Gordon. However, none of us had anticipated the hostility this legislation would encounter from the Executive Branch. They wanted money to contract with home help agencies. They wanted to fund a continuum of care that included adult congregate living facilities, adult day care, senior centers, homemaker services, hospital discharge planning. They had no use for legislators trying to solve the problem with funny money. And they knew how to deal with that kind of legislative stupidity. Use bureaucratic red tape. Get the implementation hopelessly bogged down. Then, when the legislation expires, express profound regrets that the idea, while really creative, simply wouldn't work.

I had put all my eggs in that basket, trying to get the State of Florida to move. And I had hit a brick wall. Were the skeptics right? Was the idea unworkable? Two events sent me in another direction.

A classmate from Yale Law School, John Hart Ely, was dean of Stanford Law School. Either out of pity or friendship, he invited me to share my ideas with the faculty. They listened politely, then sat back while their law-and-economics expert went after me with one question relentlessly: *What could my kind of money do that real money could not do better?* At first, I didn't take the question seriously, since it was clear to me that "real money" was not going to be available. It seemed moot. It was a stand-off—but the question haunted me. The Dean ended the debate gracefully, observing that this same skepticism had greeted my earlier proposal for neighborhood legal services—and predicting that in 10 years, they all would see this kind of money spreading across the country and perhaps across the world. He was wrong. It has taken nearly 20 years. It's just as well I didn't know that at the time.

But the question—why real money couldn't do it better—would not go away. I felt I needed an answer. If I was going to propose a new kind of money, I had better learn some economics.

My son gave me the next shove. "Dad, most of the economists in this country are mathematicians. You need to consult another tradition in economics. Why don't you try the London School of Economics?"

Next stop: LSE. It was a pivotal move.

THE LONDON SCHOOL OF ECONOMICS: THEORY IN AID OF POSSIBILITY

By the time I returned from LSE, I had an answer to the question put to me at Stanford: What can your money do that real money can't do better. But I had more than that.

The economists and political scientists at the London School of Economics had listened to this lad from the colonies and concluded that the idea was at least theoretically feasible. That was as far as they would go. But at least I hadn't committed any major fallacies.

The first breakthrough came when I understood their language enough to be able to put Time Dollars through a simple, litmus test. Did the *benefit* of earning Time Dollars equal or exceed the *cost* of earning them? I learned that *cost* didn't just mean money and *benefit* didn't just mean monetary gain either. At first, it didn't seem possible that anyone would want to spend an hour earning funny money helping someone if they could use that time to earn real money at a real job. Once I understood that personal satisfaction and self-esteem can count in the benefit column, I was home free. If Time Dollars could increase the psychological reward sufficiently, then people would work for Time Dollars. Combining the psychological reward with purchasing power worth one hour gave Time Dollars a competitive advantage over volunteering. The two combined would make helping others pay on two levels: internal and external.

The second breakthrough came as I learned more about money. It all boiled down to a very simple set of propositions. Money had certain characteristics. Each characteristic produced certain results. If you changed those characteristics, you would change the results. Therefore a new kind of money, if it was different from the old kind, could do different things. The new money might not replace the old kind. But I wasn't trying to get rid of money or replace it. I was trying to find a way to complement it. At the time, I just wanted to help address some needs and solve some problems that government didn't have enough money to solve. Only later would I find out that I was in fact tackling a far larger problem.

But at least I had an answer to my Stanford inquisitor: Money with different characteristics of course does different things. Whether it was better or worse would depend on which characteristics one chose and what one was trying to achieve with the change.

LSE gave me one other important gift: the imprimatur of legitimacy. It published a paper I had written. That, together with what I had learned, gave the idea critical momentum. The Robert Wood Johnson Foundation, a major U.S. foundation specializing in health care, had been studying my idea while I was overseas. When I returned, better equipped to talk about and defend the idea, they were willing to listen. The result was a decision to launch an experimental national initiative. The idea was suddenly hot. At least it would have its 15 minutes of fame. Whether it would have any more than that would depend on what we would learn.

Fifteen Minutes of Fame

In those post-LSE days, support came like a rising tide.

Between 1987 and 1990, the Robert Wood Johnson Foundation invested a total of $1.2 million at six sites to test whether Time Dollars could help reduce the need for nursing home care.

These programs succeeded in generating thousands of hours in service credits and new social networks that felt like extended families. By 1990, the third and final year of the Robert Wood Johnson initiative, all programs were generating at least 6,000 hours of service by elders to elders. The biggest one, Miami's, was generating over 100,000 hours by year 3.

The most in-depth study of service credit programs was conducted by

TIME DOLLARS IN A NUTSHELL

1. Members list the services they can offer and those that they need
2. All agree to both give and to receive services
3. Everyone is interviewed and provides references
4. Every hour giving help earns the giver one credit, a Time Dollar
5. Members 'buy' the services they need with their credits
6. The computer matches the task, the giver and the receiver
7. Every transaction is recorded on a computer 'time bank'
8. Members receive a regular 'bank' statement
9. One hour is one credit regardless of the skills one offers
10. Members can donate credits to friends or to the 'credit pool'
11. Everyone is seen as special with a contribution to make
12. All activities maintain set standards of care and a code of ethics

From the *Fair Shares First Annual Review* (Gloucester, United Kingdom)

Georgetown University's Center for Health Policy Studies, under contract with the Robert Wood Johnson Foundation. The reviewers concluded that the support services facilitated by the programs were "necessary to the independent functioning of an older, frailer population with potentially limited social supports." They also recognized the community-building benefits of the program, noting that the programs "have developed less as anonymous or mechanical exchanges than as community membership organizations."[1]

There was a flurry of legislative activity. Seventeen states enacted laws mandating the creation of service credit or Time Dollar programs for the elderly. Michigan actually appropriated over a quarter-million dollars each year for three years to fund a statewide Time Dollar program for the elderly. A front-page story in *The New York Times* and later a full-page piece in *Newsweek* triggered national and local media attention.

In 1992, the U.S. Administration on Aging formally endorsed Time Dollars and recommended to state and area agencies that they make use of this strategy. That year, the federal government committed $400,000 to experiments testing the concept, and Congress directed the Administration on Aging to use discretionary funds each year to "establish ... nationwide, statewide, regional, metropolitan area, county, city or community model volunteer service credit projects to demonstrate methods to improve or expand supportive services or nutrition services, or otherwise promote the wellbeing of older individuals."

That first burst of experimentation with Time Dollars generated lots of happy stories of people helping other people. Wonderful, happy memories. A special sense of being valued.

A film clip from "The Today Show" said it all. One senior, turning to her helper, says, with moist eyes, "I just love her." The Time Dollar helper, glancing to the camera man, feels compelled to explain: "More friends than volunteers."

PBS captured another scene: Two men, both retired, had lived within a block of each other all their lives but never would have known each other. Now they are a Time Dollar home repair crew, fixing old toilets with jury-rigged parts while the arthritic but beaming resident, the owner of a three-legged dog named Tripod, looks on. She has worked all day preparing a seven-course meal, served on her best china. As they take seats around her prized dining room table, festive with table cloth and candles, one of the men wisecracks, "I guess we won't have to go to McDonald's tonight."

These stories can be multiplied one-hundred thousand times in community after community. For me, one came much closer to home.

Radicchio and Social Capital

The phone rang. It was my mother declaring, *"Edgar, Time Dollars really work!"*

At 90, she reminds people of a Chinese empress: beautiful, elegant, self-possessed, always in charge, and of course brooking no deviation from the royal will. Not a woman who easily accepts help. Now, she was going to tell me about Time Dollars.

Wasting money is a no-no for my mother. Even at 90, this New York resident would rather wait in the rain or snow for a bus than waste money on a taxi. Her primary goal after fracturing her hip was to regain the ability to step up onto the bus so that she could save taxi fare going to physical therapy.

If she really needed help, though, she would much rather pay for it than be in someone's debt. She had spent weeks picking out pictures and artwork to bring beauty to people's lives in the Village Nursing Home she had helped establish. She had been a founder of the Caring Community, a wonderful support program for seniors and had been on its board for almost 20 years. But she had never accepted help from that organization. She fell and broke her hip trying to put in a light bulb herself rather than ask the apartment handyman to come do it for her.

At that point, she could afford to hire home help from an agency, and she did so. She has a wonderful capacity to create almost instantaneously a warm, bonding relationship that bridged race and class. Yet, she was using Time Dollars. I shall never forget her explanation: "Edgar, I can actually ask them to go to Balducci's for me and pick out radicchio, and chicory, and romaine lettuce! That's all I wanted; I couldn't possibly bother a home help agency and ask them to find someone who could just run that errand."

With home help, she explained, you have to hire an aide for a minimum of four hours. What do you do if you only need someone for ten or twenty minutes? If you are paying a person, you have to keep thinking up things for them to do! You can't just chat with them.

Other details followed. She had just bought a small cordless phone to have by her bedside—but she couldn't figure out how to attach it. The Time Dollar person sent by Caring Community apparently had no technophobia. She read the instruction booklet and found the recessed lip for hanging the phone vertically. For my mother, using the instant-cook, one-minute button on the microwave was a triumph. So this feat represented to her a level of technical virtuosity that ranked in the appliance world as the equivalent of a neurosurgeon's proficiency.

This woman remained fiercely proud of her independence. Her carefully guarded self-sufficiency was private space, studded with land mines, which one tried to cross at one's peril. Now, she could accept another kind of help because it didn't feel like charity. She had done her part with years of service. She knew that. Time Dollar helpers were welcome.

Matchmaking

I get drawn into abstractions, thinking about social policy and the theoretical implications of Time Dollars as a medium of exchange. But when I think of my mother, I realize that Time Dollars aren't really about money. They enable people to accept help without feeling diminished, and to give help without fear of rejection or the feeling they are doing work that is "beneath them." That's a new kind of equalizer, a social etiquette that bridges, links, and facilitates.

Modern life erects barriers of knowledge, time, physical safety and pride. Time Dollars wipes out those barriers—and others that appear more intractable.

A film crew for the TV news program "Inside Edition" made this discovery when doing a story on a Time Dollar program in Miami. One of the "stars" is Daisy Alexander, a large, elderly black woman who limps along with a cane and always has a bright, slightly mischievous smile. Daisy never finished high school, but that hasn't stopped her from doing what she wants to. She beams at the video camera, ever so proud at a chance to show what she had been teaching the kindergarten children. That's how she had been earning Time Dollars. Her words tumble out with almost breathless excitement when she instructs: "This is a goat."

"I teach them their ABCs, colors, numbers, and simple arithmetic," she says, glowing with pride.

Media people always want to show two things: how people earn Time

Fair Shares is funded by Barnwood House Trust/National Lottery/Tudor Trust/Esmee Fairbairn.

Join Fair Shares NOW. Telephone: 01452 541337 **Fax**: 01452 541352 at City Works, Alfred St, Gloucester GL1 4DF **e-mail:** fairshares@cableinet.co.uk **Website**: www.fairshares.org.uk

Cartoon by Dylan Thomas: 01407 830970. Design and artwork by The Graphics Studio, Health Promotion Gloucestershire: 01452 396134.

Dollars and how they spend them. So next we see Daisy spending her Time Dollars. A slimly built Cuban male knocks on her door and announces himself. "It's Pepe. *Como esta*?" He helps her to the car and belts her in. He turns to explain that he speaks only Spanish. "Sorry. My English, no good." Daisy responds: "You're a good amigo." Together, they walk slowly into a local Publix supermarket. Daisy picks out her groceries while Pepe pushes the cart. The commentator catches something the camera misses: people turning and watching with interest. The voice-over notes, "That's one of the unusual things about this program—the friendships it creates in this racially divided city." Time Dollar members seem oblivious to an otherwise pervasive racial divide.

We start as strangers, and commercial transactions leave us as strangers. Time Dollar exchanges are clearly different. We may start as strangers, but we end in a social network that feels like neighbors who know each other and like extended family whose members can count on each other. Barriers fall.

The sheer numbers generated by Time Dollar programs begin to define as possible what others had thought was impossible.

DATELINE 2000

This book is the culmination of twenty years struggle and effort to bring about a world in which there would, truly, be no more throw-away people. In the process of that struggle, there has emerged an understanding of something that I have called Co-Production.

Co-Production is a different imaging of the world we know, and this book is an attempt to take that imaging and make it real for others, because I am convinced that if more of us can see the world in this new way, we will change the world as we know it.

For me, Co-Production has become one seamless web—a universe whose every part is linked to every other part. In fact, the elements of Co-Production yielded themselves up slowly, piece by piece, not as the whole that I now understand them to be. One puzzle solved led, not to understanding, but instead, to another puzzle.

At the beginning, all we had was Time Dollars. They seemed to supply an all-purpose tool. The more fundamental implications of time money and time banking surfaced much more recently—with the emergence of Co-Production.

We invest dates with meaning. We want the millennium to issue in an era of unbounded promise. If we can tap vast unutilized human resources, if we can enlist that which is best in all of us, we surely hold the power to make that be so. Not just in the sphere of technology and science—but in the far more enigmatic and baffling realm of social justice.

For me, the year 2000 has a special meaning. It marks the twenty year anniversary of my admission to the Intensive Care unit.

So the numbers that follow are quite literally:

Numbers with a Heart

Worldwide Time Dollar Census: As the millennium dawned, 70 communities in Great Britain, Japan, and the United States had registered programs on the Time Dollar web page (www.timedollar.org).

Health Care for Seniors: Elderplan (rated #1 HMO in New York in 1999) recorded 97,623 Time Dollars earned by senior members serving 4,316 members through 41,985 care-giving episodes. The program yielded a 1999 Points of Light award.

Asthma Management: A Virginia HMO's asthma management program using Time Dollar members resulted in a 39 percent drop in Emergency Room visits; an 80 percent drop in in-patient days; a 74 percent drop in hospital admissions; and $80,000 saved in Year 1 and $137,500 in Year 2.

Legal Services For Communities: In exchange for Time Dollars earned by the community, Holland & Knight provided $231,000 in legal services to help local residents close crack houses, keep the neighborhood school off the closing list, and get funding released to clean up JFK Playground.

Juvenile Justice: Youth Courts run by teen jurors earning Time Dollars now handle more than one-third of all non-violent first offenders (juveniles) in Washington, D.C. Sentences include community service, restitution, jury duty, and an apology. Jurors cash in Time Dollars for a recycled computer.

Public School Tutoring: Utilizing Time Dollars, Chicago Public Schools boast the nation's largest after-school cross-age peer tutoring program. Now in its fourth year, it has spread to 25 schools; older students tutor younger students and earn Time Dollars. In 1999-2000, 1,500 students will earn enough to secure a recycled computer.

Rent in Public Housing: In Baltimore's Hope VI project, 8 Time Dollars per month are part of the rent. One hundred and fifty households are providing help to each other, to the local school, and to their community. Families use Time Dollars to buy a bus pass, discounts at shops, furniture, clothing, and membership at the Boys and Girls Club.

Citywide Neighborhood Services Program: As of November 4, 1999, the St. Louis Grace Hill Neighborhood Services program had recorded 12,378 exchanges involving 42,519 Time Dollars at 10 sites encompassing 33 neighborhoods. Projected 1999 year-end total = 70,000.

Food Bank: With monthly dues of 10 Time Dollars, a Food Bank club generated 78,000 Time Dollars by helping neighbors. Membership meant food at the end of the month in 18 Washington, D.C. public housing complexes.

In Retrospect

Each of these numbers represents a triumph of the human spirit. But numbers can lull one into false security.

In August 1992, Hurricane Andrew hit the southern tip of Florida wreaking havoc on an unprecedented scale. We jumped in to rally the membership of what was then the largest time banking program in the world. By 1994, more than three thousand members were earning over 12,500 Time Dollars per month. The 1993 total exceeded 150,000 Time Dollars, providing sustained relief for hurricane victims. At the time, that represented a kind of high water mark for Time Banking.

In the Bible, we are told of Pharaoh's dream that seven lean years would follow seven years of plenty. We had no Joseph to forewarn us. No sense of the struggle yet to come.

Chapter 2

Time Dollars Meet Co-Production

With Time Dollar programs, I was trying to demonstrate that money did not define the limits of what was possible. But ironically, the availability of money was proving to be a crucial determinant of whether they would survive.

Someone had to recruit people, sign them up, match capacity to need , monitor assignments, input the hours. The phone, the computer, the brochures, the local travel, the refreshments, the meetings—all cost money. At the beginning, when Time Dollars was spanking new, the sheer novelty could generate seed money. The real test would come when the seed money ran out and the demonstration phase ended. Unfortunately, the struggle for survival would unfold just as the political climate was about to shift.

The Lean Years

A tidal wave of conservative thinking was crashing over the nation's old verities. By 1994, the Gingrich Revolution was driving hordes of non-profits to foundation doors and program officers were reeling from the shock. They could not see the relevance of Time Dollars or its potential to mobilize the public conscience to confront real suffering and injustice.

For intellectuals and social change pacesetters, anything that remotely resembled volunteering seemed like a kind of moral opiate, a way to let government avoid responsibility, to numb the public conscience, to run from tough choices on priorities, to divert attention from runaway inequality and above all, a device to let politicians off the hook. For foundation program officers and government policymakers, Time Dollars seemed either too tame or an unwelcome corruption of volunteering. The phrase *points of light* had been tainted by its use in a political context to counter demands for more public spending and effective governmental intervention. At the same time, for volunteer devotees and community service apostles, Time Dollars bordered on the heretical, debasing the purity of the true faith by offering a reward.

Those who were trying to get Time Dollar programs off the ground and keep them running had their hands full. None of us had yet grasped the larger implications of Time Dollars. We had a new tool to do good things—but there was only a dim realization that more fundamental principles were at stake far beyond Time Dollars themselves.

Time Dollars as a strategy simply was not part of the political dialog. There had been no articulation of the larger implications of Time Dollars for the economy and social change because we hadn't fully grasped them yet. No one invoked Time Dollars in response to Charles Murray's assertion that every attempt to help people invariably creates a reward for becoming defective and dependent in order to qualify for the help.

Perhaps foolishly, those of us who were just trying to test the implications of this new currency stayed out of the political crossfire, not wanting to be tarred by partisan labels in what seemed like a sterile debate. For better or worse, we found ourselves immersed and overwhelmed in learning how best to get Time Dollar programs up and running. Pragmatic concerns, from software to staffing, to funding, pre-occupied us; we rejoiced because we saw new kinds of support systems emerging out of concrete instances of caring that turned strangers into family. We were strung out thinly. It didn't seem critical to focus on the larger implications. We were too busy, even to try.

The net result was that even though Time Dollar programs generated vast amounts of help for people by people, that success did not frequently translate into long-term funding. Those who were interested asked questions we couldn't answer. Could we show dollars saved through Time Dollars earned? Could we prove that the elderly persons helped through Time Dollars would have gone into a nursing home? Evaluators and funders wanted proof of a kind we didn't have.

Funding sources would say, "That's nice, but we can't devote our limited resources to nice things. We have to spend our money on the really tough problems: drugs, school dropouts, crime, unemployment, AIDS, health care, economic development, equal opportunity, civil rights, poverty, hunger, homelessness, cures for disease." To funding sources and policy pundits, Time Dollars just boiled down to some old people helping some other old people. If we had understood what Co-Production meant, we would have had an unstoppable answer about the relationship between what we were trying to do in communities and what government and foundation programs try to do. But it would be at least two years before we could frame the Co-Production Hypothesis—and five years before we could demonstrate that it was in fact an Imperative.

It did not help that the first Time Dollar programs focused on the elderly. Originally, this segment of society was a natural place to begin, a target of opportunity. We needed to tap unutilized time, and that's one thing the elders had a lot of. We didn't foresee that Time Dollars would come to be labeled, *For Seniors Only*. Labels can imprison an idea.

Tenacity—The Grass Roots Diet

That isn't to say that all support died. While the nation's large funding sources did not come forward or even just stay involved, an amazing number of persons sensed the catalytic potential of Time Dollars. They dug in, out of personal commitment. Time Dollar programs sprung up in more than 30 states. Some had staying power and survived. A kind of word-of-mouth underground spread the idea. After an initial grant, funding sources often evaporated. But in communities, in tiny grass-roots organizations, and among graduate students, many persisted, trying to think through how to use Time Dollars. For them, it wasn't about grants and funding. They were drawn to the idea because it affirmed the right values. The thinking seemed sound. In practice, it felt right.

But the sense of being part of an unstoppable movement, of unleashing a force with unlimited potential, shifted from a conviction to a dim hope. The excitement of being where the action is, engaged with the hot idea, the in-thing, the new idea on the block, faded. Philanthropic fashions change. There is an insatiable appetite for novelty. The moment for Time Dollars, it seemed, had come and gone.

We could not know then that new events and intellectual currents would eventually revive an insight that, however sound, appeared to have faltered. But in the mid-1990s, all we could do was hang on to a conviction that we were on to something important. Tenacity and core values had to supply the primary fuel.

Unbeknownst to us, a new ecological niche for this idea was emerging. A combination of intellectual currents and external events was altering the landscape. It would bring us back to square one. In T. S. Elliot's words, we "would arrive where we started and know the place for the first time." We would have to rediscover the world we live in, the world of family and neighborhood and community. We would have to understand the larger implications of that discovery. Until then, we would have to brace for more turndowns, more deaths of valiant but fragile programs. It looked as if we had been consigned by funding sources to a philanthropic burial ground. As rejection after rejection arrived, the air seemed to ring with the sound of a chisel striking stone for a tombstone bearing the legend, *Time Dollars 1980-1995. Been there. Done That. R.I.P.*

For the time being, all we could do was keep plugging away, pruning, refining, learning. Massive public and foundation funding was going elsewhere—but it felt like Time Dollar folk were doing the work that the communities needed to help them strengthen themselves and deal with their own problems. That seemed to be a constant. Gradually, we came to understand what that meant, why it was, and why it had to change. And the Co-Production Hypothesis was born.

LEARNING TO LISTEN

In 1996, I was still gamely peddling Time Dollars to a wide variety of agencies and organizations as the greatest invention since sliced bread. Most expressed interest. But I had become extremely familiar with the equation, *Enthusiasm ≠ Action.*

Nonetheless, I thought I was hearing something that sounded familiar, regardless of setting. A recurrent theme kept materializing in the responses—no matter what the field, what the profession, what the social problem. What kept surfacing had nothing to do with the professional, or the kind of service rendered, or the characteristics of the client, or the neighborhood, or even, the amount of money being spent. What began to feel like a universal constant kept emerging. I stopped talking about Time Dollars. I started listening.

The consistent refrain that kept surfacing in all the expressions of concern, anxiety, and frustration was *how difficult it was to get and to sustain participation from the very people being helped.*

The refrain took varied forms:

> *We can't get them to turn out for meetings, even when they know it's critical.*
>
> *We can't get them to call for an appointment—even the ones who need it most, especially the ones who need it most.*
>
> *We're not charging anything. But no one comes in for help until it's too late.*
>
> *It's virtually impossible to mobilize community support on any sustained basis. No turnout means no return.*

The more variations I heard, the more it sounded the same. Different voices, different contexts, different messages kept manifesting an unexpected common denominator. My mind kept returning to a passage from James Gleick's book, *Chaos*: "Nature had pulled back a curtain for an instant and offered a glimpse of unexpected order. What else was behind that curtain?"

The X Factor

Could there be a constant, a missing factor that cut across the full spectrum of social problems? That question triggered an informal, highly unscientific inquiry to see whether the same constant would continue to pop up in different fields. Sure enough, it was there:

> *Educators complain that they can't succeed if they can't get students to do their homework.*
>
> *Doctors and health professionals complain that they can't get patients to change their lifestyles: poor eating habits, lack of exercise, smoking.*
>
> *Police explain that there is no way they can make a neighborhood safe without getting people to organize some kind of patrol or look-out program.*
>
> *Substance abuse counselors and drug treatment programs say, "We can detox a person—but if they won't go to a support group or a twelve step program, there is no way we can keep that person off drugs or alcohol."*
>
> *Gerontologists say, "We can prescribe pills, design a diet, replace a hip, provide by-pass surgery or angioplasty—but it takes work by the patient to stay healthy, avoid depression, and reduce the risk of disability."*
>
> *Politicians and officials tell me they want to improve government efficiency, effectiveness, and accountability but that—regardless of laws passed, regulations promulgated, and money expended—without the backing and vigilance of alert civic groups, nothing changes.*
>
> *Housing authorities describe how all their efforts to keep the buildings in good shape fail because they can't get the residents involved.*
>
> *Community Development Corporation staff say, "We can build affordable housing but we can't build community by ourselves."*

It didn't matter what the problem was or what discipline the person belonged to; it became evident that they were all saying the same thing. It lacked the mathematical beauty of chaos theory, but it did seem to have a similar pervasive, predictable quality:

> *We can't succeed because we can't get the participation we need from the very people we are trying to help.*

More corroboration was to come as I started sharing these findings and enlisted others in the inquiry. At first, there were only anecdotes and hunches. These evolved in time into a kind of empirical hypothesis, which finally matured as a virtual theorem that seemed to hold true regardless of the sphere of endeavor.

There was an X-factor. We knew that but not a lot more. We didn't even know what to call it. Thus began a more systematic exploration into what was absent. There was a missing factor, *labor-from-the-consumer*, that appeared uniformly and consistently. It was the factor in every sphere of social endeavor. The convergence was compelling even though the inquiry was more intuitive than scientific.

It was clearly a factor of production. That was why we adopted the term *Co-Production.*

Co-Production worked as a label. People thought they knew what it meant. We knew we didn't. It was not self-defining, though it created the illusion of being so. We didn't know at that point what we had gained by giving the concept a name. Maybe it was universal. We know that it had to mean that program beneficiaries were part of the equation. But what else was it?

Then one of those serendipitous coincidences occurred. I was in a bookstore and the title of a book caught my eye: *The Science Class You Wish You Had.* Whether by fate, instinct, or just inveterate curiosity, I found myself drawn into the stories of great scientific discoveries by Copernicus, Galileo, Newton, Madame Curie, and Einstein. Each time, something unexplained had bothered them. The prevailing wisdom could not explain certain phenomena. They asked a new question—or an old question in a new way that no one had asked before. And they went looking for an explanation with a tenacity that would not quit.

For the first time, I had a feeling of closure about where we were. We certainly had the requisite tenacity. We still didn't have an answer. But nearly every breakthrough in knowledge had come from asking the right question.

Maybe, just maybe, we had asked the right question.

In Search of a Definition

We now had an official name for Factor X. We called it, *Co-Production.* But that didn't mean we knew what it was. *Co-* is a prefix. It connotes a relationship—a partnership. "Co" does not necessarily mean equal. The co-pilot is *not* the pilot. But both do share the cockpit—and except in an emergency, a plane can't get clearance for take-off without both on board. Combining *Co* and *Production* signaled a shift in status from subordination to some kind of parity. There was deliberate ambiguity on just how "equal" that parity was. But at the very least, inserting "co" as a prefix meant joint, mutual, and complementary.

Production represented a finding that the consumer could no longer be regarded as passive, an invisible factor to be taken for granted. We were groping to define an altered role, function, and status for the consumer. The consumer was to be involved in production—and production meant the actual creation of value.

Based on what foundations and committed professionals were telling us, Factor X would have to be more than simply a euphemism for getting free labor from the consumer to make the professional look good. It would have to be fundamental. If the need for "participation" was so critical to outcome, then Factor X would necessarily alter conventional distinctions between producers and consumers. If it could do that, it would trigger new processes and interactions. It would foster new behaviors. By creating parity for individuals and communities in their relationships with professional helpers, it gave promise of effecting systemic change. If we could understand what it was and if we could figure out how to generate it, Co-Production had the potential to unleash the capacity of disempowered groups as a critical resource and a new force. But that still left the question, Exactly what was it?

Have you ever asked a doctor what was wrong with you and been given an answer along the lines of "That's a virus," or "You have some kind of flu," or "That's chronic fatigue syndrome"? At first, you think you have actually been told something. But sooner or later, a nagging question returns: What does that mean? You work up courage to ask the doctor, "Can you do anything about it—except give it a name?" When you press for answers, when you ask what that really means in terms of treatment and recovery, you get either more gobbledygook or a candid admission that medical science still doesn't have the foggiest idea of what it means or how to deal with it. That's how it was, at first, with Co-Production. It worked as a label but lacked a clear definition.

To understand what Co-Production meant, we had to stop asking what it was. The secret to finding the "right" answer was to ask, Why are you asking the question? What is the real reason behind the inquiry? That's because the quest for Co-Production was driven by a commitment to certain core values.

Defining Co-Production By Four Core Values

It felt like the search for Quarks. Scientists didn't know exactly what those were—but they knew how they would have to function to produce certain outcomes. Co-Production was a similar construct. It would embody core values in a way that yielded certain normative outcomes. The answer came when we asked what core values would produce the outcomes people want when they tackle social problems. Time Dollar stories supplied many of the clues and many of the illustrations.

Earlier experiments with Time Dollars had demonstrated consistently that the beneficiaries of programs have capacity, are special, and can do things that they are rarely asked to do. They can contribute. They can mentor, monitor and mediate. They can provide companionship and care and collective energy. They can exchange time, tears, talents, and tools. This was the assertion that John McKnight and Jody Kretzmann had made over and over again in their book, *Building Communities from the Inside Out*: We have to start with what people can do, not with what they can't do. Once one starts by valuing what people can do, other core values precipitate out. Time Dollars had already proven to be a tool to value people. Now it would help us map the topography of Co-Production as an all-inclusive construct.

The Time Dollar stories enabled us to identify four core values:

1. **Assets. The real wealth of this society is its people. Every human being can be a builder and contributor.**
2. **Redefining Work. Work must be redefined to include whatever it takes to rear healthy children, preserve families, make neighborhoods safe and vibrant, care for the frail and vulnerable, redress injustice, and make democracy work.**
3. **Reciprocity. The impulse to give back is universal. Wherever possible, we must replace one-way acts of largesse in whatever form with two-way transactions. "You need me," becomes "We need each other."**
4. **Social Capital. Humans require a social infrastructure as essential as roads, bridges, and utility lines. Social networks require ongoing investments of social capital generated by trust, reciprocity, and civic engagement.**

That in turn led to a negative formulation—a refined definition of what Co-Production was by getting clear on what it was not, and (more importantly) what it must not be allowed to become.

Defining Co-Production by What It Is Not

Time Dollar examples helped us to be clear that Co-Production is not cheap labor. It is not a new etiquette for subordination; it is not pseudo-collaboration. It is not what Virginia Mason in her first address as CEO of the Family Resource Coalition labeled "collabo-babble."

It is all too easy for any pro-active, community-based, empowering idea to evolve into a new, specialized market niche dominated by professionals and controlled by folks who know how to secure the mega-bucks needed to stamp a brand name on an idea and go nationwide. John McKnight supplies a wonderfully acerbic description of what happened to the holistic health movement. When it first emerged, it promised to shift the focus from disease and medicine to health—real health, not doctor-defined health. Holistic health at the outset involved self-care, nutrition, meditation, fitness. Home birth and hospice movements came into being.

It did not take long before these became new profit centers for medicine. The holistic health specialist became, in McKnight's words, a "new five-in-one professional acting as doctor, nurse, psychologist, pastor, and herbalist for a single fee." Fitness became an opportunity for the development of "sports medicine and doctor-directed exercise centers." Likewise, Co-Production is clearly vulnerable to co-optation and exploitation.

The dangers are predictable:

1. Professional Monopolization

We all respect expertise. We know how often we wing it, just taking one day at a time, improvising and praying each step of the way. We wish we could take the time to learn more, to learn what others know or what we think they know. That is why so often professionals incapacitate citizen groups. Citizen action is hard work. Handing things over to a professional feels safe, sure—and easier. The result is that people buy a diagnosis of both problem and solution that is sanctified by professional expertise. By some strange coincidence, that diagnosis always seems to require a response that only the professional can supply. Lawyers are notorious for leading community groups down a litigation path that can take years and that immobilizes the group. But lawyers have no monopoly on the tendency to reconfigure problems in ways that appear to eliminate the need for citizen action or for systemic change.

2. Professional Exploitation

Volunteering can become reduced to little more than a strategy providing professionals with free labor. There is much, incredible civic activism by lone pioneers and grassroots organizations. They triumph against all odds and demonstrate incredible creativity when they become obsessed with a problem, defy apathy and take the initiative. But co-optation remains a constant danger.

Civic groups and associations want recognition. They want to feel they are doing the most valuable thing they can do. They seek opportunities to make a significant impact. And validation by professionals and agencies and government can supply what most organizations and civic activists crave: recognition for contributing in a significant way. As a result, the citizen energy needed to hold government and professionals accountable and to effect real systemic change can readily end up being siphoned off into activities that simply expand or enrich systems that are ineffective and unresponsive. Citizens and neighbors can cease to be community people drawing on their own native strengths, if they devote themselves entirely to activities that make professionals the ultimate source of approval and validity.

3. Professional Domination

Citizen participation, when sponsored and structured by professionals and organizations, is not necessarily a form of participatory empowerment. It can degenerate into busy-work that keeps citizens from taking direct political action to curb or correct systemic malfunction. All of us can be seduced by the illusion of power we get from being invited to meetings and even sitting at the table. We need to be wary of being relegated to an advisory role. All too often, we discover that we have genuine decision-making authority only with respect to trivia (for instance, the date and place of a fundraising event or public forum.) Or we discover that the important policy we labored for and voted for was, by its own general nature, one that changed nothing because it could be readily subverted or supplanted in the process of day-to-day implementation. Participation becomes debilitating when it degenerates into nitpicking debates over revenue, grant opportunities, new programs, scheduling, formal notice, agendas, reports, quorums, and parliamentary procedure.

Let the Buyer Beware

Co-Production mandates a different kind of partnership. It stems from a finding that without labor from the intended beneficiaries, nothing that professionals do can really work. Yet, writers such as Ivan Illich, Jody Kretzmann, and John McKnight would caution that in most circumstances, professionals are bad news. Keep them away—at all cost.

Co-Production may indeed be what the professionals, agencies, and organizations want. But are these writers correct? Is Co-Production simply co-optation waiting to happen?

That's not what is intended. But is Co-Production asking for trouble? Would any group trying to use Time Dollars be better off staying far away from agencies, using them only when absolutely necessary, making a total cost-benefit analysis of any contact or interaction with them, and above all, holding them at arm's length? Surely, if Co-Production came in a bottle and John McKnight were the Food and Drug Administration, it would carry an Old English Proverb as warning: *He that sups with the Devil must have a long spoon.*

For professionals committed deeply to social justice, the peril that McKnight warns against is particularly confounding. It draws into question the life choice they made when they selected what they thought was a higher calling. Reframing the question in contemporary polemical terms, we ask, Are the unintended consequences of helping necessarily hazardous to personal and civic health? If so, what are we to do? We are in a bind.

Would Co-Production-Factor-X-prove to be only one more trendy buzz-word, a fashionable chimera, a grantsmanship gimmick, the caring community's version of cold fusion in a bottle? Or was there something that could preserve the integrity of Co-Production—whatever it was?

The Missing Element: A Social Justice Perspective

In mid-1998, I was sitting in Chicago on a platform with Jody Kretzmann. Jody is John McKnight's co-author and colleague. Jody and I had been comparing notes. We had both seen how words like "strength-based" and "asset-based" had been turned into a mantra by social welfare professionals. He and McKnight knew the dangers of co-optation first hand.

Now, every program description began with mentioning "assets" as an obligatory incantation recited to prove that one was in-the-know. Use of the buzzwords certified one as morally pure and appropriately avant-garde. Behind the curtain, though, business was proceeding as usual: preserving one's turf, creating dependencies, and protecting a livelihood earned by catering to people's needs, deficiencies, and problems.

Asset-based inventories inspired by Kretzmann and McKnight have become a new public works program. All over this country, savvy agency directors are converting a genuine paradigm shift into mere busy-work: conducting an inventory of resources, cataloging assets, then distilling that inventory into an elaborate catalog demonstrating that their agency is in-the-know. Nothing happens; the catalog sits there. But it can always be pulled out and displayed prominently when funders come by, or used as a shield to ward off criticism of non-responsiveness and lack of accountability by the community.

Jody Kretzmann and I were in agreement: It was no longer tolerable for professionals to get away with simply replacing the old Needs Assessments with new Asset Inventories. What was obscene was the way in which we were throwing away, destroying, degrading, or denigrating the most precious assets we have: human beings.

Outrage as Epiphany

Jody spoke first, calling as he always does for us to tap the strengths and resources that are out there in the community, that are universal, that are part of the miracle that human beings are. But what got to me, as he was talking, was how we had both seen that brilliant work circumvented and perverted, used to get money without really altering professional practice or changing who got the dollars, who defined the problem, and who defined the response.

That was what set me off. Something must have snapped when I got up to speak. It was nothing that I had prepared. It just came out that way. There I was, standing in front of 1,600 people at the Family Resource Coalition's national convention. The folks who arranged the program had provided elaborate instructions. We had even had a kind of dry-run at breakfast to rehearse and make sure we were all on the same page. And my script had said, Edgar Cahn will talk about Co-Production.

But there I was, explaining to the audience that most of my life had been spent raising hell and suing the government on behalf of poor people. What could that possibly have to do with Time Dollars or Co-Production? But that was who I was. And I was there because I was angry about how a throw-away society treats people as throw-away objects. It wasn't logic that drove me. It was outrage. And so I spoke fueled by that anger. I never even mentioned Co-Production. Somehow, it all came together. When I sat down, it was to thunderous applause, but I didn't have the faintest idea what I had said. I just knew I had been honest about what I felt and what was possible.

It took me two days to find out what people had heard and why they had responded the way they did. In the process, I came to understand in a different way what Co-Production might really mean.

That was how I came to identify and understand the missing element behind the Co-Production Inquiry. It was a simple matter of Social Justice—the heart of my life mission. Yet, it had been missing from everything I had written, said, or seen. It was the message that people had been waiting for. No one talks about justice anymore, even though that was the very urge that had shaped so many people's choice of careers—before they got mired in budget, and caseload and quality control and continuing education credits and lay-offs. Before they forgot what they had hoped their lives would be about.

The audience's basic message that day was, "Thank you for that call for social justice. It's about time someone said what you said."

"What did I say?" I would ask.

And then they would tell me, "You said it from the heart, that the real work to be done was strengthening families and rebuilding our communities."

Or they would say, "Until I heard you, I hadn't really put two and two together. But now I see how the welfare law could end up stripping our communities of the ones we need most, the ones who have the get-up-and-go to rebuild these neighborhoods."

I had not used the term, Co-Production, in my remarks—but the feedback took my understanding to a whole other level. It said that it wasn't just a concept. It was a force, a passion for social justice that supplies a new and different kind of energy—both to community audiences and professional audiences. It reminds people why they chose the life's work they did—and why they know there may not be another chance to make real change happen. We were talking about a new kind of partnership, but it really felt more like a new kind of movement that would bring people together on common ground and out of a shared sense of necessity.

The Co-Production Imperative

Thanks to McKnight and Kretzmann, we had been emancipated from a fixation on needs and deficits. But that emancipation was being reduced, perverted, and trivialized into something else: a new accounting and inventory system. Oh, goody. It felt like being told we could shift from Peachtree or Lotus to Excel. Not exactly an offer of cosmic transformation.

Co-Production is about two additional dimensions. First it says we cannot stop at merely inventorying those assets. We must deploy them in actual transactions, in exchanges based on mutuality.

Second, if Co-Production was going to resist co-optation, it would have to embody a social justice perspective.

That realization hit like a kind of normative tsunami. It changed all the core concepts. Co-Production became an Imperative:

> ***Assets*** **became: No more throw-away people.**
>
> ***Redefining work*** **became: No more taking the contribution of women, children, families, immigrants for granted. No more free rides for the market economy extracted by subordination, discrimination, and exploitation.**
>
> ***Reciprocity*** **became: Stop creating dependencies; stop devaluing those whom you help while you profit from their troubles.**
>
> ***Social capital*** **became: No more disinvesting in families, neighborhoods and communities. No more economic and social strip-mining.**

The social justice perspective supplied an antidote to co-optation. It would function as an antitoxin that would ensure integrity, prevent trivialization and prostitution. That perspective would consistently summon the best in us. It meant that there could be no neutrality. We would have to take sides—as professionals, agencies, consumers, communities. For some that could seem threatening. For others, it would mean the realization of a dream, the dream that had taken them in the first place into the "helping professions," into public policy, into the quest for a more just or, more precisely, a less unjust society.

Chapter 3

Co-Production
An Overview

Co-Production is a construct: a framework designed to realize four core values. The construct springs from an observation that something is missing in social programs. That "something" is the contribution that the ultimate beneficiary must supply in order to achieve the end result ultimately sought by producer and consumer. It is invariably unpaid labor, not treated as work or valued as work. All too often, the participation sought by the professional is circumscribed by what the professional wants or needs. That treatment-bounded expectation disregards, dismisses or disallows the much richer, seemingly irrelevant contribution which the beneficiary could have made to create the kind of world in which both would choose to live.

Co-Production thus refers to that labor but it insists that that labor be elevated, that the capacity of the laborer be acknowledged, and that the contribution be valued. That will not occur unless the world of community and family in which that contribution will be made is first elevated to one of parity with the world of money and market in which professionals live.

Second, Co-Production is a process: whatever process is necessary to establish a parity between those two worlds. That process may be one of collaboration or confrontation. It may be smooth and cooperative or it may take the form of a dialectic that yields parity, only after a struggle because the process entails a shift in status that may be embraced or resisted.

Finally, Co-Production is a set of standards, or goals: *an asset perspective*, *redefining work*, *reciprocity* and *social capital*. We called them core values because they are, at bottom, the touchstone and litmus test against which the integrity and authenticity of the effort is judged. However idealistic the framework and however difficult the process, the core values themselves are not controversial. They have a kind of universal appeal.

Core Values as Universals

Most people subscribe to these values. I have yet to find anyone who takes issue with the proposition that human beings have the capacity to love, to communicate, to care—and that those capacities are assets.

The observation that being a parent, a citizen, a caretaker, a neighbor, a citizen is real work is hardly likely to spark violent protest.

Reciprocity is more complicated. It is not controversial. It does not polarize an audience. But the term *reciprocity* is hardly everyday language. In England, Martin Simon, who launched the first Time Bank program, found that he had to substitute terms such as "pay-back" and a folk expression, "What goes around, comes around" to convey the concept. Calvin Pearce in Chicago reacted more violently, declaring: "Reciprocity will never play on the streets." He translated it, "A two-way street beats a one-way street." Even if the word is not known, the idea of giving back, of mutuality, strikes a universal chord.

Finally, there is widespread recognition of something called community. People know that community is more than the public sector, the private sector, and the independent or non-profit sector. There is a social sphere called community that is public but not governmental. It conjures up images of the village green and the commons, the neighborhood and the town meeting. It evokes values of trust, reciprocity, and involvement. Thanks to Robert Putnam, we now cluster these together under the label, Social Capital. Regardless of the term we use, there is this sphere between private and public that supplies a kind of connective tissue. It is authentic; it transcends jargon.

Two Economies: Market and Non-Market

We all know that there is a market economy in which money drives transactions. And we know that there is another system outside the market comprised primarily of family, neighborhoods, and community. But we do not think of it explicitly as an economic system. We tend to take it for granted—until it malfunctions.

Co-Production supplies a *framework* designed to bridge market and non-market. In doing so, it elevates the function of the non-market system—clients, families, beneficiaries, community—to a level of parity that is new and different. It structures or restructures the relationship between professionals and clients, between programs and beneficiaries, between agencies and community. Graphically speaking, Co-Production is the border that surrounds, embraces and incorporates the two worlds depicted in the simple rectangle below:

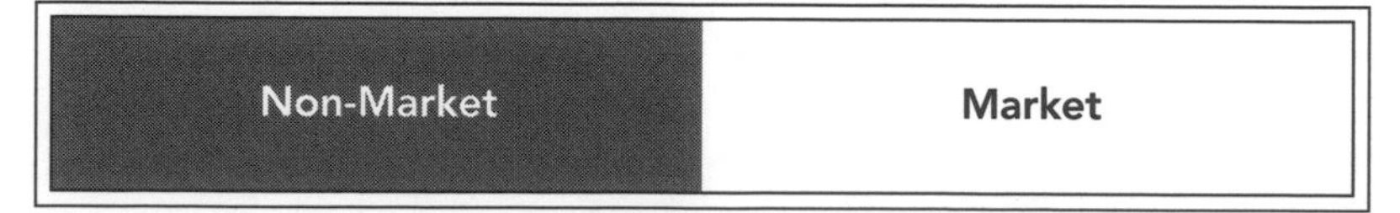

Co-Production is more than a conceptual box that encompasses both market and non-market. The line between those two worlds is both permeable and malleable. If we think of the four core values as establishing new terms of interaction between those worlds, then those values, when put into practice, will generate a dynamic that reflects a new parity in status, a new valuing of assets and contribution. Reciprocity defines part of the interaction; social capital is a by-product of exchanges in ways that can impact either world. Part III of this book examines specific, concrete examples of what that looks like and how it happens.

Two analogies supply useful parallels. First, we know we have two nervous systems, the conscious and the unconscious (or autonomic). We are most aware of what we exercise conscious control over. We actively will our arms to move, our legs to walk, our brains to focus on certain tasks. We tend to take our autonomic system for granted. It is automatic. We do not give a lot of thought to the fact that we breathe, that our heart beats, or that we are conscious—until something goes wrong. A T-shirt worn by a recovering heart patient said it all: "If I had known this body was going to have to last me this long, I would have taken better care of it." We ignore the well-being of that autonomic system at our peril.

The environment supplies the second analogy. For most of our lifetime on this planet, our species has taken the environment as a given. Clean air and water would always be available. Trees could be cut down; they would grow again. Species could be hunted; they would propagate. Only recently have we become aware that there are limits to what the environment can absorb, the extent to which it can renew itself and recycle itself, the extent to which endangered species can avoid extinction.

Just as our body needs its autonomic system and our post-industrial civilization requires the environment, so too the market economy needs a healthy non-market economy. It depends on inputs from that economy. Co-Production generates the dynamic needed to build those bridges, restructure those relationships, restore and preserve the functioning of those infirm, impaired, and fragile elements in the non-market economy.

The Multiple Levels of Co-Production

Co-Production operates at two different levels: individual and societal. The core values embodied in Co-Production move in logical progression, from individual to society, in expanding concentric circles. They convert individual capacity into contribution to others, contribution into reciprocal obligation, and reciprocal engagement into social capital.

The Individual Level

At an individual level, Co-Production is grounded on the premise that we all need to be needed and to be valued regardless of age, formal credentials, marketable skills, or barriers (be they ethnicity, gender, class, citizenship, language, or disability). Co-Production entails fulfillment of that need. One's contribution is acknowledged, recorded, and externally validated.

On the receiving end, a different outcome is sought. Individuals want to be able to secure help without acquiescing in a framework of dependence. This entails acknowledging and even embracing interdependence. But that is coupled with a need to give back, to pay one's way, to avoid being a supplicant, to resist designation as an object of charity.

Co-Production validates individual worth and contribution with a mix of psychological reward and extrinsic confirmation. Absolute self-sufficiency in total isolation is not feasible. Individuals are embedded in larger contexts. Co-Production supplies an interconnectedness based on core values. The values—an asset perspective, redefining work, reciprocity, and social capital—become fulfilled in the process of application. We have all heard the classic philosophic riddle: "Does a tree falling in the forest make a sound if no one hears it?" What do core values mean—unless they can be seen, heard, recognized, recorded, and rewarded?

The Societal Level

On a societal level, Co-Production entails a simple but profound shift in relationships. It elevates the non-market economy as an obligatory source of energy, vitality, knowledge, insight, and essential labor. For agencies, institutions, and organizations operating programs, Co-Production defines the elements needed to produce the outcomes dictated by mission and mandated by funding. There is always a persistent demand for increased effectiveness. The pressure for results may come internally or externally; it may stem from competition for scarce resources, from professional norms, or from a need to retain the confidence of political and funding constituents.

Co-Production does something else, as well. Attacks on helping professionals are in fashion. The accusations vary, ranging from siphoning off money intended to go directly to the poor, to the intentional domination of clients, to profiting from the creation of dependencies. Co-Production provides an answer by offering another role. It says: expertise is not bad; specialized knowledge and commitment are not necessarily destructive of local initiative. Co-Production provides a way in which the professional's knowledge can be converted into a catalyst that empowers. Co-Production asserts that it is possible to actualize these values in a win-win dynamic.

We find that where Co-Production is present, the end product partakes of the nature of a public good: safety, mutual support, trust, reciprocity.

The relationship between professional and non-professional shifts from one of subordination and dependency to parity, mutuality, and reciprocity. Co-Production thus emerges as a process that fosters new behaviors and that alters the conventional distinctions between producers and consumers, professionals and clients, providers and recipients, givers and takers.

A Social Justice Perspective

Co-Production is only a construct. It is no more than that. But then, justice, democracy, equality, free speech, and due process are only constructs. Before they actually existed in any form, the values they embodied had to be recognized and named. As ideals, they were no less powerful because they did not yet exist. The pressure for their creation came from the pain and suffering exacted by monarchs and tyrants to whom such concepts were anathema. A construct that is valid may nonetheless struggle to be born. Pain, deprivation, outrage have driven the movements of our age: the civil rights movement, the anti-war movement, the women's movement, the anti-apartheid movement, and the human right's movement. A kindred distress about the suffering in our midst drives Co-Production.

My father was a legal philosopher. For him, the quest to define Justice was a pre-occupation. He concluded that it took on meaning only when one confronted deprivations of justice, instances of injustice. That perception determined his definition: *"Justice means the active process of remedying or preventing what would arouse the sense of injustice."*

Co-Production may be a similar construct. The core values provide measures and tests. But in the final analysis, Co-Production may mean the active process of remedying or preventing whatever would violate our sense of social justice.

A social justice perspective elevates this principle to an Imperative. The Co-Production Imperative asserts that the market economy, resting as it does on such work, has an obligation to ensure that that work is acknowledged, honored, legitimated and compensated.

No More Throw-Away People is the ultimate Co-Production Imperative.

II.

Co-Production: Expanding the Economic Universe

Chapter 4

Beyond Economic Orthodoxy

This book is written for those who want to do something about the vast disparity between what could be and what is. That disparity translates into suffering, isolation, deprivation and inequity. It also translates into unmet need on a scale that seems incomprehensible given the vast productive capacity of the economy. And it translates into grave social problems: homelessness, substance abuse, crime, illiteracy, school drop outs. The disparity gets locked in by alienation, a sense of powerlessness, disenfranchisement and ultimately a combination of personal and civic fatalism that paralyzes individuals and nations.

In the past, those who cared about social problems developed programs to address those problems using their best professional judgment as to what would work. In recent years, there has been increased resistance ranging from skepticism to outright opposition to this approach. Critics assert: Social programs haven't worked. Salvation lies with the market, with the work ethic, and with the disciplined pursuit of self-interest. Just get people working. If they work, they earn. If they earn, they can buy whatever they need. The work ethic operating in the context of market supplies the all-purpose cure.

Any effort to expend public resources to address problems meets increased opposition. Critics offer two primary reasons. First, they assert that social programs send the wrong message. Social programs, they argue, say in effect that the way to get attention and resources is to have a problem. The more problems, the more attention you get. So helping professionals are condemned for creating or perpetuating dependencies. Both expertise and commitment are dismissed as irrelevant. Second, critics note that social programs require money and that public moneys are necessarily secured by taxing those who produce wealth. They assert that taxation for such purposes is a potentially disastrous disincentive. All money earned legally is presumed to reflect an essential and unquestionable contribution to productivity. Taxes to support social programs only increase the cost of doing business in a world where costs must be cut relentlessly in order to produce the best product for the lowest price. Taxation reduces the competitive capacity of the private sector to compete in a global economy.

Accordingly, social programs are regarded as necessary evils—concessions by the political system to special interest groups which are simply trying to bleed resources from those who produce real wealth and prosperity. No matter how benign the intent, critics stress that any endeavor to help people is doomed because those we try to help will understand that dependency pays as well or better than work. Tough Love means withholding help, denying assistance, cutting off aid as the most effective way of motivating people to become productive.

This is increasingly the prevailing ideology of both left and right, progressive and conservative.

When advocates for the poor, for children, for ethnic minorities, for the homeless, for the elderly, for inner city residents, for the hungry or unemployed or addicts or delinquents or immigrants cry out for help, market ideology supplies a two-level response. The first response is pragmatic. It asserts: Without prosperity there is nothing to share. The market and only the market can produce that prosperity. Second, the work ethic supplies the moral response to moral claims: Those who produce wealth are the only ones morally entitled to share in the wealth. If you want to eat, you must either put your money to work or go to work yourself.

Trapped within that framework, the only permissible intervention is one designed exclusively to get people to work. The function of childhood and adolescence is primarily preparation for work; the function of old age is to provide a market for goods and services based upon pensions and earnings made during a lifetime of productive employment. Beyond that, the function of old people is not to burden the economic system; restated more bluntly, the function of the elderly is to die as cheaply as possible unless they can pay their way with assets acquired by previous employment or investment.

Within this framework, it is difficult for those who care about social justice to make any headway. Anything which does not directly further market productivity and wealth production is suspect.

Breaking Out—First Steps

Viewed through the lens of Co-Production, the framework supplied by market orthodoxy is basically flawed. With all due respect for the awesome productivity and power of market, salvation cannot lie with the market.

This portion of the book, then, unabashedly deals with economics.[2] For readers who find the thought of economics daunting let me assure you: You already know what you need to know in order to understand where economic reasoning falls short.

First, let's start with work. If we accept a market definition of work, there are a few minor omissions worth noting. Work does not include: raising children, taking care of one's elder parents, keeping one's family functioning, being a good neighbor, or being a good citizen. So work includes everything—except family, community and democracy. Some of us think those are rather important. If they can't be addressed as work within the market, it is clear we need a larger framework than that supplied by market.

Second, let's look at money. It is the all-purpose medium of exchange that drives market. It is the all-purpose tool that market (including government) uses to fix anything that is broken. Yet, built into money are certain characteristics that give rise to some of the very problems we are trying to cure. Money is mobile. So it leaves the very communities we are trying to build. Money is all-purpose. So it can buy drugs and guns as well as food and shelter. Money defines price and price defines value. But the pricing system built into money assigns a high value to things that are scarce and a low value to things that are commonly available. It assigns a high value to activities that make money and a low value to activities that don't make money.

That means that the "tool" we are using to fix the problem can never adequately value certain activities until they become truly scarce: caring, learning, imparting values, sharing, neighboring, socializing, helping others. Likewise, child rearing, family building, neighborliness, altruism, and civic participation do not rank high on the money-making scale. Money devalues the very things we need most in order to fix some of our most critical problems: strengthening families, revitalizing neighborhoods, developing community, restoring civic society, making democracy work.

Returning Economics To Oikonomia

The response to prevailing market orthodoxy begins with one critically important observation. The market is only one of two separate economic systems. It is driven by money and monetary transactions. But real productivity takes place in two economic systems running side by side. We have known that since at least 347-335B.C., the period when Aristotle wrote the classic *Politics*. The word economics derives from the Greek word for *management of the household: Oikonomia*. The basic unit of this second economy is the household—but it also includes a vast array of exchange networks including kinship, neighborhood, and community. Aristotle characterized the monetary system we call market as a system of acquisition; he regarded the household as the core system for production and consumption. Ironically, we now equate economics with market. What Aristotle considered the real *Oikonomia*, we define by a negative as though it doesn't really count. We give it a throw-away name. We call it the *non-market economy*.

That non-market economy is, in fact, far more efficient than the market economy in doing certain things, among them raising children, taking care of the elderly, creating community, nurturing and maintaining civil society. That economy functions in ways that fundamentally differ from the market economy. It differs in mode of production: in lieu of specialization, it relies upon maximizing self-sufficiency. It differs in mode of distribution: in lieu of price as a mechanism to determine who gets what, it uses normative considerations like need, contribution and moral obligation. It differs in the form of compensation: in lieu of money, it relies on various forms of psychological rewards—pleasure and pain generated by love, praise, altruism, guilt, self-esteem, kinship relationships, obligation, duty, loyalty, reputation, trust, mutuality, and commitment.

The market economy takes that economy, the real *Oikonomia*, for granted. In policy and practice, it denies or ignores its existence as an authentic economy. The market views the non-market economy primarily as a present or potential consumer of its goods and services. It does not regard anyone outside the formal labor market as a producer. At the same time, the market economy enjoys huge subsidies of incalculable worth from the non-market economy. It starts with nine months of pre-natal care, continues with toilet training and teaching children to wait for the green light before crossing the street. It ends with caring for elderly parents who want to remain self-sufficient as long as possible. The market economy assumes that it can rely upon that contribution from the non-market continuing forever.

The chief message of Co-Production is that we must once again acknowledge the true significance of that non-market economy.

SHIFTING LEVELS TO FIND NEW ANSWERS

Einstein was right. "The significant problems we face cannot be solved at the same level of thinking we were at when we created them." We need a larger framework than that supplied by market and money.

We need a framework that embraces both economies, market and non-market, and that redefines the relationship between those two economies. Currently, that relationship operates on zero sum principles: if one economy gains, the other loses. They are in competition for the time and talents of every individual. What the market economy gains, the non-market economy loses. Co-Production supplies that larger framework and prescribes a way to structure that relationship so that it becomes a win-win relationship.

The framework is even-handed. It says: Play fair. It would be foolish to underestimate or undervalue the power of market, its successes, its capacity to produce goods, expertise and services that are needed, its ability to motivate creativity and to mobilize knowledge, labor, and capital. But it is equally foolish to underestimate or undervalue the economic significance and contribution of non-market. Economic analysis does so implicitly when it consigns or exiles non-market activity to the realm of values, ethics and morality—as if those had no economic implications. Alleged efficiency that takes no account of human costs, social costs, and civic costs is in fact false efficiency supplying highly deceptive and misleading measures of economic well being. That's not playing fair.

Co-Production supplies an even-handed economic framework. It makes use of conventional economic theory but it applies it to the non-market economy. Thanks to the work of economists, we now know what causes certain types of market imperfection and malfunction. Economists have developed concepts that pinpoint critical conditions required for markets to function efficiently. From the Co-Production vantage point, it is clear that economists have not done two things with their own discipline. They have *not* applied those constructs to assess or to diagnose the impact of market on the non-market economy. And they have *not* applied those basic analytic constructs to their own measuring rod, money.

As a result, economists fail to confront the extent of the subsidy that market has extracted from non-market or the extent of the damage inflicted by market on non-market. And they fail to realize the extent to which money itself has external costs that distort the results they get, the diagnoses they make, and the remedies they prescribe.

Market Externalities and Co-Production

When conventional economic theory is used to examine the impact of market on the non-market economy, the external costs cry out for acknowledgment. Externalities are a concept economists use when analyzing the impact of a transaction on people other than the buyer and the seller. Regardless of whether we know the term, we understand the concept because we have all been made aware of the impact that certain manufacturing processes have on the environment.

Externalities arise when manufacturers inflate their profits by polluting, by dumping toxic waste, by destroying the environment, by making water undrinkable and air unbreathable. The costs of environmental degradation and clean-up are not reflected in the accounting of profit and loss. They have been shunted onto others. Thus, external costs (or externalities) are costs that are generated by the production of goods or services that are not paid for by the producer.

To economists—and to the rest of us—external costs are significant.

They prevent the pricing system upon which market relies from reflecting the real costs of doing business. In this sense, they undermine the market's ability to allocate resources efficiently—supposedly the key benefit of having a market. Externalities therefore draw the attention of economists. They represent, in effect, a breakdown of the market—a "sickness in the system" which has to be constantly watched for, diagnosed, and fixed. Considerable attention has gone into exploring alternative ways to deal with them. External costs, economists agree, must either be absorbed by the manufacturer and included in the price charged consumers—or, better still, remedied and prevented.

Significant consequences follow when we bring the non-market to stage center. The Co-Production principle asserts that the non-market economy must be recognized as a real economy. It refocuses the lens of economists onto a whole range of human activity that official economic policy makers have thus far seen fit to disregard and ignore.[3] Once the non-market is brought into focus, it is clear that the concept of externalities can now be applied to the non-market economy much as it has been applied to prevent or arrest degradation of the environment. Producers in the monetary economy, both the public and private sectors, can evade the social costs as well. Healthy families, neighborhoods, communities, and civic society are the social equivalent of clean air and clean water. Once we see this, we can understand why it is critical to examine the ways in which the non-market economy is impacted by external costs imposed by the monetary economy.

In this sense, Co-Production economics necessitates a kind of ecological awakening about the non-market economy. It illuminates externalities that are as critical as those that threaten bio-diversity, deplete the ozone layer, pollute the air we breathe, and contaminate the water we drink.

But identifying the externalities is only the "diagnosis." There is also the "fix." When economists confront hidden external costs or hidden subsidies that mask true costs and inflate profit margins, they have some standard responses. They say: Pay the costs or prevent them. They say: Eliminate the subsidy or pay for it openly. Those same principles apply when subsidies from the non-market economy conceal true costs or when externalized costs result in damage to the non-market economy.

The logic of the situation thus becomes compelling: Market must pay the cost for its subsidies from non-market. Just as it must pay the price for environmental clean-ups, it must pay for the social toxicity that has been discharged, for the social equivalent of acid rain and smog and brown fields.

There is still one further step. Economists' response to pollution or toxic waste goes further than diagnosis and remedy. Paying for the clean-up is just the beginning. Changes have to be made (and paid for) to prevent further damage. Producers who have caused environmental degradation are required to pick up the tab for replanting, reforestation, and restoration of critical habitats. This prompts the question: why should the market not be responsible for the social degradation it inflicts? Why should it not pay for rebuilding a healthy, vibrant non-market economy?

A Win-Win Economics

Efficiency is another economic concept altered fundamentally when Co-Production is taken into account. Measures of growth and productivity in the market economy need to do more than incorporate previously hidden externalized social costs; they also need to incorporate the productive contribution of the non-market to the market. Thus, any assessment of efficiency is incomplete unless it also takes into account the economic health and productivity of the non-market economy.

Let us be clear. The market seeks to tap the assets of the non-market economy. But it does so selectively, opportunistically and in ways that frequently degrade the non-market. Market forces are driven by money—and money has no enduring loyalty other than to make more money. Economists have failed to take adequate account of the external costs generated by money as it functions in a global economy.

There is an alternative, however. The first step is to elevate the non-market economy to an appropriate status of parity vis-a-vis the market economy. There are practical, straightforward ways to do so. Experiments with Time Dollars prove that. Once we understand that the dense interface between market and non-market is malleable and can be consciously shaped, awesome possibilities emerge—beyond anything that money and market, by themselves, can supply.

The Co-Production principle illuminates ways to shape the interface between the two economies that ensure a "win-win" relationship. There are ways in which Co-Production can increase the well-being of both non-market and market economies. Professionals charging a fee in Time Dollars; merchants giving discounts to Time Dollar members provide a market incentive for labor done in the non-market economy while expanding the market for their own goods and services. Non-market growth can then spur market growth. Implementing Co-Production enlarges the pie in a way that enables contributors in both economies to claim their due. Defenders of expenditures on social problems need no longer be trapped in a Zero Sum game. Co-Production is Win-Win.

If social programs are refashioned as investments in non-market that will generate Co-Production, they will not reduce market efficiency. In fact, they will do the opposite. They will enhance efficiency. They will offset or correct hidden, external social costs. Regardless of how one regards the past track record of social programs, they can be restructured to enlist beneficiaries as Co-Producers. The point is that expenditures on social problems *if expressly redesigned to generate Co-Production* are not subject to the usual attack on social programs for creating dependency and rewarding deficiency.

We now have four critically important constructs that we didn't have before. First, there is the notion of a second economy—the non-market economy—which was previously unaccounted for. Second, we have the understanding that economic concepts such as externalities can be applied to the impact of market on that other economy. Third, efficiency can now be understood to necessarily incorporate elements of equity, rooted in norms of caring, decency, and trusteeship that have their base outside the market economy and that draw sustenance from family, community, and civic society. Fourth, the interface between the market and non-market economies is malleable and can be refashioned to secure a more equitable exchange. We can use those constructs to extend the reach of economic reasoning one step further.

Economics in the Service of *Oikonomia*

Co-Production offers the vision of a world that rewards decency and caring, cooperation, altruism, and collaboration as automatically as the market economy rewards self-interest, competition, aggression, and acquisitiveness. Time Dollars are a tool that can be used to supply proof that Co-Production is indeed possible. At the very least, Time Dollars supply a mechanism to implement Co-Production and they generate evidence of the new outcomes that Co-Production can yield. That evidence backs up the assertion that Co-Production makes:

We can create a society where every human being willing to help another can earn sufficient purchasing power to live decently, to develop and grow, and to pass on to the next generation a world that is better for our having been here. We can provide an opportunity for our children and our children's children to realize their potential to create, to learn, to contribute, and to dream.

This vision is within our reach.

Chapter 5

Oikonomia

THE WORLD BEYOND MARKET

We need a more complete examination of the non-market economy as an economy. We need to revise our thinking about economics in order to comprehend the pervasive and primary importance of the non-market economy. Market and non-market are not merely two separate, parallel, complementary economies. The non-market economy has a special primacy; it supplies the fundamental substratum upon which the entire market economy is built. Understanding that relationship is critical.

That examination is followed by an analysis and critique of current efforts to "fix" or strengthen the non-market economy. It condemns them as a patchwork job that is destined to fail for two reasons. First the non-market economy itself needs major restructuring to cope with the changing role of women and the prohibitions against practices of discrimination and exploitation that have subsidized that economy. Second, the fixes supplied by the market economy (including government programs) bring with them the same flaws that have produced failure in the market economy. Economists have diagnosed, analyzed, and classified classic situations where markets in practice do not deliver the benefits that market theory seems to promise. That diagnosis provides the intellectual framework for understanding how and why efforts to use professionals and specialized solutions to fix families, neighborhoods, and civil society are doomed to fail unless Co-Production is incorporated as part of those efforts.

This primer on Co-Production Economics concludes with an application of the concept of external cost to the economists' own measuring rod, money. The medium of exchange economists use as an all-purpose, neutral measuring rod turns out to have characteristics that generate massive external costs. When we become conscious of these external costs, we can begin to devise ways to create a medium of exchange that can offset or counter them. This analysis utilizes Time Dollars to illustrate what a complementary currency, operating in the non-market economy, might uniquely do to generate Co-Production and to offset some of the external costs of money.

This exposition lays the foundation for the remainder of the book: an exploration of Co-Production as (1) a framework, (2) a set of principles and (3) a process for reconstituting the interface between the market and the non-market economy.

Drawing upon a heightened awareness of the interdependence of the two economies, Co-Production emerges first as an array of specific strategies and examples designed to fulfill certain core values, and then as a moral imperative that declares: No more throw-away people.

The Second Economy

Every state is primarily composed of households. The parts of household management will correspond to the parts of which the household itself is constituted. The 'art of acquisition, as a way of acquiring property [is] distinct from the natural way of the household. It originates in exchange when exchange is conducted through the medium of currency and for profit. Acquisition for acquisition's sake shows its worst side in usury, which makes barren metal breed. — Aristotle, Politics

There is a second economy, existing all around us, that we have never fully appreciated as an economy. We call it home. The Co-Production Imperative obliges us to revisit that world.

The earth Is not flat

There is more to the economy than the market. The earth is not flat. We need a new map of the real world. The map provided by the government and prepared by economists is fatally incomplete. It defines reality exclusively in terms of money transactions. That's all the GDP measures. It is a flat earth view.

According to that map, it is growth when we build more prisons and more nursing homes, when we have to clean up toxic waste, and when a couple gets a divorce and has to hire two lawyers. There is no growth if we keep people out of trouble, seniors out of nursing homes, when we preserve the environment and save marriages. Similarly, when we measure the productive capacity in terms of our work force, we exclude about 50 percent of the population: children, teenagers, the disabled, persons on public assistance, volunteers, and seniors. Likewise, only paid work is "real" work. That excludes child rearing (that isn't paid child care), elder care (provided by family and relatives), volunteer work, community work, faith-based work, and all the civic work essential to making democracy work. Finally, if you examine the map supplied by economists, you won't find anything called *social capital.* So trust, reciprocity, and civic engagement—the connective tissue that holds an entire society together—simply do not exist.

The earth is round

There is a second economy out there. Various economists estimate that at least 40 percent of all economic activity takes place outside the so-called market economy in industrial and post-industrial economies. The percentage is higher in rural and lesser developed countries.

The productive contribution of this world is not included in any of the economists' measurements of GDP. It is called the non-market world. It is the world where most of the problems originate. It is a world where most of the problems could be solved. But first, we would have to admit the existence of that world.

We cannot begin to address fundamental problems so long as we remain trapped inside a defective framework that creates the problems. If social progress is limited to what we have money to buy, we are going to have to tolerate a great deal of needless suffering and deprivation. The only money available is whatever can be extracted by taxes and by charitable contributions from individuals, corporations, and foundations. There is a limit to what can be skimmed off the top. Global competition will squeeze what there is, relentlessly.

Non-Market as an Economic System

Both production and distribution function according to different principles in the two worlds, market and non-market. Conventional economics looks to the market to provide the keys to efficiency. In fact, the non-market world functions brilliantly on its own principles of production and distribution.

Production: In the market economy, specialization (or division of labor) is the dominant principle that generates superior efficiency. In the non-market economy, families, neighborhoods, and civil society function on different principles. Maximum self-sufficiency replaces specialization. The relevant unit for attaining self-sufficiency is not the atomized individual. It is the family, the neighborhood, the village. In the non-market economy, interdependence is a quintessential element of self-sufficiency. There is task differentiation, but nothing approaching what the market does. Specialists are a last resort.

Distribution: Distribution operates on different principles too. In the market economy, pricing provides a highly efficient, self-regulating, self-adjusting distributive system. Price adjusts supply to demand automatically and continually. What is scarce and what generates money costs more than goods or services that are commonplace and not in short supply.

Distribution within the non-market sector operates on different principles. Price is not the mechanism. No one holds the drumstick up at the dinner table and says, "What am I bid for this?" No one divides the mashed potatoes or salad up according to the market value of activities performed by different family members. Caring is not distributed based on ability to pay. Distribution stems from *normative considerations*: need, fairness, altruism, moral obligation, and contribution.

Where the non-market shines

The non-market world, within its realm, functions more efficiently than the market world. If we had to buy—at market prices—the goods and services needed in order to address social problems, we would all be in deep trouble. Let me illustrate. We have not yet contracted out one service to the market economy: brushing our teeth. But if we tried to do so, we could not have a mere neighbor do it. It would have to be done by a licensed oral hygienist. That would come to at least $50 for a visit. So we cannot even afford to address that one basic function, brushing our teeth daily, through the market.

What would it take to provide the full range of services that a family provides to raise a child? We know that feminist groups costed out the market value of a mother/housewife to be, in 1980 dollars, $66,000. Neither families nor the government can afford to buy those services at that price.

The average stipend paid a licensed foster care family is three times what is paid to a mother receiving public assistance. Increasingly, Child Protective Service agencies are turning to relatives and setting up licensed kinship care arrangements to pay relatives to raise a child. Even at that price, they are running out of available, suitable foster families. It is clear there are some things that families do more efficiently than the market.

Family is a world where even the economists admit that altruism functions to produce and distribute services *more efficiently* than self-interest. Nobel Economist Gary Becker writes: "Altruism is relatively inefficient in a market context; but altruism is more efficient than self-interest in a family context and in a non-market context.... If I am correct that altruism dominates family behavior to the same extent as selfishness dominates market transactions, then altruism is much more important in economic life than is commonly understood."[4]

No society, no matter how rich, can afford to buy at market prices those things that home and family and neighborhood supply: love, caring, wisdom, culture, knowledge, and 24-hour, 7-day-a-week support. Small investments here can leverage profound changes. If there are grounds for hope, it is because the return on investment here can equal or exceed anything the market has to offer.

When pitted against communism, the market and monetary

transactions proved superior. But the market is by no means as efficient in discharging certain functions historically performed in homes, neighborhoods, and communities; in religious, charitable and associational settings; by families, neighbors, members, and volunteers. The non-market world is the place from which to leverage change. If we want to make a difference, the place to begin is by enhancing the capacity of the non-market economy to enlist untapped resources, regain lost territory, enter into joint ventures with market specialists, and compete more effectively for the energy, talents, and commitment of people.

We need to redefine the relationship between the two economies. That is what Co-Production is all about. So far in this book, market and non-market have been presented as separate economies, existing side by side, complementing each other, and interacting with each other as if at arms length. That is only part of the story. In fact, there is a fundamentally different relationship that we need to grasp.

Chapter 6

The Non-Market Economy: More Than Equal

Most people have seen computer screens with all kinds of little icons. Each one can activate a specialized program: word processing, graphics, spreadsheets, communications programs. But we also know that underlying all of these highly specialized programs is something called an operating system that functions as a kind of master traffic cop to direct, store, and log in all the data; to read, write, and manage files; to load and execute programs.

If that operating system goes down, then none of those wonderful, powerful, specialized programs work. The operating system costs less than $100—but without it, the specialized programs that typically cost much more are useless.

SOCIETY'S OPERATING SYSTEM

Like the computer, our society boasts an array of expensive, powerful programs designed to perform very specialized tasks like educate, catch criminals, make subways and buses run, deliver medical care, conduct elections, resolve disputes, manufacture, grow and sell all kinds of things. But like the computer, our society has a basic operating system too. And if the operating system goes down, nothing works.

The core operating system of our society is the non-market economy: family, neighborhood and community. Like any operating system, if it is overloaded or hit with a power surge, or malfunctions or develops a bug, nothing works. The programs and the specialized institutions that we count on cease to function. They freeze; they crash; they malfunction.

It is safe to say that the present operating system—family, neighborhood, community— is in bad shape. We may not have a name for the virus that has hit the non-market economy. But whatever used to happen is no longer happening in many communities. The operating system is no longer reliably performing basic functions such as transmitting values, rearing children, providing support, maintaining safety, generating consensus, preserving memories, sharing limited resources. More and more, the evening news flashes messages across the screen that read like the equivalent of *Bad sector, Lost cluster, Out of memory, Lost allocation unit, Errors found, Corrections will not be written to disk.*

In our efforts to deal with social problems, programs keep crashing. We keep trying to fix them, upgrade them, re-install them. But it becomes clearer and clearer that the problem is not with the programs; it is the operating system that is malfunctioning. More and more of the things that families and neighborhoods used to do are not being done—or are getting done by much more expensive, cumbersome, specialized agencies that are not designed or staffed to handle all the things that families and neighborhoods used to do for themselves.

There were a lot of things wrong with the old operating system—but for much of the past millennium, it worked reasonably well. If we are going to be honest about it, we will have to admit that the old operating system worked as well as it did because it was heavily subsidized by the subordination of women and the exploitation of minorities, immigrants and children. It took a lot of free labor and cheap labor to keep that operating system going. As ideals of equality and opportunity emerged, as jobs opened up for women, as certain forms of discrimination and exploitation became unacceptable, that labor ceased to be available on the same quantitative and qualitative terms. The lure of the market and the apparent rewards of employment empty the kitchen table, the home, the neighborhood, whole communities, whole regions.

The arbitrary limitations built into that operating system are no longer acceptable. We need a new operating system for our society, one built on equality and reciprocity, on mutuality and caring. Co-Production supplies the framework. It initiates a critical dynamic by explicitly elevating the non-market economy to its true role as Operating System.

Why Patching Up the Old Operating System Won't Work

Let's stick with the metaphor a bit longer. If we think of the non-market economy as an operating system, the traditional operating system has limitations that are unacceptable: subordination, discrimination, exploitation. That system cannot handle the conflicting demands on working mothers any better than DOS could handle multi-tasking. It could not handle the aspirations of women, minorities, and others any better than DOS could handle graphics or multi-media. A patchwork job won't do. We need a new operating system—but that's not what we're getting.

We are currently trying to fix the old operating system with specialized programs operated by professionals supported by money and operating within the constraints of the market economy. So we ask schools to take over the role of families, police to take over the role of neighbors, the health care system to function as a support system, and specialized, public interest advocacy groups to function as the equivalent of an alert, engaged citizenry.

Fatal Flaws in the Market's "Fix"

We can't fix the operating system, the basic non-market economy, from the outside. It's a little bit like trying to fix DOS by beefing up the word-processing program. When we utilize specialized programs operating within the market economy to fix the non-market economy, they bring with them additional problems well known to economists because they are the very shortcomings that cause market failure.

Monopoly

Thanks to economists, we know what four of those problems are. One is *monopoly*. Markets fail to deliver the most and the best for the least when monopolistic power enables a producer to create scarcity in order to boost profits. We encounter the same monopolistic restrictions on supply when we rely exclusively on teachers to teach rather than enlisting parents and students as Co-Producers. We encounter the same monopolistic restrictions on supply and the same inflated costs in dealing with health care, long term care, public safety, and civil society when credentialing and licensing are used excessively and restrictively.

Co-Production supplies a remedy—but only by enlisting consumers as co-producers of health, education, safety, and civil society. So long as we relegate citizens to the passive role of consumer, we can anticipate that professionals, doing the best they can, will do unintentionally what monopolists do: limit supply to maximize economic return. Co-Production says: You cannot remedy monopoly if you approach life as a spectator sport.

Monopoly is just one of the shortcomings that a "market-oriented fix" brings to the non-market economy. Economists tell us that there are at least three others.

Imperfect information

One is *imperfect information*. The whole market system is built on the assumption that individuals acting in their own self-interest will make rational choices. That can't happen when consumers lack information about alternative sources that could meet their needs more cheaply.

When we use specialized market strategies to remedy problems in family and community, they bring with them the problem of imperfect information that plagues the market. Paid staff, no matter how professional, do not know which of your neighbors you can trust. They do not know which member of your family and friends you can rely on. They cannot tell you who is available within a block or two to help your child with homework or provide companionship to your 90 year-old grandmother who remains a steadfast chain smoker and speaks only her native tongue. They can only tell you what they know and what money can buy. Building a better information system requires Co-Production: enlisting the participants and beneficiaries to remedy the professionals' defective, imperfect information.

External costs

Another classic problem of market is the external costs that we have already examined. When one tries to remedy family and community problems with specialized professional programs, certain results are predictable:

1. The professionals get the money and take it home with them.
2. Community groups get upset because their sponsorship or endorsement was needed to get the money and they feel used.
3. Factions split the community wide open fighting for the few crumbs offered.
4. The intended beneficiary (at-risk families or targeted neighborhoods) understand that the way to get money and services is to have more and more problems.

Unless those programs are designed to trigger Co-Production, the unintended result of spending money on a problem is that the problem will grow and the numbers claiming they have the problem will multiply. That's hardly the way to "fix" the non-market economy.

Undervalued social benefits

The last problem that economists talk about is a different external problem: the unwillingness of people to use their own money to buy things like public safety, clean air, or disease control. Economists dub this problem: undervaluing external social benefits.

Everyone wants more safety, but few people want to pay more for police protection. Everyone wants roads without potholes, but few people want to pay more taxes in the hope that somehow that will happen. Everyone wants pure water coming out of their tap but no one wants to pay for upgrading waste treatment plants. We would rather buy bottled water. No one wants a flu epidemic to disable them—but that doesn't mean they are willing to spend the time or money to get a flu shot. Our tendency is to want to buy the education, the water, the protection as a private good—but how do you "buy" a safe park or a vibrant neighborhood, or a teenage culture that rejects drugs, or a flu-free work environment?

When services, funded by the government or foundations, come to the community or to a family to "fix" some aspect of the non-market economy, they encounter the same problem of "the undervaluing of social benefits." Unless one can find a way to increase the value associated with contributing, creating, or maintaining a public good, these goods will continue to be undervalued. Anything free, regardless of quality, tends to be devalued. Public goods and social goods are regarded as free. They are not—but no one actively desires to pay for them.

The reward system needed to remedy that undervaluing cannot be the same as what the market uses. Money in your hands is yours. It says: "Spend me to get the best deal you can for yourself." When we function as consumers spending our own money, we want to get what we think is the best buy for the money. Few people consider more public goods and social goods a "best buy" for themselves.

Money will not remedy this tendency to undervalue public goods. It will reinforce a market preference for private goods, for consumption, for acquisition. Professionals driving nice cars, carrying cell phones, and going home to the suburbs at 5 p.m. will have a hard time asking for sacrifices from people they are seeking to help. Who are they to preach sacrifice for the good of others? Professionals get upset when those they are trying to help don't show up for meetings or appointments. But we know who gets paid to attend those meetings and appointments and who does not. And we know whose lives have at least the structure of an eight-hour day and a regular pay check and whose do not. It will take other forms of compensation that combine the rewards of volunteering with the rewards of market in order to offset the tendency to undervalue services and participation in activities that benefit the community at large.

Trying to fix the non-market economy from the outside won't work. It means relying on money and paid specialized staff to deliver results. Instead, money will do what money does: reinforce the tendency of people to think in terms of scarcity when what is needed is love, caring, neighboring, and involvement. When money is involved, people tend to think selfishly, to ask "What's in it for me?" followed closely by the question, "What have you done for me lately?" If public goods or programs paid for by government or foundations are involved, people prefer to be free-riders, counting on others to pay the tab.

Co-Production supplies a remedy. It says: Pay for what you get by contributing what you can. It says, No more free rides. But it also says, We value what you can contribute; and we do not equate what you have to offer with how much money you can afford to pay.

We can extract one recurrent lesson from the analysis of classic flaws, endemic to market, that economists have developed: Trying to fix the operating system of our society, the non-market system, from the outside is guaranteed to bring with it all of the problems that plague the market. If we really want to fix that operating system, we need to build a new one.

It turns out, it can't be built with money alone—because money brings along its own external costs. It is time to turn a favorite analytic tool of the economists, the concept of *external costs*, on the economists' own all-purpose measuring rod, money. When we do that, a primary, but previously invisible, source of the danger of trying to fix the non-market economy from the outside emerges. If we rely exclusively or even primarily on the medium of exchange that drives market exchanges, we will have to live with the same motivation that drives market: competition, conquest, aggression, acquisition. If we want to enlist other aspects of human nature: cooperativeness, caring, and collaboration, we may need something in addition to what market and money can provide.

Chapter 7

The Dark Side of the Force: The External Costs of Money

Money originated as a practical solution to real needs. It serves a number of critically useful functions. First and foremost, it constitutes a medium of exchange—something that others will accept in return for goods and services. And that is mighty useful.

Money has other functions. It provides a standardized measure of value that enables one to compare the relative worth of different articles and services. It also provides a way to store up value so that you can save part of what you receive to use later. And for those of us who lack the cash to pay for a computer or a car or a home, it provides a way of making deferred payments over time. All of that is exceedingly useful. No one doubts that. But like most useful solutions that our species has come up with in order to address a specific need, money has a way, over time, of creating its own kind of problem. Human solutions have a tendency to outgrow their humble origins, to spread, and to take on a life of their own. Tools evolve but not without generating consequences that alter their ecosystem. The wheel, fire, tools, and weapons all provide abundant evidence. Money is no exception.

One might think of money in Darwinian terms: It has not merely survived; it has evolved. It has undergone incredible transformations—from being embedded in pelts and wampum, to being tied to commodities like gold—to taking the form of paper currency that is infinitely more portable. And now it exists as pure information, embodied in nothing more corporeal than the binary code of computer languages.

There are characteristics built into money—into its molecular structure, its genetic code or more recently its binary code. Those characteristics are exactly what make money useful. Most we take for granted as givens. They aren't. They can be changed. Some we are aware of; others are almost invisible. None comes without a cost. Part of the cost we are aware of—if only because we have to pay interest on loans and credit cards and the national debt. But many costs slip by unnoticed. We just take money—as we have always known it—for granted. It just is.

We are so immersed in a money environment that we can no more perceive how it shapes or affects our perception than a fish can imagine that water might distort the world it perceives. But each of those characteristics creates a special dynamic, alters the world in which we live and breathe and have our being.

MONEY: OUR DRUG OF CHOICE

It is important to appreciate on a gut level what it means when one says: There are external costs to money. Not just costs in the abstract, but costs that directly impact adversely on the non-market economy: on family, on neighborhoods, on community and on democracy itself. They are costs that can impair and even nullify Co-Production.

What does that really mean?

During World War II, cigarettes were used as a currency in Prisoner of War camps. Two things happened. Chain smokers became health problems for their fellow prisoners. And when the cigarettes were smoked up, trading went way down, even though prisoners had a lot to trade. The drop in trading reflected a competition between cigarettes' function as a medium of exchange to drive transactions and as a commodity to use, to smoke.

We can "modernize" that example to bring home what it means to say that money has external costs. Change the setting from a Prisoner of War camp to an inner-city neighborhood. And change the medium of exchange from cigarettes to crack cocaine.

What would happen to family, extended family, neighborhood, and community in that case? What would happen to the work ethic, to the way we value assets, to reciprocity or "pay-back," to the social capital of trust, reciprocity, and civic engagement?

We don't have to speculate. We know. People would stop spending time with their kids; they would stop going to work; they would go deep into debt; they would not have enough money for food or rent or car payments. They would lose everything they had saved up. Families would break up. Competition for drug markets would erupt into gunfire. Killings would multiply.

Use of that "currency" as a commodity would be far more important than its use as a medium of exchange to put food on the table, pay the rent, raise children, or be an informed citizen who knows about the candidates or the issues in an election.

Is it just possible that money has some of those same "external" effects on family, neighborhood, community, and democracy? Is it possible that people would neglect their children or their families just to earn money? Is it possible that an employer would sacrifice all the employees who had worked diligently over the years and relocate overseas where labor costs are lower—in return for a huge bonus? Is it possible that the political process itself could be put up for sale to the highest bidder?

We don't think of money as our Drug of Choice. But would it surprise you to know that between 80 and 90 percent of all the money made in the world has nothing to do with producing goods or services or buying capital equipment to produce goods or services? It is money making money off of money. Some have said: It is money delinked from value.

When we talk about money having external costs, there is no intention of doing away with money—and there is no need to deny that money, functioning in the market, has produced an incredible array of wonderful things to buy, has spurred inventiveness and creativity, has fueled scientific exploration and discovery. Cars have external costs; when smog becomes unbearable, we face up to it. Air conditioners have external costs; when the ozone layer is threatened, we face up to it. Money has external costs. Before we can deal with those, we need to know what they are.

What if we understood that money itself might be addictive? Would that be an external cost worth noting? Is it just possible that sometimes, reliance on money leaves no time for giving love to children or to the elderly, no time or resources for feeding hungry people, no time to invest in community or civic activity, no time to do anything but make more money and more money and more money—and then to wonder if that was enough? Does that begin to sound like an addiction?

No one that I know thinks that family is unimportant, that democracy is not precious, that safe and vibrant neighborhoods are not important, that a healthy life style does not pay off in the long run. But we just can't be bothered doing it ourselves—and we hope that we can earn enough money to find a way to enjoy all of those things.

Co-Production is rooted in certain core values that most people embrace. It says: People are the true wealth of our society. Social contribution is valuable work. Reciprocity or giving back is a fundamental principle of human life. We reap what we sow. And finally it asserts: We are not an island unto ourselves. We come together in community to care for each other, to learn from each other, to sink roots, to celebrate and, in times of woe, just to be there for each other. Those are not difficult propositions to affirm.

But suppose the medium of exchange we use had side effects, external effects that violated or nullified those values. Not completely, but enough to create civic smog, to have a toxic effect on an ozone layer called trust, to pollute the environment needed for democracy to thrive. We would not want to do away with money. It does too many useful things. But we might want to ask: How do we curb its side effects? How do we reduce or prevent those external costs?

First we need to understand the source of those external costs. They flow from particular characteristics built into money. And if they flow from those characteristics, it is worth asking: Can we undertake the equivalent of genetic engineering to create an antidote, something that can offset or balance or reduce those costs?

Anything good can become an addiction: sex, eating, drinking, exercise. Money is our "drug of choice." And we are in denial about the possibility of addiction. The first step to economic sobriety is to understand and acknowledge the external costs that flow from reliance on money as our sole medium of exchange.

The Dark Side of Money

Star Wars fans all know Darth Vader as one who has succumbed to—and indeed, embodies—the Dark Side of the Force. Like the Force, money has its own dark side.

To be sure, money has spawned some of our species' greatest achievements; it helps power our hunger for knowledge, our quest to understand the universe, our efforts to cope with disease and natural disaster and famine, our conquest of space, our understanding of the mysteries of life. But each characteristic of money that makes it useful has a Dark Side that, if left unchecked, can have undesirable and even tragic consequences.

If we look around us at the suffering, the inequity, the waste of human capacity, we have need of Obiwan's invocation: "May the Force be with you." But we need to understand the Dark Side first.

Let us turn to money—the bright side and the dark side. The good things about money are fairly obvious:

1. It confers all-purpose purchasing power. You can buy anything. Or just about anything.
2. You can use it anywhere in any country, no questions asked.
3. It is a powerful motivator. Ask any child.
4. Money is non-discriminatory. It works for one regardless of class, race, color, national origin, age, sexual preference, or disability. Money is an equal opportunity asset.
5. Money supplies the Invisible Hand of Price to deal with scarcity, to signal quality, to frame preferences, to delineate and compare options. You get what you pay for: price modulates choice.
6. Money is efficient. It facilitates transactions in a way that barter could not.
7. Money makes Money. It multiplies. Capital Growth is the key to productivity.
8. Money gives rise to legally enforceable sets of rights and duties, obligations that the law will enforce. One breaches that duty at one's peril.
9. Money provides an all-purpose measure of value, a way to assess cost/benefit.

One function of an economic system, market or non-market, is to mobilize resources productively in order to meet needs—long-term needs as well as short-term, immediate needs. Co-Production affirms the capacity of every human being to make a socially valuable contribution. We need to examine the extent to which this supposedly "value neutral" medium of exchange is inimical to the core values that comprise Co-Production. One function of a medium of exchange is to facilitate transactions that match supply with demand. Money seems to do that brilliantly in the market economy. But its success there desensitizes us to the external costs that money imposes on the non-market economy. Those external costs can translate into negative outcomes for families, neighborhoods, and civil society.

Each characteristic exacts its own cost:

CHART 1: MONEY'S EXTERNAL COSTS

$ Characteristics	Problem or External Cost of Money
All-purpose	Can buy guns, drugs, bribe officials.
Highly mobile	Money can leave neighborhoods, communities, nations too quickly.
Pricing: value of hour varies based on scarcity, skill	Caring, love, civic engagement are devalued; market pricing embodies market values. If everything has a price, everything is for sale.
Paper money	Paper money leaves no trail; the parties come and go as strangers. Trust requires memory. When money substitutes for trust, trust atrophies.
Compensation defines work force	Persons not in workforce treated as if they have nothing of value to contribute. Excludes children, elderly, disabled.
Money bears Interest	Interest and exchange rates make money a valuable commodity. Commodity value of money drives up transaction costs, rewards arbitrage and speculation on derivatives.
Money debt = legally enforceable	Breaking one's word is fine, so long as damages are paid. Obligation is based on enforceability and damages, not honor and trust. Legal remedy is often prohibitively expensive.
Taxable to support government	Tax dollars set limits on public expenditures to address social problems. Induces civic paralysis waiting for government funds.

Each of these external costs impacts directly and adversely on Co-Production: how we value people as assets, what we call work, how we reinforce reciprocity and reward contribution, and whether we are able to create social capital.

It is possible to design various kinds of money that lack some or all of these manifest advantages. Indeed, alternative currencies are now beginning to proliferate and all of them lack one or more of the advantages we have just listed. Why would anyone do that? Why would one want an inferior kind of money when the real thing is available? The *short* answer is: Each advantage, each benefit of money exacts a cost. And the cost, individually and cumulatively, can have a toxic impact on family, community, and civil society. Becoming aware of those costs is the first step toward moving beyond denial to gain greater control over our own lives and our species' destiny.

The following examination explicates the costs and canvases some of the evidence substantiating the extent of those costs.

1. All-purpose purchasing power

Money's all-purpose purchasing power may be its most useful characteristic. But if money can buy anything, it can buy our young, our elected officials, our judges, the Savings & Loan executives to whom we entrust our life savings, our most highly classified weapons systems. The all-purpose buying power of money fosters the illusion that we can buy anything: love, family, caring, friendship. There may be some things that money just can't buy—and shouldn't buy. Those things tend to be based in the non-market economy—for a reason.

2. Money's superior mobility

Money is accepted anywhere. Money knows no geographic loyalty. It goes to where it will secure the highest return. But that mobility comes with a cost. Building a community means sinking roots, making a commitment, sticking it out through hard times. Mobility impacts on sense of community and on social capital.[5] Nobody knows that better than sports fans who have seen "their" team's franchise moved to a more lucrative city.

Unencumbered by loyalty or state of origin, money is an ideally efficient medium for a global market. Yet communities of place are held together by another kind of money—social capital that creates an infrastructure of trust, reciprocity and commitment. Money flows with centrifugal force—away from community and toward optimal return. Mobility can produce hidden social costs. The young abandon the old to go "where the action is" in pursuit of opportunity and bright lights. With computerized global currency trading, the mobility of money has now taken off exponentially.[6]

Advanced skills provide less and less protection for local jobs against capital flight and business exodus.[7] One night, I called technical support at a computer company of national standing—only to find out, upon asking, that I was speaking to technicians in Costa Rica.[8]

Money's mobility, coupled with advances in data communications, make it increasingly "possible to farm out any kind of work—engineering, architecture, banking, even medicine—and get daily feedback from the most highly skilled practitioners in every field, around the world. Much has been made of the large number of high-paying jobs recently created in the United States as a result of advances in computer capabilities, but a high percentage of them are in business services and are vulnerable. In a few brief years, such jobs will easily be duplicated, at much lower prices, by individual contractors—accountants, data processors, graphic artists, brokers—anywhere in the world."[9]

Corporations have now detached themselves from their national roots, their roots in community, and their relation to workers. The only thing they remain attached to is shareholder returns, stock prices, and management compensation.[10]

Mobility comes with a cost. Mexico and Southeast Asia have learned that the hard way. For every blow to the market economy, there is some multiple impact on families, communities, and nations, particularly fragile democracies.

3. Motivation

Money motivates; there is little doubt about that. And people need motivation. But there are two kinds of motivation: external purchasing power and intrinsic or internal rewards, such as a sense of pride in having done something well or having helped another. The more we prize the external motivator, the less we pay attention to intrinsic values. The non-market economy functions heavily on those intrinsic values: moral obligation, pride in one's children, love, affection, gratitude, approval, trust, caring.

Monetary motivation has its dark side. George Soros characterized the dark side of this motivation in these words: "People rely increasingly on money as the criterion of value. What is more expensive is considered better. The value of a work of art can be judged by the price it fetches. People deserve respect and admiration because they are rich. What used to be a medium of exchange has usurped the place of fundamental values.... Society has lost its anchor."[11] His critique of money-worship can hardly be dismissed as sour grapes.

Increasingly outrageous disparities of income stem from money's function as a motivator. Money drives corporate raiders; the pursuit of more and more devours locally owned businesses, and generates massive lay-offs and massive exportation of manufacturing jobs. Increasingly, CEOs understand that they will be targeted for corporate takeovers if they build reserves, pay decent wages to employees, pursue long-term growth. The surest way for an executive to get an outrageous bonus plus stock options is to maximize short-term gain, move to where there are cheaper sources of labor, lay off loyal, productive, long-term employees, and find ways to raid pension funds and liquidate assets for immediate distribution. The impact of profit maximizing on both the market and non-market economies is immense and long lasting.

There is another dimension to money as a motivator: It rewards specialization as scarce and therefore more valuable. The runaway costs of our health care system are in part the direct result of the disparity of earnings received by general practitioners and specialists. When all care has to be purchased piece-by-piece from specialists, the cumulative cost of general coverage becomes prohibitively expensive. Specialists guard their speciality; they tend to be the last to embrace Co-Production.

4. Money as egalitarian

Money provides a uniquely nondiscriminatory, non-exclusive form of identification—pieces of paper with pictures of dead notables, credit up to an approved limit and beyond. In theory, money excludes no willing worker with time and talent. In theory, money confers equal purchasing power on all, regardless of race, class, gender, age or national origin. But the theory isn't working. Disparities of wealth have increased exponentially. The combined wealth of the top 1 percent of American families is nearly the same as that of the entire bottom 95 percent. That disparity is increasing annually at an accelerating rate. Racism, divisiveness, and class stratification are all on the upswing. In a winner-take-all society, little differences become vast differences, even life-and-death differences.[12] The vast significance attributed to infinitesmal differences in ranking based on standardized test scores illustrate a principle that has now spread to every facet of economic life.

For the non-market economy, money's egalitarianism means that the market can compete with the non-market for time and energy. Children don't have money so they can't bid for their parents' time and priorities with that medium of exchange. Family, neighborhood and community all lose out.

When businesses generate profit, the egalitarian question changes: Where does the money go? Who gets what share? Those who contribute capital or workers who contribute their skills and labor. The motivation supplied by money is the major determinant. Money is constantly in search of higher return. When the hard choices have to be made, money wins; labor loses.

The media regularly report what at first seems like a puzzling phenomenon: when workers are laid off, stock prices go up. It is clear why. The market anticipates that profits will rise if labor costs are being reduced. When projected annual profits rise, the value of shares increases by some multiple of that profit. The more workers who are laid off, the higher the bonuses that are paid to CEO's who will make the "tough decisions."[13] For workers, money's egalitarianism puts them in a worldwide race to the bottom. There is neither time nor energy to invest in family, neighborhood and civil society when one job or two still leave one hovering near the poverty line.

5. The invisible hand of price

Price brings supply into line with demand. It rations scarce supply based on ability to pay market price. It induces others to enter the market to augment supply by offering a monetary reward.

Price will always devalue what is not scarce—like air and water (until polluted) and basic tasks like caring, neighboring, citizen involvement, rearing, and learning (until we make them scarce and unavailable commodities). That means it will always devalue the universal assets upon which the non-market relies: the qualities that define our humanity. The hierarchy established by price does not typically support collaboration, cooperation, sacrifice and altruism.

Price has other drawbacks. Market wages convert price into status hierarchies that subordinate women and those tasks that women have historically done. Accepting money means accepting the status defined by the wage. That is the cost of price.

6. Money as efficient

Economists love efficiency—and for them, money provides the ultimate measure of efficiency. The issue they rarely examine is: Efficient for what purpose. Consider light bulbs; are they efficient compared to flourescent? The answer depends on what the question really means: Efficient for what? Heat or light or a sustainable environment?

How efficient is money? It measures profit but how efficient is it as a measure of equity, of value, of beauty, of justice, of the environment, of what builds and sustains family, neighborhood and community? Co-Production insists that the market pay for the external costs imposed on non-market. When rapidly accelerating disparities of income decrease opportunity, induce alienation, heighten divisiveness, and decrease trust, who pays for those "externalities."

The cumulative cost of this "efficient system" mounts. We take the money system for granted—but this efficient system employs legions of cashiers, bookkeepers, accountants, tellers, and layer upon layer of management. One must rethink the "efficiency" of our present monetary system every time a few more billion dollars get added to the cost of the Savings & Loan bail-out or the critically important bail-out of Third World country debt. How "efficient " is money when we pay more for the cost of borrowing it than we do for the car or the house it helps us buy?

7. Money makes money

In his book, *The Death of Money*, Joel Kurtzman, executive editor of the *Harvard Business Review* and former editor of the Sunday Business section of the *New York Times*, lets out a dirty little secret. Two trillion dollars change hands in world markets each day—but at most, only 20 percent of those exchanges have anything to do with goods and services. That means that 80 percent of the wealth that people are "earning" has nothing to do with goods and services.[14]

Arbitrage and hedge funds account for most of that 80 percent. Earning money now means around-the-clock gambling in a global casino that takes bets on exchange rates, mortgage rates, commodities futures, and anything else the "financial industry" can package as a "product."

Money has taken on a life of its own: its function is to reproduce for the sake of reproducing—regardless of the impact of its health on the human community. If doctors saw cells multiplying without function in the way we see money multiplying, they would have no difficulty with the diagnosis. They would call it cancer. Whether a tumor or growth is malignant or not depends upon whether it destroys other vital organs or impairs critical functions. Look at Mexico after the devaluation of the pesos, Southeast Asia after the meltdown of its currencies in 1998-99, Russia as its currency goes into free-fall. Increasingly, what we are witnessing in the world's money markets looks more and more like cancer.

The non-market economy has its own work ethic. Family and civic responsibility are real work—even if the market economy does not count them as work. When collecting dividends counts as work but changing diapers does not, the external cost to the non-market economy is clear.

8. Money's superior enforceability

Money gives you a contractual right. But the remedy is normally limited to money damages. Our legal system places no special value on keeping one's word; it is expressly designed to permit one to break one's word if one can find a more profitable deal. Legally enforceable simply means getting out of keeping your word as cheaply as possible if the opportunity arises to make more money.

The non-market economy operates on a different sense of obligation. It says: Your word is your bond. What goes around comes around. Your reputation for honoring your word is the most important asset you have. Money tends to erode the real meaning of obligation.

9. Money as the measure of value

Traditionally, money has been used as an all-purpose measure of value. It was tied to a value standard upon which all could agree—the price of gold. But on August 15, 1971, something happened to money. President Richard Nixon declared that the United States would no longer redeem dollars on demand for gold. Dollars became explicitly what some may have suspected they were all along: pictures of dead notables on high-grade paper. Once computers became commonplace, the next step was simply to eliminate the paper and store money as numbers. David Korten has summed it up: "The creation of money has been delinked from the creation of value."[15]

On October 19, 1987, the Dow Jones Industrial average fell by 22.6 percent in one day. Between August and October, investors lost a little over $1 trillion on the New York Stock Exchange. Yet, the same homes, factories, office buildings, and improved real estate existed before and after crash. When enough people started believing the crash wasn't real, it ceased to be. What does our measure of value really mean?

In his *History of Money*, Jack Weatherford writes: "Free at last from the confines of time and space, from the control of any particular government, from any collection of corporations, and even from the normal forces of the economy, money has evolved to a new level and into a totally new entity. Money will never again be what it was. ... Throughout its history, money has become steadily more abstract. By moving at the speed of light, electronic money has become the most powerful financial, political and social force in the world. Money has become even more like God: totally abstract and without corporeal body."

Ultimately, value is based on what human beings need. Money would have no meaning in a world denuded of people. When we equate money with value, everything is reversed. People become surplus, disposable, value-less. The Co-Production Imperative takes fundamental exception to the equation of money with value. It says, value starts and ends with human beings. No more throw-away people.

Imprisoning the Imagination

The real cost of money—the real price we pay—is not just interest. It is the hold that money has on our sense of what is possible, the prison it builds for our imagination.

Ask yourself: Did Einstein wait on a research grant to think about relativity? Did Moses wait on a travel grant to get out of Egypt? Did Mandela wait on campaign financing to create a break with the past that produced a 90 percent election turnout? I don't think so.

We invest money with magical powers that in truth belong to us, have always belonged to us—powers that are ours by virtue of what human beings are. We think we need money to give us permission to do what we already have the power and capacity to do.

We need to understand the dark side of money in order to break the hold it has on our thinking and the numbing it does to our moral sensibility. We need to understand how artificial, confining, and unreasonably powerful that hold is, partly to get us to break out of, through, or beyond those limits we have accepted—believing, wrongly, that they represent real external constraints.

Consider how you and I are programmed to believe in money. Most of us, for instance, would not readily go into a stranger's home or let a stranger come into our home. But there is an exception: the stranger we found through the Yellow Pages. "Come right in," we declare when we answer the doorbell. "Been waiting for you." Never saw the person in our lives before. Know nothing about them except the advertisement or listing in the Yellow Pages. But we labor under the delusion that because we will be paying them money, we can trust them.

I know, some would answer: Well, if the service or goods they provide are defective, you have a remedy. Ask the person who gives you that explanation how much he or she believes in lawyers, trusts the legal system, or can afford to pay for the services of a lawyer. I don't know many lawyers who can afford lawyers. So I don't think the availability of a legal remedy is what accounts for the faith we exhibit where money is involved. I think that in our minds, money is a substitute for trust and perhaps is even superior to mere trust—trust with a thirty-thousand mile warranty, so to speak. Money is not trust. We know that—but we don't.

Most of us have read or seen "The Wizard of Oz." And we have smiled to ourselves knowing that the lion always had courage, the tin man always had a heart, the scarecrow always had a brain. Maybe we ask ourselves: Why didn't they know that from the outset? Why did it take the Wizard?

But it does not occur to us to ask: Why were nearly all the factories in Mexico idle after the peso was devalued? How could the 1987 stock market crash eliminate nearly half the value of all property in the United States in less than a week? What does it really mean when we say, "There is a Third World debt crisis" and then change our minds: "Don't worry; there is no Third World debt crisis" or "The budget deficit must be eliminated and the national debt radically reduced—but maybe not"?

Why are the streets of Washington, D.C., and New York beginning to look more and more like scenes from Bombay and Calcutta? There is vast work to be done cleaning up our cities and cleaning up the environment. We see homeless people at highway intersections holding up cardboard signs saying "Will work for food." We know that our farms have the capacity to feed much of the rest of the world. Yet we cannot feed our own.

The ultimate cost of money is the prison we let our minds build for us.

Chapter 8

The Co-Production Antidote

Money is a human artifact. What human beings create, human beings can alter. Human beings can design it to meet their needs.

Money supplies the lens through which we compute gaps between supply and demand, between resources and needs, between what is "feasible" and what is "not feasible" because not affordable. When we see our communities failing, families falling apart, neighborhoods deteriorating, clean air and water becoming scarcer, open space disappearing, we feel helpless to address the problem because all we know is how to use money to solve it. But we do not have to stand by helpless.

Genetic Engineering of money

The implications are far-reaching. Once one changes the characteristics of money, one changes the dynamics that flow from those characteristics. It therefore becomes possible—at least in theory—to engage in a kind of genetic engineering of currency, to identify those characteristics that created harmful externalities and to substitute characteristics that might offset or remedy those externalities.

Once we understand the costs that flow from each characteristic of money, we can reduce the costs by altering the characteristics. If we understand how money creates holes in our social fabric and creates the helplessness and paralysis we experience, we can act to fix those holes and to break out of that helplessness.

That is the design process that created Time Dollars, a tax-exempt currency with far-reaching implications. The very act of creating it simultaneously provided a way to chart the existence of a world that had been there all along, but out of sight. In a scientific society, nothing exists that cannot be quantified and measured. Numbers confer reality. And Time Dollars generate numbers about activity that had not previously been counted. What those numbers reveal, document, and multiply is the extensive, ongoing activity that comprises the core transactions and supplies the actual substance of our society: the sharing, the giving, the exchange out of which families and communities are built.

Time Dollars Have a Different Genetic Code

When we alter money's characteristics, we alter the dynamics that flow from those characteristics. Every characteristic that makes conventional money valuable has a down-side, a social cost. As those social costs mount, they create social problems and social pathologies. Time Dollars are a currency designed to counter each of the adverse social consequences, the social costs that flow from conventional money. The value of money that we know best is based on scarcity. It is not clear that a system driven by scarcity is the best way to produce or distribute love, caring, trust, knowledge, or civic engagement. Let us take these changes, one by one. From one point of view, Time Dollars are a distinctly inferior currency. But each characteristic that makes them inferior can offset some of the external costs that money exacts. We can now add a new column to the two column chart on page 63 above, which showed those external costs of money. The new column shows how Time Dollar characteristics compare with money's characteristics.

CHART 2: REMEDYING MONEY'S EXTERNAL COSTS

$ Characteristics	Problem or External Cost of Money	Time Dollar Characteristics
All-purpose	Can buy guns, drugs, bribe officials.	Limited purpose
Highly mobile	Money can leave neighborhoods, communities, nations too quickly.	Locally anchored
Pricing: value of hour varies based on scarcity, skill	Caring, love, civic engagement are devalued; market pricing embodies market values. If everything has a price, everything is for sale.	All hours valued equally; compensation includes psychic reward
Paper money	Paper money leaves no trail; the parties come and go as strangers. Trust requires memory. When money substitutes for trust, trust atrophies	Electronic currency: Building trust requires memory so that present is shaped by the future

Compensation defines work force	Persons not in workforce treated as if they have nothing of value to contribute. Excludes children, elderly, disabled.	Children, elderly, disabled are contributors; earn Time Dollars
Money bears Interest	Interest and exchange rates make money a valuable commodity. Commodity value of money drives up transaction costs, rewards arbitrage and speculation on derivatives.	No interest and no comodity value make other transactions possible
Money debt = legally enforceable	Breaking one's word is fine, so long as damages are paid. Obligation is based on enforceability and damages, not honor and trust. Legal remedy is often prohibitively expensive.	Moral obligation may be safer than legal obligation. One's word is one's bond.
Taxable to support government	Tax dollars set limits on public expenditures to address social problems. Induces civic paralysis waiting for government funds.	Time Dollars reward caring and civic participation, are not taxable, virtually unlimited.

1. All-purpose purchasing power

Sorry. Time Dollars can't be traded on street corners for drugs. No Time Dollar program that we know of operates a gun shop, a crack house or a money-drop service for political favors.

From the viewpoint of all-purpose buying power, Time Dollars is a distinctly inferior currency. They can only be used to buy specific kinds of goods and services that are consciously incorporated into the binary computer code that defines the currency—things like companionship, support, caring.

Time Dollars as a currency with restricted purchasing power may be inferior for certain purposes, but it sends out a message: Maybe we don't really want all the things we value most—our future, our fate, our lives—determined by market value and up for grabs to the highest bidder. And perhaps we need a currency that, regardless of the market, enables us to use our time to secure a kind of self-sufficiency, that can't be eliminated by cutbacks in Medicare or eroded by inflation.

2. Mobility

Time Dollars are a local currency—issued locally and honored locally. If one wants to use them in another locality, one does so as part of an unofficial Time Dollar extended family that welcomes distant relatives, and not because Full Faith and Credit require it. Money flows with centrifugal force—away from community and toward optimal return. We need a local currency that will stay put as a kind of safety net, given the rate at which vast tidal waves of speculative money can wash over an entire nation, create an instant boom, and then depart overnight. Time Dollars reverse that flow. They induce a centripetal force, functioning as a reward for sinking roots, staying in place, accepting responsibility, building community, keeping family together.

We do have control over our own time; we can determine whether or not to use it to help others and whether or not we wish to earn greater security for ourselves by honoring commitments made in the past in return for similar service. Co-Production elevates the non-market economy as the only possible shelter from the vicissitudes of the global market economy. As a complementary economic system based on maximizing self-sufficiency, it represents a possible buffer in a world where money's mobility and global interdependence can mean ubiquitous vulnerability.

3. Motivation

There is no doubt that money rewards self-interest, greed, ruthlessness and material acquisition. We need an economy that rewards decency, caring, civic participation, and learning as automatically as the market now rewards unbridled self-interest, winner-take-all competition, and runaway specialization. Time Dollars devalue specialization; they assert that the most special and important thing a human being can do is to be a Human Being. That is about as unspecialized a job description as one can get. But it puts you in pretty good company—like Mother Teresa and Gandhi and Martin Luther King.

Time Dollars provide a reward for caring and decency. They reinforce the psychic rewards associated with volunteering. They provide external validation for doing the right thing. We need some kind of antidote to the motivation that enables drug dealers to buy our young, soft money to buy our elected officials, developers to despoil our environment, inside traders to extract illicit profit, and corporate raiders to pillage pension funds and company assets.

4. Egalitarian materialism

When a billion dollars entitles one to capture the media, run for president, or be regarded as a sage, maybe we need less egalitarianism. Maybe we need some elitism based on contribution, morality, and integrity. Time Dollars offers a highly selective opportunity to become a member of a highly elite, exclusionary club. Acts of caring and decency purchase privilege.

5. Price

Time Dollars reject market price as a distributive and rationing mechanism. If tough decisions had to be made about who gets and who does not, two simple principles would suffice: those with greatest need would get a priority and those who had contributed by helping others would get a priority. If that sounds utopian, ask yourself if your parents or grandparents ever went without so that you could go to bed with a full stomach—or get a college education.

There is no single characteristic of Time Dollars that distresses economists more than the absence of price as a rationing mechanism, as a way to determine who gets what. One teenager from Anacostia in Washington, D.C., was earning Time Dollars doing yard work for elderly homeowners. The Time Dollars meant a lot, he said, because otherwise his buddies would think he was a chump. He could give them as a present to his grandmother. Challenging him for helping his grandmother was a no-no. Earning something he could only give away gave him status. Market wages would have subjected him to peer ridicule from those who are making far more dealing drugs. Price may not be all it is cracked up to be.

6. Efficiency

Money may be very efficient in distinguishing the haves from the have-nots. It seems to be singularly inefficient in bridging that divide or in enabling society to place value on what it says it values: caring, neighboring, rearing children, civic participation, learning, and building community. Recent debates over the GDP as an adequate measure of our real economic status have begun to focus on all the gaps in the models that rely exclusively on monetary transactions as indicators of growth and progress.

There is one thing that Time Dollars do far more efficiently than money. No monetary system provides a gauge for the extraordinary wealth of human talent for which the market finds no use or the vast unmet need that our system finds it convenient to ignore. The omission of all non-monetarized economic activity of family, neighborhood and community represents one of the largest failures in the money-based national accounting system. The item is not small. One recent estimate projected the market value of help given within family by and for seniors at more than $196 billion. Is that kind of omission what we mean by efficiency?

7. Money makes money

Time Dollars generate no interest. But they are inflation proof. An hour will still equal an hour, regardless of what the Federal Reserve does. If you ask what is the global economy's most important economic product, then forget cars or food or computers. If money is the exclusive measure of value, then the most important product that the global economy produces is money.

> $800 billion worth of dollars, marks and yen changes hands every day in the cash and futures markets of the world. That amount is more than twenty-five times more money than is exchanged each day in all international trade transactions.

That estimate does not come from some fuzzy New Age visionary. The author is Joel Kurtzman of the *Harvard Business Review* and the *New York Times*. He writes:

> That money is mostly involved in nothing more than making money. It is an ocean of money. One day's worth of trading is more than all Canadians, together with all their industries, mines, and businesses, earn in a year.[16]

There used to be an ad that ran, " We make money the old fashioned way. We earn it." The money that money makes has a cost: in social cohesion, in growing inequality, in the demise of a living wage, in opportunity denied, in breakdown of community, in moral values, in the viability of democracy, and even in the sustainability of life on this planet. Maybe we need to find another way to make money. The old fashioned way. Co-Production does that. It honors contribution as work.

8. Superior enforceability

Time Dollars do not create an enforceable legal obligation. IRS rulings consistently single out the absence of a legal right to enforce a Time Dollar obligation as the basis for the tax-exempt rulings that Time Dollar programs have secured.[17] Time Dollars are only backed by a promise, by trust, and by a moral principle of reciprocity. The IRS has no interest in mere moral commitments. But ask yourself one question: Which would you rather rely on, a lawsuit or a moral commitment, if what you really needed and wanted was companionship and caring? "You pays your money and you takes your choice."

9. All purpose measure of value

Money emphasizes and exaggerates relative worth. A currency that treats all human time as equal makes a very different statement about value. The value of helping another is not measured by market wage; and one's own value, as a human being, is not measured by marketable skills. We have always known that but, in a world dominated by money, such assertions sound fuzzy, moralistic and rhetorical when confronted with the demand, Show me the money.

Broken Tablets

Time Dollars enable us to develop an awareness of the extent to which money distorts our calculations as to what is possible. It distorts our view of what people can do, what people are willing to do, whom you can trust, what motivates people, what human nature is—and what it is possible for us to achieve. The extent to which artificial boundaries are built into money—into its genetic structure—becomes clear when we alter the currency we use. We find that a different world and a different set of possibilities emerge.

Time Dollars are practical—like Frequent Flyer miles or discounts for being a member of Triple-A or AARP. They generate numbers. The exchanges that take place are just as real as an exchange driven by money or barter. That supplies critical, empirical "proof" to the assertion made by Co-Production that the non-market economy is a real economy, and that work done in the non-market economy can confer power in either economy, market or non-market.

At a minimum, Time Dollars actually function as a tax-exempt barter currency to generate exchanges in the non-market economy. They make it possible to go beyond charity and beyond volunteering. They confer a reward: access to surplus goods secured as a charitable donation from the market economy without undermining market price. As the examples in this book confirm, Time Dollars are already being used to access food, clothing, computers, legal services, health care services, housing, rides to the store, and even enrollment in college courses.

If nothing else, Time Dollars take Co-Production out of the realm of speculation and theory. They demonstrate that we can create a medium of exchange that makes Co-Production practical as a win-win strategy that taps assets and generates productivity beyond that which money and market have been able to do. From that point of view, they are simply a new tool, available as a kind of "appropriate technology" to enable the non-market economy to compete for a larger share of energy, time and talent and to enlist the capacity of those whom the market devalues or excludes.

They are more than a practical tool, however. We worship money. Our vision—intellectual, emotional, moral—our perception of what we call reality has been distorted by examining everything through the lens of money. For want of an alternative way of measuring and counting, we have become unaware of the appalling price we pay for exclusive reliance on that measuring rod. The Golden Calf returns.

When Moses came down from Sinai the first time, he brought with him a set of tablets. The second commandment was: Thou shall have no other gods before Me. Upon finding his people worshiping a Golden Calf, he smashed the tablets—only to be given a second set.

One set of broken tablets is enough. Time Dollars say: Reject the Golden Calf. We have each other.

Co-Production says: Amen.

Chapter 9

Mastering the Rules that Govern the Rules for Changing the Rules

In law, there are rules. There are rules for changing the rules, for enacting laws and promulgating regulations. There are still other rules that govern the rules for changing the rules. The written or unwritten Constitution of a nation supplies those rules. And finally, there are rules for changing the Constitution itself, for amending the Constitution, for changing the entire law-making structure of a society. Those ultimate rules include procedures for amending themselves, for reshaping the rules that shape the rules that determine how the rules we live by are made.

It is clear that in different spheres of human activity, our species has moved systematically to gain control over that ultimate set of rules: the rules that determine the rules for changing the rules.

In genetic engineering, we see that happening. The timetable keeps accelerating. In short order, scientists will have been able to locate and plot all the important genes in the human genome. It is clear that as we learn to manipulate the human genetic code, we gain an unprecedented power over the rules that govern the rules: for healing, for genetically altering human beings, for taking control of evolution itself.

Much the same process is unfolding in the realm of knowledge and information technology. We have watched as all human activity and knowledge have been reduced by binary code to combinations of zero and one, how an operating system shapes and controls the manipulation of that code. And we have seen a battle emerge for control and ownership of the platform, the basic linguistic system for transmitting all knowledge and information.

Early in the debate over the copyright implications of Windows, one protagonist declared, “How can anyone claim ownership of the alphabet, the basic building block of language, of communication?" But even that analogy falls short of what is really at stake: the rules for determining what alphabet is used by our species—and the rules for changing the alphabet and the rules that govern the rules for changing the alphabet.

When it comes to language, we control the rules that govern the rules for changing the rules. Actually it is not clear whether we control them or they control us. But we certainly have a sense of how dramatically that level of elemental control has altered our lives and transformed our world.

The creation of new forms of money—whether it is Time Dollars or e-commerce—represents a similar and equally fundamental form of control over the rules that govern the rules for changing the rules. The sphere is not biology or information; the sphere is all human interaction, all exchange transactions.

Money in all its forms, tangible or digital, is simply a medium of exchange. The money we are most familiar with has built into it characteristics that reward one aspect of our nature: the competitive, acquisitive aspect. Time Dollars are a currency designed to reward the other aspect of our nature: the cooperative, caring, altruistic aspect. Some contend that this social, cooperative aspect is genetically encoded in all of us. Some contend that it is gender-based or at least gender linked. Regardless, it is a fundamental part of our nature—and it clearly has value for our survival as a species.

Co-Production is really a call for restoring balance—balance between the two economies, market and non-market; balance between the two sides of our nature, competitive and cooperative. Time Dollars are simply a tool for restoring that balance. They are doubtless the first, primitive generation, an attempt to manipulate the characteristics of money in a way that shapes the dynamics that flow from those characteristics.

Even at this first, primitive stage, this genetic engineering of money has demonstrated that we can exercise a new control over the rules governing the rules in human interaction. We already know that this new medium of exchange can help us rebuild the family, transform our neighborhoods into community, and redefine work so as to value a much broader range of social contribution.

This book invites you to expand the frontier of knowledge. It holds open the possibility that we can gain a new level of control over the terms of human interaction and human exchange by finding a way to reward our best and noblest impulses: caring, loving, learning, sharing, celebrating, valuing. At stake is control over the rules that govern the rules for all human interaction.

III.

Co-Production:

The Core Values

Chapter 10

The Parable of the Squares and the Blobs

David Matthews, President of the Kettering Foundation, once disclosed a dilemma that had preoccupied a group of foundation executives for several years. They would come together regularly to ponder a phenomenon they had all noted: Every time foundations picked a problem to target, the problem seemed to get worse!

Over time, the group developed its own analysis of what they saw happening. They labeled the institutions and organizations that they funded *Squares*. Hospitals, universities, community service organizations, volunteer organizations were all "Squares."

They labeled the people in community who clustered informally into affinity groups and grass roots associations *Blobs*. The Blobs seemed to have the energy, the vitality, the contacts, the gossip, the networks that were needed to deal with the problems. But the money invariably went to the Squares because the Squares knew how to manage it, account for it, spend it. They had the accountants, the bookkeeping, that tax-exemptions, the equipment, the institutional capacity, the expertise and the presumptive competence.

The problem was that no matter how much the Squares promised to reach out in the community and get at the root causes of the problems, the Squares never got there. They really weren't able to get to where the problems were or mobilize the energy of the community. A gulf separated the Squares from the Blobs.

The logical response of the foundations was to try to create a kind of neutral buffer zone to bridge that gulf. So they started funding Partnerships and Collaboratives. In order to get the grants, foundations insisted that the Squares partner with the Blobs. But regardless of the formal partnerships, the Squares kept the money and dominated the scene—throwing a few crumbs to the Blobs, putting a few representatives on the Board, hiring some "natives" as outreach workers. But the partnership approach didn't seem to pay off as a way to capture the energy of the Blobs.

The next step was an obvious one: Give at least some of the money directly to the Blobs to solve the problem. But when that was attempted in the form of grants and sub-contracts, something strange occurred: The Blobs were required to turn into little Squares in order to get the money and account for it. That required a major investment in training and technical assistance. Grass roots groups were taught to develop mission statements and strategic plans in order to remain "true" to mission. Neighborhood leaders were trained in how to be Board members, how to conduct "proper" meetings, how to write and amend by-laws, and what their responsibilities were as Board members. They needed a corporate charter, by-laws, a tax-exempt status, and an adequate accounting system. By the time those groups and those leaders jumped through all those hoops, they had ceased to be Blobs. Handling all the reporting requirements and other accountability demands meant there was no time or energy to be what they had been.

Now Kettering and other foundations are funding research on neighborhood transformation and promoting new forms of community dialog. They are trying to find ways to reach into community more effectively, to bridge that gap, how to "create even stronger ties to rank-and-file citizens." Official foundation pronouncements declare they "must embrace fundamentally new notions of what it means to *work with* communities." They just can't figure out how to do that.

Resolving the Square/Blob Impasse

The Square/Blob Impasse encountered by foundations has a familiar ring. It restates the search for Factor X. And Factor X is Co-Production. The Blobs have something the Squares need if the Squares are to make effective use of their specialized expertise and their institutional resources. But the whole reason for tapping it is to create a better world for both Squares and Blobs. That means a partnership, a joint undertaking that puts the Blob world on a par with the Square world. The question is: How to do that?

Why not enable the Blobs to earn dollars for the Blob Association by being Blobs and doing what only Blobs can do—without turning them into Squares? Time Dollars supply one way to do that. Blobs could earn Time Dollars being Blobs. For every hundred or thousand Time Dollars that Blobs earned helping each other, the Association could gain access to a certain percentage of a grant. Those Time Dollars could be treated as earning the actual dollars by satisfying an "in-kind" match requirement.

We also can borrow from something that is familiar to all of us: the walkathon, in which people walk miles to earn money for a cause. To be sure, this is just a one-time event. It mobilizes people by enabling them to make a contribution by rewarding them for what they can do: walk. The same principle applies to Blobs. For every hour of work spent as a contributing Blob, an agreed-upon number of dollars would flow into the Blob Association's bank account. Time Dollars provide an easy way to do that, because they value what Blobs can do without requiring the Blob to stop being a Blob and without getting into issues of minimum wage.

If funders really value what Blobs can do, they don't have to give them a grant and turn them into accountants. If they earn the Time Dollars by being Blobs, it's like a walkathon. Walkers do not receive minimum wage. The purpose is to create a way in which people can raise money for a cause or an organization. You start with what people can do, not what they can't do. Walkathons do not require walkers to be jumpers or sprinters. It's enough that they can do what they do.

As the Blobs generate the funding by being Blobs, they collectively can determine what to do with the money they have earned for their organization, without having to turn into little Squares. Time Dollars enable Blobs to function as earners in their own right. The Blob Association can then have the choice of buying what it needs from the Squares.

Framework, Process, and Four Core Values

Co-Production turns out to provide a resolution to the Square/Blob Impasse. But look at what that tells us about Co-Production. It is more than a word.

It is a framework, a process, and a set of core values that define outcomes.

As a framework, Co-Production simply embraces two worlds: market and non-market that declares: the earth is round; the economy includes all productive activity, regardless of sphere. As a process, Co-Production involves a transformation that bridges, and links two now-separate worlds. That process can be collaborative or it can inform a dialectic that yields a new synthesis. But above all, it means persistence coupled with a willingness to hear the bad news as well as the good, to avoid believing one's own propaganda. Each world comes with its own perspective, its own definition of reality; each will need to learn how to see through each other's eyes, walk in each others footsteps. Sometimes, the process is painless, the transition fluid; sometimes, not. But failure is not an option.

As a set of *principles*, Co-Production is comprised of four core values. We will start with an affirmative statement of each, knowing that the real crucible comes when each core value is reframed from a social justice perspective. Part III of this of the book explores each of those core values:

- **The asset perspective means more than simply inventorying Blob assets. It means those assets must be deployed in actual transactions, in exchanges based on mutuality.**
- **Redefining work means acknowledging, recording and compensating the full range of socially useful contributions made by Blobs. It means rethinking how one defines the labor force and how one defines work.**
- **Reciprocity means that the Squares must stop congratulating themselves for their unilateral acts of charity, of service, of largesse. Walking the talk means going the next step. It means embedding reciprocity in all transactions as a way of saying and meaning "We need each other."**
- **Social capital means more than a buzz word, more than invoking the mantra: It takes a village to raise a child. It means being willing to ask: what does it take to build, to restore, to sustain that village? It means building an infrastructure of trust and reciprocity and engagement, often in situations where distrust and alienation hold sway.**

The following chapters explore each Core Value in turn.

Chapter 11 Core Value One: An Asset Perspective

People are assets. It's about time we valued them for what they can do.

We—and particularly, helping professionals—are used to asking what we can do to help, how we can be useful. If that is our only question, it means we are starting from the wrong perspective, the perspective of need, of deficiency. After all, that's what we know how to do. We need to be needed.

Why does it matter whether we call the glass half empty or half full? What is wrong with pre-occupation with the empty half? Fixation on what we don't have, on how we would like others to be, on variables beyond our control doesn't solve anything. All too often, it is a way to avoid accountability for doing what one can with what one has.

There is a sign posted at gasoline pumps: Do not top off. Do not keep trying to fill the tank to the brim. It wastes a precious resource. Worse, it can create hazardous, inflammable conditions. A deficit perspective can prove incendiary. An asset perspective says: Maybe we already have enough to get where we are going.

Co-Production asserts that real change takes place when we focus less on our own need to be needed and more on outcomes that can only be secured by enlisting those we are trying to help.

When we shift to an Asset Perspective, some basic principles come into play.

Principle 1. People are assets.

Principle 2. There is always a way to use an asset.

Principle 3. We have enough if we use what we have.

Principle 4. Use it or lose it.

Principle 5. Lamenting that a glass is half empty will not fill it.

Principle 6. Don't build on quicksand.

Principle 7. Counting what people do makes people count.

Principle 8. People as assets require a new accounting system.

The Basic Principles

Principle 1. People Are Assets.

We all know how to do more than others know we can do. We may have resumes. But how much does a resume really tell about all that a person can do? Does it tell anyone that a person knows how to cook scrambled eggs without burning them, can wire a lamp, is really good at finding sales, can charm information out of anyone on the telephone, or can usually figure out where something is in the computer that no one else can find?

Now turn that around. If others know so little about us, how much do you really think we know about others—what they like to do or know how to do? It's a version of *Don't Ask, Don't Tell:* If we don't ask, they don't tell. And if we don't ask in the right way, we still won't know.

Last summer, I met with a group of teenagers who were going to serve on a Time Dollar Youth Court, earning Time Dollars. I was trying to explain to them how Time Dollars worked:

"Tell me what skills you have." Blank stares and glazed eyes from a dozen teenagers.

"Let's start all over again. How many of you have a younger brother or sister? How many of you have a grandparent who is still alive? Let's see hands." Hands went up all around the room. I actually got eye contact.

"Name just one thing you've done for your mom or dad, grandmother or grandfather, any brother or sister. Just one thing."

Sheet after sheet of newsprint got tacked up with masking tape. The list of what these kids could do covered two walls: painting and dry wall, fixing cars, teaching boxing and karate, speaking Spanish, woodwork, shooting baskets left- and right-handed, cooking all kinds of special dishes, shopping, doing hair and fancy nails, sewing, babysitting, helping with homework, reading Bible stories, fixing bikes.

Principle 2. There Is Always a Way.

There is always a way to use an asset. Using what we have takes being proactive. I am a member of a sub-species of humans that loves to go to hardware stores—when there is something to fix, and when there is nothing to fix. More often than not, there is nothing that does exactly what we want. We have to improvise—and that's a challenge that turns us on, that grabs us and doesn't let go. So we are constantly scanning the shelves to see if there is something we can put together with something else in a way that isn't obvious but that our instincts tell us will work. We are always making a mental inventory of what is out there, because we know, sooner or later, we will find a use for it. And even if no one else knows how clever we are, we will know.

The same principle applies to human beings. It isn't always obvious. We have to find new ways, or very old ways, of putting people to use doing things for each other. It takes ingenuity and creativity, but it's something we can do if we are determined.

Marion Kane, President of the Maine Community Foundation, tells a story about a remarkable woman in a small town in southern Georgia and a client named Joe. This woman worked for an agency charged with serving mentally retarded persons. The agency decided it was too focused on deficiencies and that it needed to think about the gifts, contributions, and capacities of the people who were its charges. So this woman began spending time with the people the agency had once called "clients" to see if she could understand what gifts they had to offer. In Marion's words:

> *At age 29, Joe had no place in society. Every day he went home from the agency to a pig farm, where he did two things: he fed the pigs twice a day, and he sat in the living room and listened to the radio. (He couldn't see to watch television.)*
>
> *After four days at Joe's house, the woman still hadn't found his gift. But on the fifth day, she realized what his gift was. He listens to the radio.*
>
> *She found out that three people in town spend their time listening to the radio and get paid for it: the sheriff's office, the police department, and the civil defense office. She picked the civil defense office and told the dispatcher, "I have somebody here who likes to listen to the radio as much as you do. I'd like to introduce you to him." And so she introduced Joe to the dispatcher, and they put a chair on the other side of the desk where from then on, Joe sat every day, listening to the radio.*
>
> *That little house is also the neighborhood community center. Everybody came to know Joe, and he became a part of the neighborhood.*
>
> *Joe began to go downtown at noon to eat at the diner. One day, the owner of the diner said, "Hey Joe, what's happening?" Joe looked at him and said, "The Smith house over in Boonesville burned down this morning. And out on Route 90 at that turnoff where you can have picnics, there was a drug bust. And Mr. Schiller over in Athens had a heart attack."*

> *Everybody in the diner stopped talking and looked around at Joe. They couldn't believe it. They realized that Joe knew the answer to the question, "What's happening?" because he listened to the radio all morning.*

Marion visited the Georgia town and the woman who introduced Joe's gift of listening to the radio in the community. She continues,

> *I saw an incredible thing there. All day, everyone who ran into Joe came over to him to ask what was happening. And I realized that I was in the only town in the United States that now has a town crier!*
>
> *The woman told me she was planning to take Joe over to the newspaper editor. It had occurred to her that in this little town with a little newspaper and one editor, the editor couldn't possibly know all of "what's happening." But by noon, Joe knew. And if Joe could go over and talk to the editor every noon, the grasp, the breadth, the knowledge of the newspaper and what it could report would expand overnight.*

Joe is now a stringer for the local gazette. He contributes in many ways to the community because somebody knew that community is about capacities, contributions, and hospitalities—not about deficiencies, needs, and services.

The world doesn't always say, "You're exactly what I need"—any more than pieces in a hardware store jump up and say, "Take me and put me together with something over there." Making use of human assets is not a neutral, objective process. It is contextual, and it is guided by purpose, by a determination to count assets. Mechanical methods of making an asset inventory often omit real strengths. In England, for instance, the Fairshares Program listed assets that are often overlooked: on call at unsocial hours, spreading news, providing local knowledge, organizing social events, surfing the net, and plant watering.

An asset perspective means finding ways for people who don't think they have skills to discover their own strengths. As one woman in Tacoma, Washington, told me: "I didn't know how much I knew until I was helping someone who didn't know what I know." Assets don't fit normal categories. They come out the way they come out. We learn about them by putting them to use.

Principle 3. We Have Enough—If We Use What We Have.

In 1996, several newspapers ran front-page coverage of the story of one senior citizen whose adult child had placed him in a wheel chair, rolled him to some race track, and then disappeared, abandoning him. But how different is this action from the fate to which elderly people regularly find themselves relegated?

In September 1999, *The New York Times* reported a new survey that found that older adults have a difficult time finding meaningful volunteer opportunities and that they feel that their skills are not valued by organizations.

> *"People are tired of stuffing envelopes," Mr Freedman [president of Civic Ventures, a nonprofit organization in California dedicated to expanding the social contribution of older Americans] said, adding that his own grandmother, a retired store manager, was frustrated by the only volunteer job she could find, pushing a gift cart in a Philadelphia hospital.* [18]

Take a minute to consider what we don't use. According to best estimates, when one counts the number of people who have lived to be over age sixty since the beginning of recorded history, slightly over half of them are alive *right now*. This is the greatest reserve of knowledge, experience, caring time, and untapped energy in the history of the world.

Those over sixty have lived through more than a half-century of change—change that has accelerated at an unprecedented rate throughout their lives. Persons we label "elderly" have lived through at least one World War; the Cold War; manned space flight; the discovery of DNA, the genetic Rosetta stone; the Civil Rights, Environmental, and Feminist Movements; the fall of the Berlin Wall; the end of Apartheid; and the first three decades of the Information Age.

Is it so difficult to conceive of the possibility that such a being might be able to make some insightful contribution to the deliberative processes needed to shape the future?

We all want our children to cherish certain values, to experience love and patience and understanding. We want our nation to learn from the past, to avoid repeating mistakes. Is it inconceivable that memory might be an asset in an Information Age, or experience an asset in a Knowledge Age?

It takes a deficit mentality to turn such an asset into a problem of catastrophic proportions with dire fiscal implications. The message we implicitly send to the elderly is that their primary responsibility is to die cheaply without bankrupting the country by running up Medicare and Medicaid costs. That mentality perceives seniors as a liability—except to the extent they have accessible cash and represent a potentially expanding market niche. Yet a recent economic study computed that these seniors whom we classify as "not in the labor force" are making life-giving contributions of care for others. The study made a conservative estimate of the value of that work:

> *This study explores the current market value of the care provided by unpaid family members and friends to ill and disabled adults. Using large national data sets, we estimate that the national economic value of informal care giving was $196 billion in 1997. This figure dwarfs national spending for formal home health care ($32 billion) and nursing home care ($83 billion).* [19]

In our post-industrial society, we proclaim that brain power is more important than muscle power. Our elders may lack muscle power, physical agility, and dexterity. But when it comes to cumulative wisdom and insight based upon having seen repetitious patterns of human folly and human courage, they represent a national treasure and a triumph of the species over brute force and the vicissitudes of nature.

We claim to prize democracy. But we are just too busy to make democracy work, so we accept low voter turnout, and we let special interest groups control the political process and block campaign finance reform. Our elders may be the only ones with the personal time necessary to discharge the full responsibilities of citizenship.

I recently attended a meeting on neighborhood revitalization in Washington, D.C. The Mayor had issued a call to begin a neighborhood-based process that would lead to a summit—and he had made a public commitment to shape his budget requests in response to that process. Chairing the meeting were two young men, hired through a contract to organize neighborhoods and manage the meetings. My eyeball census told me that with the exception of those two at the head table, there was no one in the room under sixty. Apparently no one else had the time to care. And no one else was willing to give this new mayor the benefit of the doubt and try to make the process work, one more time.

There was plenty of cynicism, backed by ample experience with past administrations. But there was also an incorrigible optimism, edged by realism. One gentleman stood up, after listening to the grumbling and objections, and told the group: "This process is going to move forward; this train is on the tracks and moving. Either we get on—or we lose the ability to chart its course." Later I asked him what he did apart from attending community meetings. He handed me a business card that read, Arendt-Fox. In Washington, that is a known name, one of the powerhouse law firms for which the city is famous. This grey-haired anonymous community person had retired but still retained an office. In "retirement," he was determined to focus his energy on making Washington, D.C., a liveable city.

At the 1998 White House Conference on Aging, Arthur Fleming declared, "Older persons need a dream as well as a memory." What dream would be worthy of pursuit as we advance in years?

"I am what survives of me" was the way Erik Erikson framed it. A foster grandmother, helping others raise their children, said it her way: "I need to give what it is I have to give, and love is what I have to give."

We have enough. We need to use what we have.

Principle 4. Use It or Lose It.

At the end of one extended "leadership training" program that had focused on subjects such as budgeting practices and Robert's Rules of Order, one elderly gentleman raised his hand. For him, the pivotal question of the entire program turned on the answer to one simple question: *Who is Robert?*

Given the talents involved in genuine community leadership, how much sense does it take to invest large amounts of resources trying to turn grassroots people into parliamentarians or accountants? Even if we assume that capacity to run a meeting, develop an agenda, and handle disputes is important, in their absence these "deficiencies" are often used as the basis for deferring implementation of a program. "Training" can be used to postpone any shift in governance power until the money is virtually all gone. Technical assistance can involve a fixation on what people can't do and don't know how to do—rather than building on what they can do immediately.

Much of technical assistance and training is justified as "teaching a person to fish." It represents an investment in capacity building. An asset perspective does not dispute that training and knowledge are valuable. It does, however, question whether there is an implicit devaluing of what people can already do, and an unnecessary delay in getting on with critical objectives.

When the first Time Dollar programs were started, many administrators postponed any actual service until a training program could be developed to teach Time Dollar members how to help elderly persons and how to recognize certain conditions. Consistently, the training sessions resulted in a loss of 50 percent or more of those who wanted to participate. When questioned, people said: they had lived a long life; and didn't need to be put on hold to learn how to give companionship to another human being.

After that pattern emerged again and again, there was a shift, first initiated in Miami by Ana Miyares. Apart from an initial orientation session, Ana decided to match people offering to help with people needing help within 72 hours of the time they signed up. This generated some expressions of shock and dismay from consultants, framed in terms of quality control and concern for the elderly person being helped. Ana converted the "training" into pot luck lunches with speakers — but more often than not, the sessions turned into mutual brainstorming about how to solve particular problems and needs and how to swap knowledge about resources.

Community folks have grave reservations about the so-called technical assistance they get. They are polite; they go through the motions; they try to learn Robert's Rules. But privately, they wonder about whether those who are giving the training could have survived the situations with which they have had to cope.

Valuing people as they are means no longer trying to turn seasoned community activists into a mirror image of oneself. The hard work is figuring out how to tap what they know how to do, how to value them as they are, how to fill in for what they don't know, and how to make do with what they have.

Principle 5. Lamenting That a Glass Is Half Empty Will Not Fill It.

All over the country, Children's Protective Service agencies are putting more and more children in foster care as the volume of cases involving neglect and abuse grows. In a meeting with one of those agencies, I took the risk of proposing that the families they were helping could provide help to other families and earn Time Dollars. The initial reaction was, *We couldn't ask one of those families to earn Time Dollars helping someone else; they are dysfunctional!* I found myself responding,

> *I was a dysfunctional parent. My kids knew all my hot buttons—and they knew just when and how to press them to set me off. But I was brilliant with other people's kids. I don't know any dysfunctional family that can't cook a meal for some other dysfunctional family. Or if they can't do that, they can do something: give them a ride, escort some senior to church. Everyone can do something. It all depends on how commodious the circle is in which you can exhibit functionality. Draw it small enough and we are all dysfunctional; draw it expansively, and nearly everybody becomes functional.*

People go into the helping professions because they want to help others. But that means they are looking at people through one very narrow lens: "Do you have a need that I can help to fill?" That's not evil. But it is the equivalent of always looking at the empty part of the glass.

As an attorney, I am a helping professional. My job is to ask, "Do you have a problem that I can help you with?" We all get satisfaction out of that. We also get money, because that's what we are paid to do. And that has consequences. As John McKnight points out, behind the mask of love is economic need, our own economic need. In fact, the more we can make people feel incomplete, in need, lacking and deficient, the more we can sell to them. If you want to make sales, creating dependency is good business. Drug dealers know that. Madison Avenue knows that. Helping professionals know that. If we want to fulfill our own commitment to make a difference in the lives of others, we need to find a way to use our expertise to unleash the capacity of the person we are helping.

Principle 6. Don't Build on Quicksand.

A focus on present capacity supplies a foundation; a focus on incapacity builds on quicksand. Clients and communities have decades of experience in being labeled "at risk," disadvantaged, target populations, urban renewal sites. Sometimes the language gets more positive: model cities, empowerment zones, collaboratives, neighborhood transformation, community-building, or Hope I, II, III, IV, V, VI, *ad infinitem.* But the bottom line is always the same: you get resources by presenting your needs. You learn how to package them creatively for different audiences.

The typical Needs Assessment or Problem Statement (the type required by foundations) finds what one might expect: unemployment, truancy, broken families, gangs, slum housing, illiteracy, crime, child abuse, graffiti, mental disability, lead poisoning, drop-outs, and an impossibly heavy caseload for some beleaguered helping professional. Focusing on needs or problems means focusing on deficiencies rather than strengths, resources, and capacities. The deficit perspective prevails as the default mode of defining reality. It is fashionable to pay lip service to assets—but without internalizing how wrong-headed a deficit perspective can be or doing the hard work of figuring out how a true asset perspective would be operationalized.

Classifying a community or a family in terms of needs and problems can define a problem too narrowly or isolate one aspect of it, and leads to fragmentation. This impedes an appreciation of the interconnectedness of problems and the interconnectedness of solutions. In that way, it short-circuits a number of problem-solving options. Each individual problem is likely to be "owned" by an agency or a profession. The problems may be symptoms of a more fundamental disenfranchisement or of widespread system malfunction. A piecemeal response may blind one to the need for collective action or systemic change.

That is just the beginning. Funding invariably seems to go to professionals and agencies who "own" the problem, define the "proper" intervention, and therefore own the resources needed for the solution. In order to secure resources, leaders demonstrate leadership by defining their communities in terms of problems and needs and by characterizing constituents in terms of deficiency and incapacity. A needs assessment shifts power to the professionals and away from neighbor-to-neighbor relationships. Key survival relationships become those controlled by experts—the social worker, health provider, funder. Improvement is dangerous; it can bring about a loss of funding. Continued funding depends on a problem getting worse, becoming more intractable.

Other destructive consequences follow. A needs assessment tends to focus all funding on survival rather than capacity building. Once on that treadmill, it is almost impossible to get off; all energy is invested in simply staying where one is.

Less obvious but equally destructive is the fact that no matter how accurate it is, a needs analysis actually impairs accurate assessment and diagnosis of a problem because needs are normally defined in terms of individuals, or at most, families. A needs analysis overlooks the important role of groups, associations, and organizations. As a result, real developmental activity and authentic capacity-building are omitted, defined out of the plan. With the entire focus on individuals or families, success in meeting a need translates into Exodus—moving to a better place—rather than building that community and transforming it into a place to live and contribute.

If all we do is look for needs and deficiencies, we will never break even. A zillion half-empty glasses will not get us there. We won't make up the losses on volume.

There is a singularly useful definition of insanity, attributed to Einstein: *Insanity is doing the same thing over and over again, and each time, hoping for a different result.*

The Social Justice perspective on Assets declares: *Stop the insanity. Enough is enough. No more throw-away people.*

When one takes that mandate seriously, all of these principles come into play. And the impossible starts to happen.

Principle 7. Counting Counts.

We live in a world where nothing exists without numbers. If you can't count it, if you don't record it, then it never happened.

The Scottish have a saying: "You don't make sheep any fatter by weighing them." But that doesn't seem to be the case with Time Dollars. Basically, Time Dollars just count the hours people put in. But even when people don't spend the Time Dollars they earn, something else happens. Observers note that turnover in Time Dollar programs is far lower than in volunteer programs. It was less than 10 percent in all of the original programs, and less than 3 percent in the largest Miami-based program. The only thing we did differently was to count. And people earned the Time Dollars without stopping whatever volunteering they were already doing.

These sheep got fatter when they were weighed. The act of measurement, of inquiry, had somehow altered what we were studying. How could that be?

Many people have had the experience of talking to someone who suddenly grabs a pad and starts writing. This gives one the feeling that what one is saying is really valued—this person is taking it down because they are going to use it. Recording something makes a difference. It confers value. It invests an act or a statement with a degree of permanence. It means that what is learned or done will not be forgotten. It just might shape the future.

The philosopher-scientist Werner Heisenberg articulated an insight known as the Complementarity Principle. It asserts that measurement is not neutral and external. The scientist, in making measurements, interacts with the observed object and thus causes it to be revealed not as it is in itself but as a function of measurement. Applied to assets, Heisenberg's principle means that the act of measuring alters the nature of what is measured. We had actually been making the sheep fatter by measuring them. Measurement and recording are not neutral actions. Counting what people do is a way of valuing what they do. The act of measuring can alter reality.

Principle 8. People as assets require a new accounting system.

An asset perspective means enabling human beings for whom the market economy has no use to redefine themselves as contributors. That requires more than a static inventory. It requires a dynamic information system constantly updated by live transactions.

An asset defines itself and realizes itself in the context of a transaction, in the act of helping another, meeting a need, filling a void. Time Dollar programs utilize computer software that lists members' skills and capacities. When a member needs help, a call is made to the Time Dollar coordinator who checks to see who can provide the service at the time requested. The coordinator checks with the member and confirms the match. When the job has been done, the helper is credited and the person helped is debited. Thus Time Dollars provide a first prototype of one such information system about what neighbors can do and what neighbors need. An asset perspective means finding a way to convert latent capacity into kinetic energy.

A user-friendly information and accounting system serves two functions. First, it makes knowledge of what people can do into a shared resource. Information is wealth. Shared information is shared wealth of a new kind. This is one kind of wealth that is not diminished by sharing. In fact, it is increased.

Most of us do not know what our neighbors can do. And we won't ask. But when that information is in a data base, we don't mind phoning up and saying,"Do you have anyone in the computer who could take care of my dog this weekend or help my child with homework?" That's not a question we are going to go up and down the street asking. Nor is it information that would normally be volunteered by a neighbor in casual conversation. Information systems create a new social etiquette that breaks down old barriers. Any e-mail user knows that.

Merely the issuing of Time Dollar bank statements operates as a kind of reward. Those of us who enrolled in frequent flier miles programs know how pleased we are to see the mileage grow, even if we know we may not be able to use those miles for months or even years. And if we can, we keep using the same airline because we like to see the miles accumulate.

The Information Age is teaching us that information stored and constantly updated is a new form of wealth. Every time one visits a Web site, it becomes more valuable to potential advertisers. Each click can increase the value of a site, so much so that free Internet service is now being financed by advertisers counting on volume visits.

Time Dollars do the same for actual visits and phone visiting. Elderplan, the Brooklyn HMO, is finding out how valuable Time Dollars can be. Each visit swells the visitor's bank account at the same time that it promotes health, reduces depression, and brings down the cost of medical care. Time Dollars started with the elderly—because the elderly had time. Funding was available to try to tap that time to reduce the need for costly and often de-humanizing institutionalization of frail elderly persons. In February 1987, *The New York Times* carried this front-page Time Dollar story:

> *Seventy-year-old Ella Amaker and 73-year-old Leona Downs need each other. Mrs. Amaker, a retired government worker, does household chores for Mrs. Down, who can move about only by leaning on a walker. Mrs. Downs, a widow who says she is allergic to nursing homes, is able to drive a car and proudly says she "helps a lot of folks worse off than I am." Her battered eight-year-old sedan is available when Mrs. Amaker has to make a trip to the store.*

These are not one-way transactions; each act embeds the participant in an ongoing relationship. A Time Dollar earned means a new Time Dollar is available to spend. Helping another means you can count on someone to return the help. The help will not necessarily come from the person whom you were helping; in all likelihood, it will be someone else. But each hour given in turn triggers an hour of payback—in an unending loop of transactions. Acts of giving cease to be simply isolated, unilateral transactions. They create a living tableau of that old song, "May the circle be unbroken."

Newsweek magazine picked up that element in a 1990 story entitled, "Credit for Good Deeds":

> *Elsa Martinez sat in her bed in the Cedars Medical Center in Miami last month, her eyes watering, her lower lip drooping. Doctors had told her she had a brain tumor. Still, the 64-year former garment worker smiled when four women entered her room with flowers and reassuring faces. Martinez had earned the right not to die alone.*
>
> *The visitors were not family or longtime friends but participants in an unusual program based on the barter of volunteer services. For several months Martinez had helped other seniors by shopping, cleaning and driving them around—earning along the way 20 hours of "service credits." Last year Martinez broke her leg and began "spending" the credits. Daily visitors, each earning points themselves, came to help her with chores. "When you're sick, they come," she whispered from her hospital bed. Her new friends kept coming until, three weeks ago, Martinez died.*

Elsa Martinez had "pre-paid" for her care and support with care. In this and countless other cases, returning the help just seems to flow naturally. Such stories abound.

Juan, a Time Dollar visitor, rescued José from near-suicidal depression by quietly playing Solitaire so ineptly that José felt obliged first to intervene:

> *No. Not that card. This one. Move the black nine and then you can shift the eight from there, the seven from here and that way you can lay down the red ten you just turned over on the top of the deck.*

After that, José taught Juan poker. The two became a formidable team, regularly making the rounds to senior centers, winning tournaments—but more important, bringing laughter and love.

An asset perspective values just being there. Playing Solitaire badly represents an asset. It takes a dynamic accounting system such as Time Dollars to convert that kind of asset into purchasing power. The bank statements report who helped whom, how, when, and for how long—the moral equivalent of frequent flier miles for a life's journey.

All of us have seen family trees: one generation begets the next. It is much the same, but more so, with lives we have touched. One good deed, dropped in a still pond, sends out ripples of concentric circles: then a second and a third do likewise until, cumulatively, wavelets intersect in lines of moving light.

It is not beyond us to imagine that the day will come when computers can tap multi-generational data banks to produce graphic representations of acts of caring. Transactions would form an intricate tracery, begetting relationships that branch into a kind of extended family tree, or form fractal images of complex symmetry reminiscent of the inner lives of snow crystals.

Chapter 12
Assets: A Social Justice Perspective

> *The secret to the success of the program is its ability to make use of Chicago's most undervalued assets: throw-away kids, throw-away parents, and throw-away computers.* — Calvin Pearce

SCHOOLS AND THROW-AWAY KIDS

At night, Calvin Pearce is an engineer who maintains all systems for the giant communications firm, Ameritech. By day, he runs the Time Dollar Cross-Age Peer Tutoring program in Chicago.

Back in 1995, when Mayor Richard Daley decided to reform public education, he appointed his chief budget officer, Paul Vallas, to be the CEO. Chicago's record at that point was just as bad as Washington, D.C.'s—and Washington, D.C., ranked 51st in the nation.

I asked Paul Vallas how he was going to change that: "You have the same kids, the same teachers, same buildings, same textbooks, same families. What's going to change?"

I had a problem with his solution: bringing in 10,000 tutors from the outside. The research shows that outside tutors help individuals, but they don't necessarily change the system. What Dr. James Comer points out is that kids don't learn because they are afraid of rejection from their peers. It's dangerous to seek the approval of a teacher. You get labeled a nerd—or worse.

So I said, "The research shows that cross-age peer tutoring works—older kids tutoring younger kids. Give me some of the schools in one of your most troubled neighborhoods on the South Side. Give me schools in Englewood."

Englewood had been dubbed a killing zone. We had to make it safe for a kid to be caught learning. The quickest way to do that was to get older kids to reward younger kids with praise for getting right answers. That would make it better than safe to learn; that would buy them approval and (as we found out) actual physical protection.

So Vallas gave us a chance. The first year, five elementary schools in Englewood; the next year, ten, because the first year was so successful. Now it's up to twenty-five schools.

That first year, when I walked through the school cafeteria at Parker, there were 200 kids after school. The principal used a bullhorn to quiet them and then handed out assignments. After that, all one heard was a quiet buzz—lots of kids talking quietly to each other—but no yelling, no running up and down the aisles. Just kids really interested in what they were doing.

I went up to a kid who was simultaneously grading a math quiz, checking the answers on a science test, and testing his tutee on spelling. "How do you do all of that?" I asked, "That's real multi-tasking." He looked at me with a "What's your problem" look, as if to say, "Isn't that the way everyone does it?"

Later on, I sat with a group of older students who had been tutors, to find out what they had learned when helping the younger kids.

The first one said, "I learned that when my tutee asked me a question, I had better write it down, to make sure I answered it."

A second hand went up. "I learned that when I asked my tutee a question, I had to make him repeat the question first before he answered it."

A third didn't wait to be recognized. "I learned some of these kids are hard-headed." And I thought, this one will empathize with his teacher much more now.

A fourth very shy, thin girl in the front row looked up from under long lashes and said hesitantly, "I learned that when my kid did her homework well, I should stick a label on the paper and write, 'You are a smart kid,' so that she could take it home and show it to her mother."

And a fifth kid then poked out his chest and said: "I learned there are words inside of words."

I thought, "That's deep."

Later, the school psychologist told me this was the first time she could remember that the school system had spent any money on just plain "ordinary" kids—not problem kids, just kids trying to hang in there and do what they were told to do.

That had never occurred to me. At the beginning, the principals all asked whether we wanted just the bright students, the honor students, as tutors. Sylvan Learning Centers had been awarded a huge contract, and their approach was to try to take the brightest students and teach them how to tutor. It didn't work, but we didn't know that at the time. We just said "No."

So we got anyone who volunteered and stuck it out. Some had already been classified special education kids, attention deficit kids, problem kids. But everyone flocked to us because we made an offer: We promised a recycled computer to every student who earned 100 Time Dollars in the tutoring program. A lot of the kids who volunteered had already been programmed by the system to believe that they were no rocket scientists. They already knew how the system viewed them: They just didn't have it and would never make it.

The decision to accept all who volunteered proved to be a special blessing—though we can claim no credit for that. When these kids, whose self-esteem was at rock bottom, looked at a homework assignment for a first or second grader, it looked easy to them. And so they figured that if they could do it, anyone could do it. The result was that they imposed high expectations on the first and second graders.

Remember, these are the throw-away kids. Suddenly, they had become educators, teachers—co-producers of learning. And they had something that no teacher, no adult, has. They are peers—and better yet, older peers. Every kid seems to want praise and approval and acceptance from an older kid.

The older kids made it fun to learn. We found out from the principals that attendance actually went up on days when after-school tutoring took place. Kids came to school in order to tutor or be tutored.

The older kids also made it safe to learn, on two levels. Peer acceptance was either automatic or irrelevant. Either peer rejection didn't happen, or it lost its power to prevent learning when something better—an older kid's praise, approval and friendship—could be earned by learning, performing, trying over and over again. Peer tutoring made learning safe in a different way. The bullying and after-school fighting stopped. It was to be expected that tutors wouldn't beat up their tutees; what we hadn't anticipated was that they wouldn't let anyone else do that, either. Learning bought you a protector. Not bad.

Something else was happening, as well. Some of these not-so-special older students started to get good grades for the first time. It takes higher-order skills to teach lower-order skills. So these older kids were not only brushing up on their basics and building a better foundation; they were doing problem solving, practicing communication skills, framing and testing hypotheses as to what it would take to get their tutee to learn. Small wonder that those skills began to show up in their own studies.

Parents were another "throw-away" player. For most of them, coming to school was associated with unpleasant memories—from their own childhood as students, and again as parents being given bad news about their kids. So the rules for participation were written to require a parental contribution. Even after earning 100 Time Dollars, no child could take home a computer until a parent had earned 8 Time Dollars. You had better believe that no parent knew any peace at home—until they had done what they needed to do. But the joy on these parents' faces, and their sense of pride in having helped their child get a computer, spoke volumes—to us and to their kids.

One mother told me that the only time she had been to the school before that was to get bad reports on her child's performance and that until now she had dreaded coming to the school. Now, she had come to help out. She felt enormous pride in seeing her own child helping younger children. And her job had been simply to walk up and down the aisle to see if anyone needed help.

One seventh-grader's mother had died two months before it was time for him to get his computer. He hadn't seen his father for six years, but he was so determined to claim what he had earned that he hunted him down. The father, proud to be reunited with his son, earned the eight Time Dollars needed. He didn't stop there, though; he decided to take over as parent, full time, permanently.

The first year, we lost one kid to a gang shooting. His parents came to us with two requests: Would we be sure to include in the boy's obituary that he was a tutor and was working to earn a computer?—because that's how they felt he would have wanted to be remembered. And would we let his younger brother take over where he left off? They wanted those Time Dollars to be a kind of legacy so that the younger brother could finish earning the computer by building on the Time Dollars his older brother had earned. You never know what's going to hit you hardest, the triumph or the tears. But you know that there's no going back.

The tangible reward itself seemed to have a special poetry to it. We rounded up old computers that no one else wanted from military bases, insurance companies, law firms and wherever we could find them. First it was 286s, then 386s; now it's 486s and 586s. Y2K has turned a stream into a torrent. And as the new 64-bit operating system comes on line, kids will just have to make do with throw-away Pentium MMX's. Those throw-away computers can help bridge the great and growing digital divide between the haves and the have-nots in this new Information Age.

The real reward, though, is not the computer but what earning that computer symbolizes. It says, *You can create for yourself a new future—by helping others*. It means that we have the power to reclaim throw-away kids, throw-away parents, and throw-away computers—and to create a genuine learning community with no limits. That's happening. It's powered by kids and computers and parents helping oversee their kids' functioning as educators. All paid for by the Chicago Public School System, and embraced by teachers and principals who say it's just what they needed, just what was missing.

These kids have changed from passive consumers (or non-consumers) of education into active co-producers. They have reconfigured the world of relevant approval: Their praise and acceptance were sufficiently powerful to overcome fear of peer rejection as a deterrent to learning. Even better, somehow that deterrent never materialized. They had made coming to school, and learning, safe.

When kids, older and younger, became co-producers, they changed the product, the production process, and the production work force. Kids were no longer merely future adults. The focus was not on what they lacked. They were not empty vessels to fill, cracked vessels to repair, or defective merchandise that the public school triage system relegated to the scrap heap. They were producers, earners, learners, mentors. And they had proof. In fact, they had three kinds of proof: a Time Dollar bank statement recording their hours; a computer, a symbol of approval so important and so valid that even their parents had been willing to earn some Time Dollars to get it and bring it home; and one or more new buddies—a tutor they could look up to, or a tutee they could point to whom they had helped and would protect.

In a landmark Supreme Court case, Justice Potter Stewart declared that even if he could not define Obscenity, he knew it when he saw it. The Time Dollar Cross-Age Peer Tutoring program meets that intuitive knowledge standard. We may still be groping for a satisfactory definition of Co-Production, but we know Assets and we know Co-Production when we see them. And we've seen them both in action in Chicago.

Courts and Throw-Away Juveniles

> Question by Time Dollar Youth Court juror: *Where will you be in five years?*
>
> Answer by Respondent: *Dead or locked up.*

In Washington, D.C., over 50 percent of young black males between the ages of 18 and 24 are currently under court jurisdiction, in prison, on parole, or on probation. The so-called juvenile justice system is the feeder, the supply line. The journey starts with a juvenile's first brush with the law and the response he gets. Typically, the prosecutor's office simply "No papers" the case. After all, overburdened prosecutors have more important things to worry about than a mere first offense. They have to deal with hardened criminals, repeat offenders.

But that first "No Paper" sends a message that young people read loud and clear: "You get three freebies before anyone takes you seriously." And every one knows that doesn't mean three illegal acts. It means three times getting caught.

That's how the journey begins. By the third arrest, a formal juvenile proceeding functions more as a rite of passage. For male teenagers it is almost a macho ritual, a test of manhood, not a chance to choose a different path. Without meaning to, the juvenile justice system has been turning young kids into hardened criminals faster than any gang in town.

When I shared that observation in 1995 with D.C. Superior Court's

Chief Judge, Eugene Hamilton, his response was an immediate and direct challenge: "What can you do about it? And how fast can you do it?"

Before I knew it, the Time Dollar Institute was in the business of planning and launching a Youth Court. In April 1996, the D.C. Superior Court authorized a Time Dollar Youth Court as a way to divert non-violent first offenders from entering the juvenile justice system. First offenders come before a jury of their peers—who have the authority to sentence them to community service, restitution, counseling, an apology, and jury duty. Community service includes being an after-school tutor, helping at D.C. Kitchen to feed the homeless, assignments to resident councils in public housing, and placements with churches helping seniors. To date, jury pools have been set up at six public housing complexes, a public school, and a special charter school for youngsters living in shelters and half-way houses. Because jury duty is now a mandatory element of each sentence, there are additional juries composed 100 percent of delinquents serving that portion of their sentence. All jurors earn Time Dollars for jury duty, mentoring, and training, and they can redeem those Time Dollars for a recycled computer. The volume has increased so that now, with between seven and ten hearings a week, the Time Dollar Youth Court is handling more than one-third of the first-time juvenile offenders in the District.

Initially, the question we asked ourselves was this: *How do you turn a youth's first brush with the law into a turning point that heads him or her down a different path?*

We thought of the problem we were tackling as kids who were lost, who had made bad decisions. In retrospect, we should have appreciated that we were not dealing with isolated instances of deviant behavior. Projections based on current trends predict that between 80 and 90 percent of African American males will be under court jurisdiction before they reach the age of 30.[20] That makes so-called "deviant behavior" look like a dominant culture.

When we trained the first group of jurors, a young man who had spent some time in prison summed up his life choices and his preferences in words that still haunt me:

> *"I'd rather be carried by six than judged by twelve."*

Death was less to be feared than the life this young man could envision. Our job was to create a different set of options by creating a new sub-culture—a place where it is safe to say to a peer something as simple as, "Don't do something stupid." We had to teach—or more accurately, we had to enable young people to confront their peers with the obvious: "You knew when you got into that car that there was no way that Mercedes belonged to him."

Or to say out loud, "If you hang out at that corner, you know that sooner or later you're going to get busted. And with that crowd, someone is bound to be carrying some drugs."

Young people think those thoughts. They just don't get reinforced or affirmed for saying them. Indeed, those are things you had better not say if you want peer acceptance. Creating a Youth Court means creating a world where young people are supported and affirmed for saying what they know: "Don't hurt someone. Don't take something that isn't yours. Don't take that kind of risk."

Being part of the Youth Court makes it permissible to say those things. It vests those kids with a responsibility to tell it like it is—to kids whom they have never seen before. That takes more than teaching. It takes creating an environment that supports those values.

Co-Production is not just juvenile justice with the added component of teenagers supplying some consumer labor. There is another element—the consumer perspective that transforms the process. Teenagers know what it is like to be a teenager. They tell us they are tired of having adults tell them, "I was a teenager once myself." They want to be listened to and heard. In the present system, they think of themselves not so much as consumers of justice as consumers of injustice. Consider the following story.

A young man appears before a jury of his peers, charged, according to the police report, with having slashed the tires on his teacher's Lexus because she kept him after school for failing to hand in his homework. The teenage jury hears the young man explain that he knows he did wrong—but he lost control because he had begged the teacher to allow him to leave for ten minutes in order to bring his younger brother and sister safely home across gang territory from a neighboring school. That was his "job." He had promised his mother and father that they could count on him. And being kept in after school put his younger brother and sister in real physical danger. He was beside himself with rage, shame that he had let his parents down, and fear for his brother's and sister's safety.

When the teen jury returned from its deliberations, they charged the Time Dollar staff with a task that they felt was every bit as important as their sentence. They said, "Get him another teacher. A teacher who doesn't understand what this kid was going through has no business being his teacher." They could understand his rage at being forced to let his parents down and put his own brother and sister at risk. But they didn't let him off the hook when they handed down a three part sentence:

1. Write a letter of apology to the teacher and make a good faith payback of at least $30 that you personally earned.

2. Write a letter of apology to your younger brother and sister, explaining to them why, despite the provocation, this was no way to act. They look up to you; you need to put them straight that acting out this way is not right.

3. Hang out a minimum of 20 hours at a boys club over the next month. You need to be a kid and spend some time just being with your own age group.

Co-Production has a very special meaning when in the past, being targeted by remedial social programs meant that you were disrespected, written off, and generally (or specifically) found wanting by society. In that context, Co-Production is more than a contributory role. It amounts to a declaration of principle: *No more throw-away kids. No more throw-away people.*

The Time Dollar Institute learned quickly there is one thing we do not have to teach these kids. They already know how to care for each other, to reach out to each other. At one of the very first Youth Court hearings when we were just beginning to find out what kids could do for kids, we watched the foreperson of the jury—herself a single mom who had been through her own hell—trying to get some answers from a teenager who had taken someone's car to go joyriding at 2 a.m. The kid knew how to stonewall. He sat hunched over, eyes on the floor. You could barely hear his answers.

> *"Yes. I took the car."*
>
> *"Yes. It was 2 in the morning."*
>
> *"Yes. I go to school." (The jury knew that wasn't true.)*
>
> *"I do okay." (Again, not true.)*

Juror frustration was building. The young woman serving as jury foreperson made a direct personal plea: "We are only trying to do what we can do. The only way we can do anything is if you help us. You help us. We can help you. With you just sitting there just chilling, being quiet, you know, it's not going to do nothing."

Finally, his mother broke in. "Basically, Ronald's a good child. Since he can't speak up, I'll speak up for him so you all can help him. We're in an area where there's nothing but drugs. Nothing but killing. No positive role models around there. His oldest brother has been killed and basically Ronnie has been a troubled child because his brother died in front of him."

She went on to explain that since then, Ronnie doesn't trust anyone and won't open up to anyone. The jury went into momentary shock. But not the foreperson. She just took over, and everything changed because of what she had to give and what it cost her to give it.

"I could understand exactly why he get into trouble." Her voice slowed, halted, then deepened as she choked up, "I seen my own mother get killed. It's hard growing up, knowing all these things that you know and experiencing the things that you experience not because its your choice. It's because things are going to happen that are meant to happen." Tears streamed down her face as she added, "We're here to help. But we can't help you if you don't help us."

And then she just lost it. She stopped being a jury foreperson and just reached out to him. Without any authorization whatsoever, without seeking permission, she simply extended a welcome to a very special program that had helped her as a single mother get past drugs and find an inner spiritual strength: "We would be more than happy to have you come there with us if you want to. I'll talk to you about that after this. Just want to wish you the best. God bless you."

These are the kids whom so-called experts are now labeling "super-predators." People don't look these kids in the eyes when they meet them. They walk the other way. But these kids care for each other, even when they are strangers.

Recently, I met with a group who had been serving as jurors. They told me they wanted to know what happened to the kids who came before them, what happened after they pronounced sentence. Then one of them made an offer: "I'd like to be assigned as a buddy to stick with one."

All the others nodded in agreement. They would, too. I asked, "Wouldn't you be afraid? After all, you are the ones who sentenced them." They shook their heads, "No." After all, one explained, "We're jurors." They were absolutely convinced that this status protected them. They were equally clear that their job was somehow incomplete unless they took personal responsibility to do whatever they could for the kids they had sentenced.

The jurors know something about the Co-Production of real justice that the system needs to learn and internalize. They know it ultimately means: No more throw-away kids.

Child Support and Throw-Away Fathers

> *You are observing the only method of rehabilitation that we are sure works. These men are aging. When they reach a certain time in their late twenties or early thirties, they will stop engaging in the behavior that brought them here.* — Statement by prison warden to John McKnight

John McKnight recounts his visit to a correctional facility. There, in one vast room, more than a thousand inmates spent virtually all their time watching TV, playing cards, or just staring into space.

McKnight recognized what he was actually observing: the newest form of an age-old tradition—the tradition of human sacrifice. But unlike our predecessors, we have no excuse, no exonerating rationalization. McKnight points out that others at least had some rationale purporting to justify what they were doing: The Mayans were sacrificing virgins to appease their gods; the Puritans claimed they were burning witches; the Nazis claimed they were practicing ethnic cleansing. But what about us? asks McKnight. We lack the myths, the rationales. Our human sacrifices, he charges, are "creations of a world we made, rather than a world of devils, witches, virgins, and gods."

Throw-away fathers are the latest sacrificial offering, according to a new demonology called welfare reform. Soon, jails and prisons will be populated by a special breed of criminals on the run: deadbeat fathers. On June 8, 1998, *The Washington Post* ran a front-page story explaining that the welfare law "ushered in an unprecedented crackdown on absent dads. Fifty new regulations are locking in across the country, dictating that states track down the fathers of children on welfare; establish legal paternity, follow them from employer to employer and from state to state, and go after them with threats of jail time for those who don't comply."

The welfare law has conscripted the mothers in this massive national man hunt: If the mother wants to receive public assistance, she is required to supply the state with information needed to hunt down the father and extract child support payments from him. It does not pay for a father to surface. Federal law authorizes garnishment of up to 65 percent of wages to pay arrears.

The June 8 *Post* story gives a glowing description of a model program, noting that one participant in this program has nine children, another has eight. The average participant earns $7 an hour.

The predictable reaction for fathers is hide, run, evade. The future governmental response is equally predictable. Vast investments will be made in technology—national fingerprint, voice and retinal identification data bases, backed by extensive and expensive DNA testing. Political rhetoric will stamp these as essential tools for compelling what will euphemistically be dubbed "responsible fatherhood."

Fortunes will be made. Ross Perot made his billions as a "private sector" contractor developing computerized systems for Medicare and Medicaid. There are billions more to be made in this national manhunt to establish paternity and enforce paternal responsibility. It has little to do with promoting authentic parenting.

There is a special irony in characterizing these programs as "responsible fatherhood programs." If the mother is or ever was on welfare, the money doesn't help the mother or the child. It never gets to them. The state grabs it to recoup past expenditures. This is not about parenting. It's about recouping money. All across this country, large sums of federal money are being spent on "responsible fatherhood" programs. *The Washington Post* story boils it down to the real bottom line when it focuses on the accumulated debt represented in one small room in Trenton where twelve men are meeting: "Altogether, this small room probably contains $100,000 in child support debts. They are whittled away in $5- to $50-a-week bites garnished from irregular paychecks earned in telemarketing, operating machines, and working as laborers and clerks."

The *Post* story carries the headline, "Helping Absent Dads Take Responsibility." But the end of the article features a story about one father, Ronald Highsmith, that makes it clear that these efforts are not really about taking responsibility for parenting or raising children: Highsmith is unemployed, has sickle cell anemia and is searching for a job. In the mean time, he says, he offers to help his children's mothers with babysitting.

> *"All three mothers are working, they need help. I am not giving as much money as I want, but I can give time," he said. Unfortunately for Highsmith, his offers of child care don't count as child support.*
>
> *Much of what Highsmith owes stems from arrears he couldn't pay because he was in jail, charged with assault.*
>
> *It never occurred to him that he was expected to notify the family court judge when he was in prison so that his child support payments would be suspended. And so all the time he was incarcerated, he was falling further behind, since federal law prohibits judges from forgiving arrearages retroactively.*

The message sent to biological fathers is simple: You have no function and no value except as a money-making machine for the state welfare agency. We will hold your child and your woman hostage and will take away their means of sustenance if they do not turn you in. Your sole function is to serve as a cash cow if we can catch you or as fugitive from the law if we can't. In this process, the woman and child simply serve as means to an end for the state in its role of collection agency.

Responsible fatherhood programs are important and powerful. But so-called welfare reform can co-opt and subvert "responsible fatherhood" into a new weapon that a recent book has characterized as part of "the war on parents." Within the legal apparatus created by "welfare reform," the state has no interest in the father being a parent. Indentured servitude for past debt suits its needs much better.

What would we do if we really wanted to hold fathers accountable for parenting and for financial support? What would we do if we really wanted to strengthen families, if we wanted to encourage fathers to have contact with their children, if we wanted men to take an active role in their children's upbringing?

If we thought of these fathers as assets, we would ask: What can they do—right now, just as they are? Aren't we overlooking the obvious?

Children want to grow up in neighborhoods where it is safe to play on the sidewalks. Children in the first grade need to have mastered the alphabet and learned how to read enough simple words and sentences to be ready to go on to second grade. Children like recreation and sports and the outdoors. They want to develop their talents in art, dancing, handicrafts, hobbies, and sports, and to learn how to give to others less fortunate through various kinds of community service.

Why can't the fathers be the ones to make these things possible? Why can't they be matched to do what they can do now, just as they are? There are things that the Ronnie Highsmiths of the world can do, right now.

Time Dollars make it possible to provide a form of compensation and monitoring. Nothing prevents us from creating a form of amnesty earned with Time Dollars. Fathers who are making current support payments could earn a moratorium on past debt with Time Dollars earned by helping make neighborhoods safe, enriching child day care, supervising recreation and sports in neighborhood parks and playgrounds, renovating boarded-up crack houses, or teaching the alphabet and basic reading to first graders.

There is no reason why community-based Time Dollar enterprises could not employ these fathers part time in security patrols, tutoring, playgrounds, and licensed child care centers. All across this nation, affluent neighborhoods are hiring private security guards to function as observers and community ambassadors to maintain a vigilant watch that effectively deters crime. Newspapers report that in major urban centers, crime dropped nearly 20 percent when private security guards started patrolling neighborhoods, working out of the police station and communicating with officers by radio.

In New York, Tacoma, Portland, and Washington, D.C., Business Improvement Districts are using resources raised from local businesses to pay for enhanced security. Crime has dropped—and according to private realtors, market value of housing and property has soared. There is no reason why we could not establish neighborhood improvement districts and empower residents to tax themselves in either dollars or Time Dollars. And there is no reason why we could not enable fathers like Ronnie Highsmith to earn a moratorium on back payments by helping make the neighborhoods in which their kids live safer, the schools better, and the child care better, more affordable and available longer hours.

We can anticipate opposition. It may not come out in the open. It is more likely to take refuge behind expressions of concern about licensing, quality control, liability, and lack of credentials. But there is no reason why a Ronald Highsmith could not do what middle class parents are doing all across this country when they coach soccer teams, supervise computer literacy training, volunteer as tutors in grades 1-3, and help Habitat for Humanity build new housing for low income families.

Time Dollars supply a medium of exchange that can enable us to value such contribution, manage the labor supply—and recycle throw-aways and castaways as a national resource. An abundance of fathers is either a problem or an opportunity. Since when did a supply of human beings with the capacity to love, to learn, to play, to build become only a problem, a deficit, a liability?

Chapter 13

Core Value Two: Redefining Work

Wanted: *Parents willing to bear, rear, and educate children for the next generation of Social Security taxpayers, and to carry on the American culture of learning and progress. Quality children preferred. Large commitment of time required. At least one parent must work a double shift and/or sacrifice tenure and upward mobility in the job market. Salary: $0. Pension benefits: $0. Profits and dividends: $0.* —Sylvia Ann Hewlett and Cornel West, The War on Parents

"In any other industry, if you remove a million employees without reducing the job requirements very much, nobody would deny that the industry is woefully shorthanded. If we take a million women out of a million households to work outside the home, and replace them with precious little in child-care services, few babysitters and little more grandparenting, then the parenting "industry" is woefully shorthanded (and television sets and the streets are overworked). This is not an argument for women to stay home to do the parenting but for someone to do more of it." — Amitai Etzioni, An Immodest Agenda

We are operating with a strange definition of work. If it earns money, it is work. If it doesn't earn money, it isn't work.

Elsewhere, this book takes note of the fact that better than 80 percent of all money "earned" has nothing to do with producing goods or services or even purchasing or building capital equipment that in turn will produce goods and services. Depending upon what figures you look at, between 80 and 90 percent of all money made in the world is money making money off of money. We hide that fact behind a euphemism by saying that the financial markets of the world are "putting money to work." Some would say that sounds exactly like what goes on in casinos: putting money to work and hoping it brings a return. But on a global scale, we don't call it gambling. We call it investment.

This chapter is not about that aspect of money. It is about how we need to redefine work to capture and reward the activity that we actually need, day to day, as a society. In a sense, then, it is about work as we used to think of it before money became "delinked" from value.

In "olden days," and still for purposes of political rhetoric and public policy, we define "real work" as work done in the market economy for market wages. We have other meanings of work, of course—when we garden or clean up the house, for instance, we say that was hard work. But we are talking about our aching backs, not about what work means in terms of the so-called "work ethic."

To the extent that work is equated with work in the market at market wages, it is a seriously flawed definition. It sufficed for a long time. It no longer does. We have to understand how defective it is, in order to understand why a redefinition is essential and what principles need to structure and be embodied in that redefinition.

We are used to equating work with employment in the market economy. "Real work" means a "real job" for "real money." We do not appreciate that we have accepted a definition of work that does not do what we need it to do. We have internalized a market definition geared exclusively to employment in the market economy.

Colonizing the Non-Market Economy

We have talked of the two economies. By the market economy, I mean the monetarized economy where goods and services are produced and exchanged for money. Then there is a second economy, the non-market economy where goods and services are produced and exchanged in transactions driven primarily by relationships (family and neighborhood), emotions (love and gratitude) and values (parental, spiritual, or civic obligation) that are non-monetary.

Government, business and professionals (regardless of who pays them) are all part of that first, monetarized world. Accordingly, I shall be using the term *market economy* to include all sectors—public, private, and non-profit—as an all-inclusive term because of the central role that money plays as compensation for labor.

The history of the past century or more is the history of the market economy taking over functions previously performed by the family, kinship groups, neighborhoods, and non-market institutions—because of seemingly superior efficiency. We have contracted out as many of the functions of the informal economy, the non-market economy as we can. McDonald's now provides the meals; Kindercare the day care; public and private schools the education (such as it is); Nintendo the child care and entertainment; Holiday Spa and Gold's Gym the exercise; insurance companies the protection; Medicare and Medicaid the nursing care—and on and on the list goes. The Baby M case involving pregnancy for hire marks the outer limits of entrepreneurial zeal by the market economy.

The superior efficiency of the market turns out either to be illusory—or to have hidden costs. It assumes continued uncompensated contribution and support from the very non-market institutions the market is undermining. Employers assume that employees can manage their private lives and live in neighborhoods where they can raise their children and from which they can commute safety. Government assumes and counts on some minimal degree of participation from families, neighborhoods, communities, and constituencies. All rely on a hidden, largely unacknowledged labor subsidy from home, neighborhood, and community.

Increasingly we are coming to realize that the household economy, the non-market economy cannot keep contracting out functions to the market economy without dangerous repercussions. Everywhere one turns, institutions, organizations, businesses, and enterprises in the market economy are crying out for more and more help from the non-market economy:

- Schools cannot educate without the help of parents.
- Delinquency, drop-out rates and teen pregnancies cannot be checked without help from home and peers.
- Drugs cannot be curtailed without parental involvement or peer support.
- Health requires prevention, maintenance, nutrition, exercise, rest, peer support.
- Crime cannot be prevented without neighborhood watch committees.
- The elderly cannot be cared for without help from family and spouse, from relatives and neighbors.
- Raising children requires more than commercial child care, even if one can afford the best.
- Civic health, local government and the democratic process all rest on effective citizen participation.

The market economy peddles products that purport to be real substitutes for what families, extended families, and communities produce; they are not. At best, they complement and enrich. At worst, they provide the illusion of adequacy—with the real cost for what is lacking emerging later, with a much higher price tag.

If there is money to be made or public funds to be secured, the market economy (including those public institutions it supports through taxes) will keep trying to expropriate functions from the household economy, regardless of consequences. When it fails, the blame is shifted. And when it cannot discharge those functions it has already absorbed, it calls out for a rescue mission from—of all places—the household economy it has virtually cannibalized.

As we contracted out function after function, we left emotional ties, relationships, and values without function, without soil. And such values, it turns out, do not grow hydroponically. People need to be needed by each other in order to reinforce bonds of love and affection. Alvin Toffler summed it up brilliantly in The Third Wave:

> *What remained when all these tasks were exteriorized was the "nuclear family" held together less by the functions its members performed as a unit than by fragile psychological bonds that are all too easily snapped.*

Regaining Lost Turf

To rebuild family and community, we will have to restore functions to home, family, and neighborhood—functions that they may no longer be able to discharge. Many households are now fragile; they lack the critical mass needed to discharge the functions that two parent families and extended families used to. We need to do better. Thumping the table and lecturing on moral responsibility won't magically restore capacity. If we are serious about reducing dependence on the market, it will mean building new forms of extended families, kinship care-networks, and informal support systems that function much as families did in bygone eras. It will take some resources—dollars and human time.

The question is: Where—in which economy—would an investment give greater return? The return from the market economy will be determined by the amount of money available for payment at market prices to social workers, hospitals, schools, child care centers, police officers, lawyers, doctors, and administrators.

The return from the non-market economy will depend upon a combination of factors. Money will be only one determinant. But there will be others that determine how much caring, health, safety, learning, and development is generated. Trust, cohesion, moral obligations, kinship relations, neighborliness, community bonds, tradition, culture, and community standing will all shape the return on investments designed to address social and economic needs.

In the market, you get what you pay for—if all goes well. But that's all you get. But what do you get in a community where neighbors say, "If I have milk and they have cereal, we have breakfast"? What do you get when no police are present when a neighbor separates two children fighting and sends both on their way—or stops a child about to scrawl graffiti on a wall and says, "We don't do that here"?

We have to choose which kind of return we want and where we wish to invest resources. A market definition of "work" specifies one choice. The redefinition of work implicit in Co-Production and the need to secure involvement by beneficiaries of programs and consumers of services points in another direction. It looks to use limited dollar resources to expand non-market involvement, either alone or in new forms of collaboration with the market.

Unfortunately, if all we have is dollars to reward the behavior and generate the growth we want to promote, we can't get from here to there. Money defines value in market terms; money conveys information only about what is being sold to strangers; money promotes certification, specialization, and division of labor. Money equates value with market price. Functions performed in the home—rearing, nurturing, learning, valuing and caring—are simply "unskilled labor."

Unless done for money, the market economy does not consider any of the following to be work: raising children, maintaining a functioning family, taking care of elder parents, being a neighbor, and engaging in the civic activity needed to make democracy work. What do we mean by productive work? Can we permit the market to dictate what we consider to be real work? Alvin Toffler goads the CEO's of Fortune 500 companies into rethinking the meaning of work with this question: "How productive would your work force be—if they were not toilet-trained?"

Redefining work means curbing the unbridled expansionism of the monetarized economy, rebuilding the non-market economy, and establishing new and more equitable partnerships between the two economies.

First, we need to be more specific about the ways in which the definition of "real work" fails.

Work—A Flawed Definition

The current definition of "real work" in terms of work done in the market economy for market wages is flawed. It fails on at least six counts.

1. The definition is incomplete

It excludes the vast range of social contribution made in the non-market economy by families, seniors, children, and neighbors.

After serving nine years as the Chairperson of the New Zealand Parliament's Public Expenditure Committee, Marilyn Waring provides this description of the way in which government economists dismiss what women do:

> *Cathy, a young, middle-class North American housewife, spends her days preparing food, setting the table, serving meals, clearing food and dishes from the table, washing dishes, dressing and diapering her children, disciplining children, taking the children to day-care or to school, disposing of garbage, dusting, gathering clothes for washing, doing the laundry, going to the gas station and the supermarket, repairing household items, ironing, keeping an eye on or playing with the children, making beds, paying bills, caring for pets and plants, putting away toys, books and clothes, sewing or mending or knitting, talking with door-to-door salespeople, answering the telephone, vacuuming, sweeping and washing floors, cutting the grass, weeding, and shoveling snow, cleaning the bathroom and the kitchen, and putting her children to bed. Cathy has to face the fact that she fills her time in a totally unproductive manner. She, too, is economically inactive, and economists record her as unoccupied.*

Raising children is work. Maintaining households and neighborhoods where children and families can live safely is work. Citizen action to fight crime, industrial pollution, degradation of the environment, depletion of the ozone layer is work. Holding officials accountable and being an informed citizen is work. We don't count any of that as work for purposes of national economic policy. Recently, an organization, Redefining Progress, attempted to assign a dollar value to such items. Volunteer work in the 1990's was estimated annually at a value fluctuating between $48 and 58 *billion*. Household work in 1994 was pegged at a total value of $1,233.8 *billion*.

2. The definition devalues real work

No society can afford to buy at market prices the services that the non-market economy has historically provided. If we were to attempt to buy the services at market prices that the family (and primarily the mother) has supplied, it would cost a pretty penny. Efforts to calculate replacement cost put the value of services provided by a homemaker at $44,000. More recently, that estimate was revised using 1980 dollars. Total value equaled $66,000.

Estimates vary about the care that keeps seniors out of nursing homes. Typically, it is estimated that about 80 percent comes from family members, relatives, neighbors, and friends. A recent study evaluating the dollar value of that care sets it at $196 billion, approximately six times what this nation now spends in public or private funds on home maker services.

There will never be enough money for the real work that needs doing: strengthening families, rearing children, enabling the elderly to remain self-sufficient, rebuilding communities, creating opportunity, nurturing a civic culture, engaging citizens in the work of democracy.

3. The definition misleads through omission

A market definition of work disallows, deletes, and denies the public value of work done for one's own family. It characterizes work done at home and in the neighborhood as private goods, devoid of public value and social benefit. Conventional market thinking asserts that raising your child only benefits you.

Arguably, there may have been some validity to that in bygone ages when children helped harvest the crops, or at the beginning of the Industrial Revolution when children could bring home wages if sent off to factories and put to work in coal mines. That logic, if it ever held, does so no longer. But it is convenient to pretend that it still does.

Children are not *private goods*. The economist Nancy Folbre, points out that the public at large has a major stake in the future productivity of children. In a scholarly article bearing the startling title, "Children as Public Goods," Folbre exposes how the market definition of work undervalues the benefit all of us are relying upon: a solvent nation and a viable Social Security system.[21]

Her premise is straightforward: Every citizen of the United States enjoys "significant claims upon the earnings of future working-age adults through Social Security and public debt." It follows, she argues, that if the public at large has a stake in every child's future earnings, then rearing children amounts to the production of "public goods" and that "individuals who devote relatively little time or energy to child-rearing are free-riding on parental labor."

That supplies the basis for a more sweeping challenge to her own profession:

Economists need to analyze the contribution of non-market labor to the development of human capital: as children become increasingly public goods, parenting becomes an increasingly public service.

In short, if we need a future work force that is able to pay for Social Security and Medicare and to pay off the vast public debt that our generation tripled in the 1980s, we had better invest in the parenting needed to produce that earning capacity.

A market definition of work views children only as private goods. We go on pretending that raising children is "your business," not "our business." That children are raised by parents, not by a village, that children will "absorb" what they need from home and from the social environment—and then, that they will automatically be ready to acquire the skills that one day will make them truly "marketable." That is still the way we regard child rearing and family. Maintaining a family and raising children don't exist as real work.

We live with that logic. We are unaware that a trap has been sprung. We are saying, "It is none of my business how you raise your children." We are saying that the development of the entire next generation—its education, its values, its life style—is purely a matter of private concern. We are making a choice about investment in prevention, and development without knowing it. And we will find ourselves declaring indignantly and self-righteously that we should not have to help bear the cost or compensate families for doing something that is for their own benefit, and that is exclusively their responsibility. After all, if they couldn't carry it, we will say, they shouldn't have brought children into the world. We do not want to ask for whom the bell tolls. We know how to deal with those responsibilities ourselves: We can send our children to private schools, take them to see the doctors of our choice, hire therapists when things go wrong.

That is how our social policy looks at families and child rearing. Children are what economists label "private goods"—presumably of use and benefit exclusively for "private consumption." Jonathan Swift would have applauded that conclusion. His advice, back in the 1800s, was to sell them as tasty morsels, delicacies for the wealthy[22] to eat. Sell them young. It costs money to feed them—so sell them as soon as they are weaned.

To economists, children are simply market commodities. Government regulation gets in the way. The eminent jurist, David Posner (once a leading candidate for the Supreme Court and more recently court-appointed arbiter of the anti-trust action against Microsoft) applies economic theory to reduce the need for foster care. His advice: Put the babies up for sale. The market is far more efficient than adoption agencies and foster care.

Raising children is work. We have to decide which, of two economies, should do the job—market or non-market. To make that choice wisely and to justify the resources needed, we might have to know real costs and real benefits. Making those calculations will vary depending upon whether we acknowledge that raising children generates a public good and creates an external social benefit.

If we deny and disregard the public benefit element, we will not be willing to share the cost of basics like child care. If we refuse to acknowledge that the public has a stake in how adequately families discharge their essential functions, we will not be willing to help foot the bill or supply the resources needed to supplement what families can do by themselves. We will not be willing to find any way to compensate non-market workers. If we deny that we benefit, we have no obligation to pay based on benefit received.

4. The definition yields bizarre results

The exclusions from "work" yield strange, unanticipated, and unwanted consequences. Consider the following scene:

Imagine 15 women sitting in rocking chairs in a circle, each with her own baby on her lap. That is *not* work.

Now imagine that an instruction is given: "Hand your baby to the person on your left."

Now that *is* work.

Something is wrong with that logic.

This definition of work yields a strange and unwanted consequence. It leaves us with only one way in which child rearing can be considered to be productive work. *Strangers must raise our children.* Then it is work.

That makes no sense. It describes accurately the path the government has embraced. It is the definition that is embodied in law, in public policy. We take the child away from the parent or we send the parent away from the child. That's the only way the market knows how to make child rearing work.

It is a one-two punch. Children's Protective Service agencies are in charge of removing the child from the parents; the welfare authorities are in charge of sending the mother away from the child.

Neglect and abuse cases soar. The automatic solution is out-of-home placement. Foster care has more than doubled. Like prisons and nursing homes, Children Protective Service agencies are a major growth industry.

Next come the welfare officials. Their job has become to send the mothers to work, any work, work away from their children. Low-paying, dead-end jobs in neighborhoods far from where they live are just fine. Eliminate the prior "right" to child care. Cut funds and slots for subsidized child care—pitting those coming off welfare against those who have barely managed to stay off welfare by virtue of the subsidy. It won't be long before we see welfare "success stories" ending more and more frequently with the mother losing her child because of neglect.

5. The price tag is too high

Allowing the market to define work leads to prohibitive costs. In 1995, federal and state spending on investigations, casework services, foster care, and adoption assistance exceeded $11.2 billion. That figure does not include local funds or funds spent on individual cases by the courts, law enforcement, schools, or the health and mental health care systems.

We pay considerabl / more to foster families to raise other people's children than we provide in public assistance for single mothers to raise their own. The federal government spent about $11,698 per child on foster care maintenance and administrative costs—but only $1,012 for each person receiving AFDC. That means it costs 11 times more for the federal government to provide foster care than to provide basic income maintenance. When one adds in state costs, the average government cost of supporting an individual on welfare was $2,499—while the cost of operating the foster care system was $21,902 per child.[23]

There are other costs. The caseload of Children Protective Services has more than doubled. A half million children are now in foster care—an increase of nearly 50 percent in one decade. The agencies charged with investigation were falling dramatically farther behind. Child Protective Service agencies investigated only 28 percent of the recognized children who met the government's Harm Standard—a significant decrease from the

44 percent investigated in 1986. Schools identified the largest number of maltreated children but only 16 percent of these children were investigated.

The market has its own definition of work. That definition is inadequate, exclusionary, incomplete—and expensive. That flaw generates major external costs. We need to redefine work—to break out of the box that market logic creates.

6. The definition masks inadequate performance

The current definition of work is seductively fraudulent—with catastrophic long-term consequences. Our faith in money and what money can buy has programmed us with a filter that masks defective performance and misrepresentation by the market. The terrible truth is that youngsters removed to foster care are "*ten times more likely to be maltreated while in the custody of the state than in their own homes.*"[24] Investigations of foster care conditions have turned up cases of babies tethered to hospital cribs, eleven-year-olds warehoused in drug-infested group shelters, and fifteen-year-olds shipped off to correctional facilities where they are mixed with hardcore juvenile offenders. In addition, innumerable foster children are beaten, raped, or starved by individual foster parents in family "homes."

Children in foster care often undergo multiple placements and the child learns not to become attached for fear of moving again. Confused self-identity, defensiveness, fearfulness, lack of trust are predictable responses with long-term consequences. Foster care funding ends at age 18. When the money ends, the care stops. "We can't dump them fast enough at 18," is how Robin Nixon, director of Youth Services at the Child Welfare League of America once put it.

The most recent study of "foster care" alumni tells us what we are really buying.[25] Within 12 to 18 months after leaving the foster care system, 33 percent were receiving public assistance, one-fifth of the females had given birth, and more than one-quarter of the boys had been incarcerated. Twenty-six percent of the males and 15 percent of the females had been beaten or injured. Ten percent of the females had been raped. Thirty-seven percent had not finished high school. *Forty percent of the nation's homeless are former foster children.*[26]

If that's what the market definition of work gives us, it's a pretty defective product. The hidden costs keep coming due. The definition has to be replaced. The new definition must, at least, meet the standard imposed on commercial goods, which defines "marketable" as "usable for the purpose for which it is sold." This definition fails even that test.

There is an old proverb, attributed of course to the ubiquitous but anonymous ancient Chinese Philosopher. "If we don't change course, we are likely to end up where we are headed."

Welfare reform has set the real stage for rethinking what we will call work. This nation once provided entitlements to mothers of single children based on need. It was called Aid to Families with Dependent Children (AFDC). AFDC incorporated the old definition of work. But at least it said, if you must go to work, the government will guarantee child care.

AFDC never called raising children a job. As a result, it could never condition payment on competent parenting performance. AFDC never asked, insisted, or enabled parents to learn how to do that job or helped them build the kind of support system simply needed to function as a family in a changing world.

Then came welfare reform. It embraced the old definition with a vengeance. It said, you must go to work—but it stripped away the right to child care. It elevated and enshrined the market definition of work and it demoted child care to the status of a trivial personal problem, a mere cost of doing real work in the real world. Studies consistently confirm that for those seeking to get off welfare, affordable quality child care doesn't exist. If we even equate licensed care with quality care (an assumption that continuous newspaper exposés disprove), there is only enough for between 11 percent and 50 percent of those in need of it. There was (and is) latitude for another vastly different definition but consistently, welfare administrators have turned their back on that option.

Politicians are heralding welfare reform as a huge success. They have moved vast numbers off welfare, even though most are still in poverty or near poverty level. But from the politician's stand point, the shift represents an accomplishment. Families are subsisting on private sector paychecks, not taxpayer moneys.

The victory celebrations are premature. Most of the low-wage jobs that are available leave families financially worse off than they were on welfare. As implementation advances, the obstacles mount: addiction, lack of adequate transportation and affordable child care, domestic violence, and mental illness. Initial apparent success in reducing welfare caseloads is beginning to prove somewhat illusory.

The first hard data coming in show that much of the initial drop in welfare rolls stems from sanctions, not jobs. The majority of those who are getting off welfare are sliding back into poverty when the short-term transition benefits end. And even the basic transition benefits that were promised are not being provided. Success, to the extent that there is any, stems in part from the healthy state of the economy. A downturn could have devastating effects on job search, placement, and retention.

Even with unprecedented prosperity over an unprecedented stretch of years, something disturbing is happening: Hunger and homelessness have increased in cities for 15 consecutive years. A survey of 26 cities by the U.S. Conference of Mayors found that the demand for emergency food and shelter had increased in most of those cities between 1997 and 1999. Once confined to large cities, the phenomenon is now spreading to small towns. Burlington, Vermont with a population over 40,000 has seen a 400 percent rise over four years in the number of families seeking emergency housing.

The Mayor, Peter Clavelle notes, "Many of these families have wage earners. There are people working full time who are homeless." The political game is tax cuts. The mayor of Boston, Thomas Menino, reports, "We have a game going on in government today—who can out-tax-cut who."

We do not want to go where this road leads. The faster we succeed in moving the most work-ready, upwardly mobile welfare mothers into jobs, the faster we disinvest in families and communities. A daily commute to low-wage, entry-level jobs will deplete disadvantaged neighborhoods of their most precious resource: indigenous leaders, community spokespersons, role models, caring parents, entrepreneurs, and norm-setters. If this is success, why are the numbers of homeless and hungry people rising faster than they have since 1994?

This definition of work is like a loan with a huge balloon payment. We may not like what happens when it comes due.

The real issue is a choice of economic system: market or non-market. We have to decide which economy we prefer to rely on when it comes to the basics—children, elders, community, civil society, democracy. Is it all for sale to the highest bidder? Are we sure we want market values to determine both production and distribution when it comes to rearing our children, caring for our parents, protecting our democracy? Implicitly redefining work means asking, Which side are we on when it comes to the things we value most? Where do we start? Market or Non-Market? And what partnerships and joint ventures involving both economies might work most efficiently and equitably?

Redefining work means taking back the power to define what we value and to define how we use words. We cannot permit the market economy to have the final say in defining "productive" work. We must find a way to value social contribution devalued by the market including child rearing, eldercare, learning, neighboring, and civic engagement. Work must be—and can be—redefined to include whatever it takes to rear healthy children, preserve families, make neighborhoods safe and vibrant, care for the frail and vulnerable, redress injustice, and make democracy work.

We Need a Definition of Work that Works.

The inadequacy of the market definition supplies the specifications. The new definition must be one that mobilizes capacity, links capacity to need, rewards contribution, builds the village, minimizes cost, and avoids hidden cost.

There is a line drawing, by the artist Ben Shawn, of a man's face with a gag over his mouth. The inscription reads, "You have not convinced a man because you have silenced him."

Every time it comes down to the redefinition of work, I hit a wall. I win the argument—but that's all.

Time and again, I have asked: "How essential is this participation you are seeking to get from the client? How critical is his or her involvement to the outcome you are funded to get?"

The answer is always the same:

"It's absolutely essential. Without their participation, we can't succeed."

The follow-up question is where I lose them:

"If you say it's so important. If it's absolutely essential to achieve what you're being paid to do, why do you call it participation? Why don't you call it work?"

At that point, their eyes glaze over. The brain shuts down.

Immediately, we are back in the zero-sum game of market, money, and scarcity. Work means "they" get money. There simply is no way one can get enough money to pay everyone for the labor that is needed—and even trying it a teeny-tiny bit would create a dangerous, life-threatening precedent.

In that mindset, it is hard to get recognition or acknowledgment of the fact that if success is dependent on that labor, then an unwillingness to call it work necessarily means one is counting on getting it free. One can bargain about hiring one or two outreach workers from the community, putting a few "client-consumers" on an advisory committee—but calling it work, never.

Co-Production means we have to think outside that box.

In Either Economy, Work Is Work

If we need the work, we had better acknowledge that that's what it is.

While working on a Ph.D. and holding down a teaching fellowship at Yale, I worked the night shift in a factory, crafted silver jewelry, and was the janitor of an apartment house. I have never been afraid of hard work or long hours. But I have never been as flat-out exhausted and wiped out as the summer when my wife, after one year of law school, became the sole wage earner. I was a doctoral candidate; she was a law student. It was clear that my market value was less than hers—so fiscal logic dictated that I take care of our two sons, ages 1 and 2. Each day stretched on and on. I would watch the clock, waiting as the hours passed, for her to come home. Children are perpetual motion machines. Try keeping up with a twelve-month-old baby and a two-year-old toddler simultaneously. That summer, "Wait till your mother gets home" served as an all-purpose threat, bribe, and delaying tactic. I remember thinking, No wonder they find women have the stamina to make better astronauts.

I heard the same admission from Geoffery Canada. His book *Fist, Stick, Knife, Gun* rattles off spellbinding stories about growing up mastering the fine art of violence in Harlem. As both the book and media coverage reveal, he regularly puts his own life on the line, time after time, to intervene to prevent street fights and confrontations from escalating to epidemic proportions. Canada was the featured keynote speaker at the 1998 closing plenary session of the Family Resource Coalition. He arrived twenty minutes late and noticeably out of breath. But the audience had no trouble buying his explanation or his apology. "I just spent two hours taking care of my youngest child. Anyone who doesn't know that is the toughest job on earth has never had to do it."

Going to work, even the work he did, was a piece of cake by comparison.

If We Need It, We Must Compensate It.

Activity that creates value for others or for society is work. We tend to think there are only two alternatives: volunteering and market wages. We are wrong. And we tend to equate volunteering with working for nothing. Again we are wrong.

Co-Production supplies a context requiring proof that some alternative is possible. Time Dollars supply that proof. They are one such alternative. They are a hybrid that combines volunteering and wages. At the London School of Economics, Nicholas Barr, a protégé of Richard Titmuss, the great pioneer thinker on altruism, had made a theoretical prediction: When you combine two rewards, psychological and monetary, the more you can intensify the psychological reward, the less important the monetary one will be.

One phenomenon that disturbed the first coordinators of Time Dollar programs was that many Time Dollars were not getting spent. Yet, even though people did not spend down their Time Dollar bank account, they continued to earn Time Dollars. The turnover or burn out or attrition rate was far lower than volunteer programs in the same communities. We were watching Barr's prediction at work: The conferring of Time Dollars intensified the psychological rewards associated with volunteering. The greater that reinforcement, the less important the actual purchasing power associated with Time Dollars.

In fact, people were getting what they wanted without spending the Time Dollars. Some were buying a kind of insurance they hoped they would not have to use. They were getting the assurance that insurance provides. Some were buying access to a social setting, a new group of friends, strangers whom they could trust. Just being part of Time Dollars engaged them in a social network of exchanges that provided that access. For some, it was a way of filling their lives with special social events—because most programs had regular meetings or pot luck luncheons or birthday celebrations. Gar Alperovitz, an iconoclastic thinker about what he calls The Third Way, says that the volume of unspent Time Dollars is really a measure of the unmet need for community that Time Dollars are filling.

Compensation Need Not Mean Market Wages.

If we refuse to accept the market definition of work, we do not have to accept the market definition of compensation. Different rewards are appropriate for different tasks by different groups in different settings.

The issue of compensation breaks down into three separate questions. First, what alternatives are there to monetary compensation that might function as an adequate incentive or reward? Second, to the extent that there are dollar costs, who will pay them on an ongoing, sustained basis? Third, to what extent do the dollar costs reintroduce the limits of scale that come from reliance on dollars?

Time Dollar programs have had to wrestle with these questions; new possibilities are emerging constantly.

Alternatives to Market Wages

First, there are meaningful forms of reward that reinforce altruism directly. Elderplan, a Social Health Maintenance Organization, offers its members an opportunity to buy gifts of 15 home-delivered meals to be given by the donor to a home-bound senior. Blue Cross–Blue Shield of Pittsburgh enabled its members to buy $10 gift certificates from local grocery stores for needy families. At other Health Maintenance Organization sites, there is discussion about enabling members who earned Time Dollars to buy health care coverage for women in shelters or others who are presently uninsured.

Second, there are goodies of significant market value that can be secured as donations or by outright purchase: tickets to movies, to lectures and museums, discounted rates for shopping trips or tours and even cruise ships. One housing developer enabled families to cash in their Time Dollars for a lecture at the Smithsonian by novelist, Terry McMillan, and for a two-week summer camp for the children. In different cities, cruise lines and tour buses have given special rates for Time Dollar groups. Finally, there are social events and pot-lucks made available for Time Dollars, embedding the tangible incentive in a social setting.

In Maine, Time Dollars can be used for everything from massages, to dance lessons and oil changes. Those are either secured as member-to-member exchanges—or "awards" donated by members. Time Dollars can be used to purchase tickets to the Portland Symphony; the Symphony is awarding Time Dollars for helping in the music filing library. Portland's Adult Education program accepts Time Dollars as tuition payment for all its classes and allows Maine Time Dollar members to use their auto mechanics and carpentry workshop to provide oil changes. In return, Maine Time Dollar members act as tutors and teachers assistants or provide child care during some of the classes.

In St. Louis, Grace Hill Neighborhood Services has long operated Time Dollar stores, stocked with contributed merchandise ranging from food to soap to toys and educational materials.

In Miami, St. Louis, and Washington, D.C., food banks will honor Time Dollars and enable people earning those Time Dollars to purchase food. In Miami, they dedicate a portion of the food earned for use in monthly pot-luck meals for all Time Dollar members.

In Washington, D.C., the Time Dollar Institute spent $100 a month through a church ministerial alliance. That bought four tons of food each month. And that food, bought for that little bit of money, generated over 78,000 hours of labor, neighbors helping neighbors in 18 public housing complexes.

The Chicago Peer Tutoring program spends between $20,000 and $30,000 annually enabling participants to cash in their Time Dollars. At the end of the year, every Time Dollar earned has been spent—to redeem a recycled computer for every participant.

Who Pays for Rewards That Cost Money?

This brings us to the second question. Who pays the actual dollar costs? Recycled computers cost money to collect, overhaul, store, and distribute. More than 20 percent of the funds received from the Chicago Public Schools goes into getting working computers into homes in order to bridge the Digital Divide. The Time Dollar Institute says to the Chicago Public School system, that's part of the cost to the school system of buying Co-Production. It's a bargain. At the last distribution of computers in 1999, Paul Vallas, the CEO of the Chicago Public Schools, said he wanted to see a Time Dollar store where every student engaged in service learning and every student doing mentoring could buy tickets to sporting events, seats at concerts, T-shirts, computers, upgrades, modems, and e-mail and educational software. He knows it's a bargain too.

Elderplan, an unusual Social Health Maintenance Organization in Brooklyn, has taken the Co-Production principle even further, embedding it first in its premium structure, and later, in an extensive Credit Shop Catalog full of health-related items that can be bought with Time Dollars. Ever since 1987, Elderplan has been putting Co-Production into practice. It says, We need our consumers, the elderly, to be co-producers of health—and we are committed to finding ways that can effectively compensate them for the contribution they make. From 1987 till 1998, seniors who earned Time Dollars helping other elders in their Member-to-Member program could cash them in for a 25 percent discount on their health insurance premiums.

Then, in 1998, Elderplan's competitors eliminated premiums. They decided to compete for market share by sole reliance on federal Medicare payments without any dollar premium payments by subscribers. Elderplan had no choice: it did the same. No one paid a premium—and that wiped out the premium redemption option for Time Dollar members.

Elderplan had to go back to square one to figure out how best to reward people in its Time Dollar Member-to-Member program. The result was a brand new feature: a Time Dollar Credit Shop complete with catalog. The catalog advertises an array of goodies: a bathtub spa, a digital blood pressure monitor, a foot massager—all health- and well-being-related products. The choice didn't end there. Members could alternatively spend their Time Dollars to buy a ticket to a special luncheon for themselves and a companion. Or they could spend it to get a round trip taxi ride to the destination of their choice. It was a big gamble. But it proved very popular. In the first six months 70 percent of members made a purchase. Membership is up; morale is up. And national recognition is way up—a PBS special, national media coverage, and the designation of a special President's Points of Light award. Elderplan is on a roll.

In the Year 2000, as a millennium kick-off, Elderplan added an option for members who wanted to use their Time Dollars to help others. That's when it introduced the redemption option of 15 home-delivered meals for seniors to double the altruistic "bang for the buck" of each Time Dollar. Elderplan also convinced some lawyers to write wills, advanced directives, and living wills in return for Time Dollars. All of this costs money.

The big-ticket items cost Elderplan anywhere between $50 and $100. Do the arithmetic on that for 500 members. That means that Elderplan is spending somewhere between $25,000 and $50,000 a year on Time Dollar redemption items alone. That is on top of staff costs. Co-Production is worth real money to Elderplan. We will see why and how when we get to Reciprocity. The only point being made here is that if we acknowledge that consumer labor is valuable work, it doesn't come without some dollar costs. Elderplan has faced up to that squarely. It is willing to pay for it. It is a path-setter.

The Issue of Scale

Are there limits? Can we really get away with insisting that work is work regardless of the economy where it takes place and that if the work has value, there needs to be some form of compensation? There may be limits, right now, in the number of people willing to do this. But there is no limit to how far it can go in generating exchanges that confer value for value.

Start with this proposition: If for every hour you will give, you could get another hour of some one else's time, someone whom you could trust, would that be a beginning? Millions of transactions over the past 12 years, millions of Time Dollars earned and spent say, Yes, that might be a beginning.

Suppose there were surplus: surplus food and clothes, surplus building supplies and surplus labor, surplus recycled computers and surplus used cars, surplus tools and surplus hands to use the tools. Do you think that

that surplus might provide an incentive for people to help others? Do you think there is enough surplus or enough surplus capacity to feed, clothe, house, transport, educate, and care for every one in this affluent land? Suppose they could acquire what they needed with a currency earned by helping others? Would that be a beginning?

Time Dollars, surplus, and e-commerce

We know that there are goods and services in ample supply. We know that there are people who want those things, need those things, and will contribute their labor to get them. The market does not put supply and demand together for vast numbers of people and for vast amounts of merchandise and unused productive capacity. But we also know that new web-based technology has introduced revolutionary new speed and efficiency to create a new sector of the economy, e-commerce almost overnight.

Co-Production provides an engine that can drive a different kind of e-commerce, one that puts people together in new kinds of families, one that enables these new families to feed and care for each other, to teach each other, to support each other, and to enable each other to secure the essentials and cope with life's certain uncertainties.

Those who understand the implications of the new technology understand that, if put to work with vision, we might see a surge of growth in the non-market economy that vastly overshadows even the most spectacular expansions in the market economy. The search for creative ways to cash in Time Dollars is leading the Time Dollar Institute to use the Internet to launch a Time Dollar Web store utilizing donated merchandise. The prototype is now on the Web site, available only to people in St. Louis, using specially designed software showing actual photos of donated winter coats, Disney T-shirts, belts, shoes, computer equipment, golf clubs, printers, and more. It can be accessed through the Time Dollar web page, www.timedollar.org.

Two organizations called NAEIR (the National Association for the Exchange of Industrial Resources) and Gifts-in-Kind are demonstrating that there are literally millions and millions of dollars worth of merchandise corporations will donate in order to secure both good will and an above-cost federal tax deduction. NAEIR has successfully collected and placed over $800 million worth of new, top-quality donated products: office supplies, toys and games, tools, computers and computer software, personal care products, janitorial supplies, sporting goods, books, tapes, CDs, classroom materials, and clothing. Both Gifts-in-Kind and NAEIR are very explicit: Merchandise donated cannot be bartered or sold. Fortunately, the Internal Revenue Service has been both clear and consistent in its ruling: Time Dollar exchanges do not constitute commercial barter.

If we are serious about redefining work, we have to start valuing the work that enables families to function and neighborhoods to remain vibrant. We have to start rewarding the labor from the non-market economy that every specialized institution in the monetary economy desperately needs. And we need a way to put the two together.

Co-production, computers, and compensation

Time Dollars would not have been possible before the age of computers. Matching people up and keeping track of the records would have been too time-consuming, too laborious, and too expensive. The power of the personal computer and the extraordinary genius of one dedicated programmer, Kent Gordon, has made it possible to develop the first, second, and third generations of programs used by ordinary people in England, Japan, and the United States to keep track of the donations and the exchanges of time.

That same technology, taken to the next stage, can do far more. The real issue is how we redefine work to create the world we want—and how we secure the relatively small sums of money, on a continuing basis, to pay the dollar costs needed to build the bridges between work in the non-market economy and the goods and services produced in abundance in the market economy.

Co-Production provides the impetus to redefine work in a way that can secure those resources. Co-Production answers the question: Who will buy the labor produced in the non-market economy? Who will fork over either the money or the goods needed for survival in return for that labor?

Co-Production supplies the response: The organizations and agencies most likely to value that labor are those that are funded to address social problems that can only be ameliorated if they can get that labor as Co-Production. Redefining Work sets that process in motion. As we shall see, Reciprocity takes it from there. The potential is unlimited—in theory. In practice, we know that redefining work entails a major shift in how people think about work and whether redefining work is perceived as a threat to their own status and economic security.

Chapter 14

Redefining Work: A Social Justice Perspective

The perspective of social justice recasts the redefinition of work. It escalates the issue to a level where hanging on to the past becomes morally indefensible and a shift in framework becomes obligatory.

We have to say, in the context of social justice, *No More*:

- **No more taking the contribution of the client community for granted.**
- **No more taking women's labor, exacted by subordination, for granted.**
- **No more taking money given to rebuild the non-market economy and turning it exclusively into salaries in the market economy.**
- **No more free rides for the market economy.**

That can feel very threatening unless one is willing to think in terms of win-win rather than zero-sum scenarios.

We have taken the work of women and the vitality of neighborhoods for granted in much the same way that we took clean air and water for granted—until we learned the truth the hard way: that there was a limit to how much toxicity the environment can absorb. In much the same way, we counted on the assumption that we could get cheap labor from overseas—until a woman, nominated to be Attorney General, found out that she would not be confirmed as chief law enforcer because of her own failure to pay her foreign baby sitter what federal law required. Cheap labor, secured by subordination, exploitation and discrimination, is no longer the infinitely renewable resource it once seemed to be. Work is work.

If we want it, we had better find a way to pay for it. Those in the market will tell us that they are the only ones qualified to raise children. Somehow the species survived before the Ph.D in Child Development was invented. Those in the market tell you they are the only ones qualified to nurse the sick. Do you know who delivers the vast preponderance of health care to the sick? We call them mothers. The list goes on: who provides the bulk of drug treatment for addicts? Other addicts and former addicts in twelve-step programs. Who cares for the elderly? Family.

We need to rethink how and where real work is done. The market supplies specialized knowledge and expertise. Knowledge is not bad; it is good. Expertise is not bad; it is vital. We do not need to demonize those who possess it—but we do have to enlist them in a way that enables them to cope with their own fears by holding out the possibility that they can in fact realize their dream of using that knowledge as catalyst to make a meaningful contribution to the world.

Believing in clients, recipients, at-risk groups does not mean we must require them to start from ignorance, devoid of all accumulated knowledge, and reinvent the wheel. We need professionals and we should value what they have to offer. At the same time, we must be clear that professionals will not raise children—families will. And despite their flaws, we should affirm the capacity of "uncertified" and "unlicensed" parents, mentors, caregivers, tutors, peer support groups, and neighborhood block associations to do what they do supremely—and indeed, uniquely—well.

Co-Production translates into a mandate to create new hybrids that make use of both and that do not give all the resources to the professionals while dumping the face-to-face work on family, neighbors, friends. They need resources too—and they need compensation in some form. We have to stop pretending that work in either economy, market or non-market, can be done without resources.

If work is work, then redefining work means identifying the functional roles and tasks and making use of whichever economy is best suited to do the job at lowest cost, with least scarcity without loss of quality. That means spending money and committing resources in the non-market economy as well as the market economy in order to get the job done right.

Expect Opposition

If we expect to redefine work, we need to expect opposition. The market does not surrender turf gracefully or easily.

Jill Kinney, the legendary founder of Homebuilders, learned this the hard way.

In 1974, Jill was director of a family crisis program at Catholic Children's Services. At the time, she had only two choices when faced with a crisis: remove the child or try to prop the family up with services that she knew were both inadequate and inconvenient.

She knew that raising children was work. And she knew the services she could supply wouldn't help.

"When a family is in turmoil, they don't want you once a week on Wednesday. They want you when they are feeling the pain." Telling a family in crisis to make three different appointments at different times and at far away places was not her idea of what the job meant.

The product was no good, so she came up with a new product: highly trained Homebuilders, social workers on call twenty-four hours a day, seven days a week. With a caseload of no more than two to three families, they could respond effectively to a full range of needs. Lisbeth Schorr singled out Homebuilders in her book, *Within Our Reach* as an outstanding example of what she called, "Strengthening Families from the Outside." If intensive intervention meant scrubbing floors and buying blankets, then that's what the Homebuilder does. The payoff was astounding. Schorr writes:

> *In the first six years of Homebuilders in Tacoma, placement became unnecessary for 92 percent of the client families, which involved 849 children originally headed for foster care or other out-of-home placement. In the most recent evaluation, which followed the families for a longer period, 90 percent of the children helped by Homebuilders were still with their families.*

The cost ran an average of $2,600 per family in 1985, a pittance compared with the cost of foster care, group care, or psychiatric hospitalization.

Jill's design was built on some rock-bottom principles. She knew who had to raise children. It was families. The competing products (foster care or weekly appointments with professionals scattered all over town) were no good. She didn't try to sell a product that replaced parents. She sold an intensive intervention strategy designed to strengthen families, to help them do what they could do best. She didn't want to create dependencies so she put a time limit on the intervention. After that, the family had to go it alone, cold turkey. She did not view the family as the problem; she viewed the family as part of the solution. And she clearly understood that there was social benefit to doing the job right, both to avoid out-of-home placement and to save a family at the point of disintegration.

By 1987, at least eight states were experimenting with large-scale implementations of Homebuilders. And an unknown number of local agencies were doing so, often with contracts for technical assistance from Homebuilders. Family preservation became the magic bullet to stop out-of-home placement. Jill was hot, a national and international celebrity.

Confronting the Credentialing Question

She made three mistakes. First, she stayed honest. She knew that this was no magic bullet, that there were situations where this kind of intervention, no matter how intensive, was too little, too late, and too short. She knew when and where programs claiming they were modeled after Homebuilders were really diluted, watered down versions without what Lisbeth Schorr called the "painstakingly thought-out, carefully crafted, amply supervised set of intensive interventions backed up by services from other agencies...."

Second, she figured out that there were two economies: the world of the professionals and the world of the family. And she started taking this last lesson seriously. She started asking, which economy could do the best job. And she concluded, in a lot of the families she had known, the economy of the neighborhood, of the extended family, of informal networks was the better economy to handle a variety of cases. And she knew it didn't take a social work degree to scrub floors, buy blankets, apply for food stamps or take a child to a doctor's appointment. She knew that when Homebuilders left these families, they did not have a support system, an extended family in place and that they were often too fragile to make it without some kind of informal support system. She knew that some of the problems that precipitated family crises were not the family's fault; schools, police, landlords, merchants can all trigger crises. The Homebuilder was not necessarily going to solve problems that stemmed from racism, poverty, lawlessness by government officials, and neighborhood deterioration.

Her third mistake was going public with those perceptions and trying to do something about the problem. That's when family preservation crossed the line. It ceased being what professionals did. It became redefining work. That's when Jill hit the trip wire called professional oblivion. That's when she discovered what it felt like to go from guru to taboo person. At that point, all one can do is switch fuel tanks—and fly without reserves on high-octane social justice fuel. Jill had dared to suggest that professionals from the outside were not necessarily the way to go—that in many situations, local people, natural helpers as she called them, could do the job better.

Jill had learned this last lesson too well. She would pay a heavy price for those mistakes. She dared to suggest that the Homebuilders formula she had created was not a magic bullet, that maybe more than 4–6 weeks of intensive help was needed by some—and that exclusive emphasis on the family ignored the possibility of weaving a network of informal support for that family from neighbors, relatives, extended family—and ultimately from the village. Suddenly Jill was no longer welcome at Homebuilders. She was banished—professionally excommunicated. But she could not be stopped.

Jill dared to observe that many of the tasks performed by Homebuilders do not require a Master's in Social Work. And she could prove it because she wrote the book on what Homebuilders do: provide transportation; help the client find a job; provide recreational activities; do housework and house cleaning with the client; help the client obtain financial assistance (through, for example, AFDC or SSI), utility benefits or services, medical or dental services (for instance, visiting nurses); provide food, toys, or recreational equipment; help the client obtain food, legal aid, housing, childcare or babysitting services, and clothing; move the client to a new dwelling; provide childcare and babysitting, a job, clothing; and help the client obtain furniture or other household goods.

Then Jill took what she thought was a logical step: develop a cadre of Natural Helpers without MSWs and even without Bachelor's degrees. She didn't stop there.

In her classic text, *Keeping Families Together*, she had shared an observation:

> *Clients are often the most willing to share information when the two of us are involved in concrete tasks, such as washing dishes or waiting in line at the welfare office. Teenagers are famous for opening up while being driven in a car.*

Why were social workers the only ones licensed to use that insight? Why not train people without graduate or even college degrees to use that knowledge? From a profit-and-loss perspective, that was a threatening idea. How could anyone without a Master's in Social Work bill an hour of washing dishes as a professional consult?

Old friends and professional acquaintances became concerned. Jill had obviously lost sight of what others thought should be her true purpose in life: to find a new way to bring revenue to her agency and to generate employment for more and more licensed social workers.

Jill Kinney does not follow market logic. She marches to a different drummer. You know it by the leap of faith in family, in parents, in people that is continually at odds with a bias in favor of professionals. You know it because it gets results that everybody had said you couldn't get. You know it because it doesn't invoke professional expertise and agency jurisdiction to avoid responsibility. You also know it by contrast, by what came before it, by how different it is from whatever has been accepted as the industry standard—the standard that Jill Kinney herself created.

It Can Be Done

Redefining work is possible. It will take a struggle. For those willing to undertake the struggle, there are some principles to be learned, some mistakes to avoid, some risks that one had best confront.

Abriendo Puertas in East Little Havana now has one of the most significant Time Dollar programs in the country. It didn't come easily. It had to fight for existence and fight for resources and fight to ensure its own integrity. There are lessons to be learned from that story, lessons applicable to almost every site.

In Miami, the Annie Casey Foundation had made a multi-year, multi-million dollar investment to transform urban mental health services for Latino children. The proposal had met Foundation specifications—but then proposals always do. It promised to shift mental health from a medical treatment model to a holistic model that addressed prevention and education as well as crises—and it promised to enlist the community in an effort to create a neighborhood environment designed to support the development of mental health. All the trappings needed were there: evidence of grassroots support, plans for a parents council, commitments to community empowerment.

The best laid plans: Predictable disasters

By the time the grant had passed the midway mark, significantly more than half the money was spent—and it was clear when one looked at the program, the staffing, and the budget that a medical model had been imported with dedicated therapists treating families, one at a time and trying, against the odds, to do their best. Professional services and staffing were absorbing most of the funding. The system change that had been promised to the community and envisioned by funders simply wasn't happening.

The community was angry. Its support had been critical in getting the grant. And now people felt used. They had been promised all kinds of changes, and those somehow always took a back seat.

To be sure, there was a token family council. But that was window dressing. The bulk of the dollars either went to other agencies that formed a kind of social service cartel or to staff where professional salaries ate up most of the money. In response to some griping, two community people had been hired as family outreach workers. They were in charge of a program with the authentic sounding name: Madrinas and Padrinos. But those hired felt largely powerless.

Community people, mainly parents who had come into the center for services or who had been involved in the planning, fell to fighting among themselves, squabbling over who would get the crumbs dropped from the table of professionals. Not a nice picture.

There were lots of meetings. Community people were told they were being trained to assume governing authority—but first they had to learn how to do budgeting and interpret by-laws. It seemed likely that by the time they were ready, they would inherit an organization with no grant money left.

Hostility escalated. There were lots of meetings. Interaction became a battle of attrition. Professionals win those battles. They earn their salaries coming to meetings. That's their job. Community folks have to sacrifice, find baby sitters, change appointments—and somehow free-up time in lives where the only certainty is an unexpected crisis.

When parents come as supplicants to bargain, they normally demand what community people know how to demand: money and a voice in decision-making. Professionals, trying desperately to meet vast unmet needs in an unfriendly world are trapped. Ever since the participatory revolution of the 1960's, professionals, caught in dysfunctional organizations, have learned how to function as flack-catchers. They say the right things or at least, they avoid saying the wrong things. They exude concern and respect; they express regret; sometimes they even acknowledge error (but only past error). They create a few seats on some Board for unlettered community representatives. They commit some funding to leadership training and social events. In return, they secure anywhere from six months to two years of passivity—while the leadership training goes on, and the leadership is co-opted by serving on boards, appearing at foundation luncheons, and traveling to distant places for conferences.

Turning the corner: Demanding co-production

In Miami, something different happened. Foundation officials shared information about Time Dollars with the executive director and her staff. The information seemed interesting and possibly useful; it sounded a lot like what they had written in the grant that they would do. They welcomed Time Dollars—possibly because they thought they had no choice, given foundation endorsement. And they shared a presentation on Time Dollars with parents, hoping that it would placate them.

The parents sensed that this was something different. They said this was something they wanted to learn about. So they got a commitment to receive whatever training could be provided in how to set up a Time Dollar program.

In less than a year and a half, the results were impressive. The Parents Council learned how to make effective use of its seats on the decision-making board. Two full-time positions have been created and budgeted: a parent coordinator and a Time Dollar coordinator have been recruited, hired and brought on board. Parents have had to approve all hires. The person hired as Time Dollar volunteer coordinator is a parent who had been the most outspoken, most divisive, most abrasive community member hell bent on discrediting the program at the beginning. Now she is a fierce advocate and a fierce organizer.

All this happened once parents realized that using Time Dollars meant they had something to bring to the table: They and they alone could mobilize parents and the community. They and they alone could provide the informal support that fragile and dysfunctional families needed to complement the therapy. They and they alone could hold the social events to which others would come. And they were the ones whom the program knew to showcase when foundations and officials visited. In effect, they were the real work force needed to deliver the needed system reform. Only they could supply the labor and the interaction needed to shift from a medical model of mental health to a community-based holistic model. A new director had the savvy to understand the value of what had been created. She knew how to build on it and she understood that it would take money to staff this Co-Production and to reward this special work force: the co-producers of community mental health.

The parents as co-producers

The parents have used their status as co-producers to define a role that would build and strengthen their constituency. Everyone coming into the center for services is referred to the Parent Coordinator who undertakes to enroll the "client" as a member of a social Time Dollar club. It's an easy sell. The dues are in Time Dollars; the benefits are clear: a birthday party for anyone in the family born that month, a monthly pot luck, access to food from the food bank, computer classes, English classes, and art classes for the children. The Time Dollar club may not look like a work force but it is. Its function is to take in strangers and turn them, first into non-strangers, then into trusted friends and finally into extended family. That's Co-Production of mental health.

The Time Dollar club in turn is identifying members who know how to cook special ethnic foods; the objective is to launch an ethnic catering business that can sell its wares to community nonprofits and agencies needing to demonstrate their support of community self-help efforts. One unstated agenda is lurking in the background: Undocumented aliens cannot be legally hired as employees for a job. But nothing prevents them from helping cook meals in the catering business and being paid for the meals they deliver. This strategy originated from a source that requested confidentiality. But it evidences the value of combining professional sophistication with community savvy. It takes ongoing innovation to build bridges between the dollar economy of professional service providers and the non-dollar economy of community.

One other Co-Production innovation is critical: the professional therapists are being trained to include Time Dollar assignments in their treatment plans. Therapists are beginning to understand that they can be more effective if the family engages its friends as part of a formal Time Dollar support system. That rewards the friends for helping; it gives the family and the therapist a ready-made team to help guide, support, and if need be, intervene—at hours when the office is closed, in places professionals don't go on days when professionals don't work. The earlier dialectic of conflict and opposition appears to be history.

Two results are incontrovertible. For the first time ever, the foundation awarded prizes to its outstanding programs. Abriendo Puertas received a half-million dollar award. The feature cited most was the role of the parents and the community. Second, there has been an increasing realization that services to families and children are insufficient if one does not simultaneously endeavor to transform the neighborhood that provides the total environment in which families live. Abriendo Puertas is now moving in that direction; having enlisted the parents as co-producers, it has a capability that it didn't have and didn't even realize it needed. And the parents now have an identity that is different from simply being on a Board and different from having two neighborhood people hired. They are now players on whatever the next stage is. They know what they bring to the table, and they know its worth—and their own.

Tomorrow's Battlefield: Revisiting Welfare–to–Work

In the issue of welfare–to–work, redefining work takes center stage.

In the United States and Europe, the redefinition of work is the key to addressing the issue of public assistance and statutory entitlements. The debate over public assistance is, in reality, a debate over who should share in the abundance that is produced by the market economy, but which is made possible by virtue of an enormous subsidy from the non-market economy and from the tangle of property rights that governments create and protect.

That debate over public assistance is still curtailed and hampered by a framework that offers only two alternatives: work in the market economy or be dependent on public assistance. We are groping to find our way. In the poet's words, we find ourselves between two worlds, one not yet dead, the other struggling to be born.

The real work that remains to be done is not yet regarded as work. We all know what it is: raising children, strengthening families, educating the young, building vibrant neighborhoods, and caring for the elderly. It includes preserving the environment, getting engaged in the political process, using technology wisely, striving to make equal justice a reality and gaining public acceptance of lifestyles that promote fitness, health, and vitality.

The needs are well known. And the price of failure is expensive. It means more jails, more nursing homes, more foster care, more police, lower property values, more special education, and more school drop-outs. What we lack is a clear understanding that people, all people, are assets—and a definition of work that enables us to enlist those assets in the building of a healthy, sustainable society.

No society can buy at market prices what families and neighborhoods traditionally produce. We face wonderful challenges: how to make productive use of the last 20–30 years of our lives, and how to impart to the young the ability to learn how to learn, to care, to share, and to love and to be loved. All of us have common tasks: how to value the legacy of the past, how to function as custodians of the planet, how to master the vast new domains of knowledge, and how to exercise our franchise as citizens of our communities, our nations, and of the world.

There is no room for any of these within the limited definition of work that the market imposes. As the welfare debate moves on, the challenge will be to find ways to enlist and tap the vast human assets that we now make objects of charity or that we toss on the scrap heap. Specialization will not do it. General capacity as a human being will. Combining both, we have the knowledge and the capacity to build a great civilization—but we do so with the basic protoplasm of our humanity. The market with its awesome specialization is at best complementary. It supplies means—but cannot prescribe ends.

The market cannot answer the question of why we are here and what kind of world we wish to leave behind. That is the real work of our species.

Chapter 15

Core Value Three: Reciprocity

> *The central assumption is that service is a unilateral process. I, the professional, produce. You the client, consume.* — John McKnight[27]
>
> *"Reciprocity" will never play on the street. "A two way street beats a one way street" they'll understand that.* — Calvin Pearce on Reciprocity

What goes around comes around is a law of nature in the Co-Production universe.

Reciprocity can be the most powerful catalyst in a world where we interact as strangers. We do not start with a clean slate; we come into the world nine months in debt. Reciprocity would seem to be our birthright.

The Story of George

George was my client. He had applied for federal disability benefits and been turned down twice. His last chance was an appeal to an administrative law judge—and that case came to me and my students in the law school clinic.

It took a lot of hours to get ready for the hearing. At the age of 37, George had the build of a weight lifter. In fact, when questioned by the administrative law judge, he admitted he could press 200 pounds. He could easily lift a refrigerator. But you wouldn't want him to—because he might forget that that's what he was holding.

George was a schizophrenic, with nearly 19 years of residential and outpatient treatment at St. Elizabeth's, Washington, D.C.'s institution for the mentally ill. He had flunked every sheltered workshop program the

District had. He couldn't hold down the simplest job. When the judge got the full picture, he found George to be legally disabled, unfit for employment in the market economy.

Still, here I was reminding George of what we had said when the legal clinic at the University of the District of Columbia (U.D.C.) School of Law took his case: "Remember, we said we would ask you to pay back, hour for hour, the time we put in? Me and the law students?"

He probably had no recollection of what he had promised, but he answered Yes—because he understood that was the expected answer. George is a gentle soul. He is happiest on a farm when he can earn some pocket change grooming horses. But he spends a lot of his life in pain—afraid to get out of bed in the morning, afraid to get on the subway or bus, especially during rush hour.

I explained to George that this coming weekend, I had planned to go down to the SHARE warehouse to help distribute food to Time Dollar members who had put in their two hours of volunteer work and had paid the $14—to get $40 worth of food. That's a nationwide program. In the District, it reaches over 14,000 people. Many of them are seniors who can't lift the heavy bags of potatoes, or help break down the cartons loaded with cans and fresh produce that come in, at the beginning of the month.

"George," I asked, "could you do that for me? I really need someone to take my place." You should have seen the look of sheer joy on George's face when he realized that he could do something that really mattered to his lawyer and to the law students who had helped him out. That had to be the right message: "We need your help, just as you needed ours."

George called the next two mornings at 6:30 a.m. to make sure that arrangements had been made to give him a ride to the warehouse out on Kenilworth Avenue. And a man who could not hold down a job in a sheltered workshop worked all day, from dawn to dusk, lifting bags of potatoes, breaking down boxes, distributing groceries to seniors, carrying their bags to waiting cars or vans.

Why Reciprocity?

Colleagues and friends have challenged me: How dare I charge indigent clients for legal services? I tell them: I can keep a person from being evicted, but I can't make where they are living a place I would want to live and raise my children. That means I have a choice. My life can be a series of well-intentioned but inconsequential victories that make no real difference in the lives of others. Or I can acknowledge that I need what my clients can do in their community as badly as they need what I can do in the court room. If my work is to have meaning, I need to acknowledge that I need them as badly as they need me.

Reciprocity is not a "closed loop." It means contributing, but that payback need not be directly to those providing the help—in this case, to me, my students, or the law school that provided the service. It can be to a larger, shared vision of the world we all want to create.

Time Dollars supply a mechanism. They have reciprocity built in: I help you; you give back by helping someone else; and sooner or later, down the line, that comes back to me. Time Dollars facilitate reciprocity. They make it simple to institute reciprocity.

But reciprocity is more than a way of doing business. It is not just a means; it is an end, a core value. We have to probe further to see what confers on reciprocity a different status, the status of an essential element, an obligatory component of the Co-Production Imperative.

Lessons Learned

> reci-proc-ity *1 reciprocal state or relationship; mutual action, dependence, etc. 2 the act of reciprocating; mutual exchange.*
> —Webster's New World Dictionary

Webster's Dictionary does not give us much help in understanding how powerful a concept Reciprocity becomes in the context of Co-Production. Its definitions are rather circular—which I suppose is fitting since the spirit of the word is circular. "What goes around comes around" captures the spirit and meaning of reciprocity better than Webster.

Lesson 1. Reciprocity reinforces self-esteem.

Lesson 2. Reciprocity bridges the two worlds, market and non-market. It enables each to secure help from the other.

Lesson 3. Reciprocity multiplies the value of each hour given, stimulating greater generosity.

Lesson 4. Reciprocity converts the rendition of professional service into a catalyst that empowers the recipient.

Lesson 5. Reciprocity alters the status of a recipient from "charity supplicant" to paying customer.

Lesson 6. Reciprocity turns an isolated exchange transaction into an ongoing relationship.

Lesson 7. Reciprocity structures the Co-Production relationship between market and non-market economies.

Lesson 8. Reciprocity supplies the funding rationale, strategy, and imperative to underwrite the cost of Co-Production.

Lesson 1. Reciprocity reinforces self-esteem.

Reciprocity obliges a recipient of service to contribute in order to be a paying customer. It imputes a value to that contribution equal in worth to anything received by the consumer (receiver). In doing so, it makes an important statement to that person about his or her own self-worth.

Free services can send an unintended message: if you have no money, you have nothing I need, want, or value. That can't be the right message. I may have done more for George's sense of self-esteem by asking him to help me than I did in winning disability status for him. Despite a legally compelling impairment, George knew he was helping me out of a bind. We all occasionally think we need to clone ourselves. Maybe we don't need to, if we practice reciprocity.

Other lessons about reciprocity emerge from other Time Dollar stories. In 1996, MANNA, a community development corporation that builds low-income housing in Washington, asked me if my law school's clinic could provide them with some legal help. Their problem? It turned out to be four problems. They wanted crack houses condemned and torn down in the neighborhoods they were trying to upgrade. They suspected police corruption in the protection of crack dealers because flash radio announcements of an impending police raid consistently preceded the raid itself. They wanted legal help getting the local elementary school removed from the list of schools targeted for closing by school officials. And they wanted the money appropriated to clean up JFK Playground—once the pride of the nation's capital, but now taken over by drug dealers. Congress had appropriated money to renovate it, repair the equipment, and staff the facility, but they could not get the money released.

"You don't need a law school clinic," I told them. "You need one of Washington's major, blue chip law firms. They know just how to bring power to bear. They do it for wealthy corporations all the time." The reaction I got was one of despair; they thought I was rejecting their plea for help. I reassured them, "I think I can get you a major law firm, if you will authorize me to offer a retainer in Time Dollars along with a commitment to pay for every hour of legal services in Time Dollars." They thought I was joking. They just knew there was no chance of getting that kind of deal, so they didn't hesitate to give me the go-ahead. Behind the smiles on their faces one could sense both hope and skepticism as if to say, Sure, I could have all the fairy dust I wanted.

Two weeks later, they were sitting down in the suave Pennsylvania Avenue offices of Holland & Knight, working out the details of the retainer. A year and one-half later, all but one of the targeted crack houses is closed; the school is off the closing list; there has been a continuing shake-up of the police department; and the funds for John F. Kennedy Playground have been released.

In 1998, Holland & Knight lawyers, working on behalf of MANNA and the residents of the Shaw neighborhood, accrued $231,000 worth of billable hours. The entire bill has been paid—in Time Dollars, earned by residents doing clean-up, providing escort for seniors, helping paint the elementary school, tutoring after school, campaigning for street lights, landscaping, and cleaning up the playground. The accounts balanced: One hour of community time in return for one hour of lawyer time.

Lesson 2. Reciprocity bridges the two worlds, market and non-market. It enables each to secure help from the other.

Holland & Knight lawyers may want to relate to the problems of the District—but often feel unable to. Race and class and geography separate, so that a city with more powerbrokers than any place in the world is deemed unworthy of home rule, incapable of representing itself or solving its own problems. The lawyers appreciated that this work was different from other pro bono (free) work they have done. They know they can write by-laws for community groups, draft wills, secure uncontested divorces till the cows come home, and nothing changes. The need is unending—like a huge black hole consuming all energy and matter. *Pro bono* work can feel trivial, given the magnitude of the problems. The Time Dollar contract enabled these lawyers to contribute in a way that made a quantifiable, verifiable difference.

Lesson 3. Reciprocity multiplies the value of each hour given, stimulating greater generosity.

Lawyers who under other circumstances might have been reluctant to commit themselves to *pro bono* work were willing and even enthusiastic about doing so, knowing that every hour of legal work would generate an hour of self-help in the community. That's what sold Holland & Knight. And that's clearly part of what impelled the American Bar Association to give national recognition to Holland & Knight for its outstanding *pro bono* work. Injecting reciprocity can expand the supply of scarce, expensive specialized services.

Lesson 4. Reciprocity converts the rendering of professional service into a catalyst that empowers the recipient.

Professionals face a major dilemma. They know that their expertise and status can create a paralyzing dependency. The challenge is to turn the rendering of professional service and the utilization of their expertise into a transaction that empowers the client or recipient. Reciprocity provides an answer. If one charges a fee in Time Dollars for professional services, then the professional practice may not need to change. It can function as a catalyst. At a minimum, professional advice need not become a form of domination that creates paralyzing dependency.

Simply charging a fee in Time Dollars can empower the client in two ways. It acknowledges that the client's time and efforts have a value equal to that of the professional. And, if the Time Dollars are to be earned in a manner that is mutually determined, the fee establishes a framework that enlists client and professional in partnering around a shared objective. When a fee is paid in money, that connection and that partnership won't happen. There is no necessary connection between what you buy and how you earned the money to pay for it. That's true of most professional services: law, medicine, education, therapy. That changes when professionals charge a fee in Time Dollars, with an understanding that the Time Dollars are to be earned in a way that advances some shared vision of the world. In the case of Holland & Knight, the fee was to be earned in various community-building initiatives organized by the client securing the legal services. The shared vision stemmed from the client's agenda, and not from the attorney.

Note that this form of Co-Production does not require the professionals to stop being professionals. The lawyers do not have to become social workers, community organizers or volunteer coordinators. They are not even obliged to alter the way they do what they do. Reciprocity simply says: Charge a fee, but in Time Dollars. For lawyers, at least private practitioners, that does not appear to take any major retraining effort. They seem to know how to bill for services rendered. In this case, the fee reshapes the interchange between market and non-market.

Lesson 5. Reciprocity alters the status of a recipient from "charity supplicant" to paying customer.

The simple change in transaction from pro bono charity case to Time Dollar fee case alters the lawyer-client relationship subtly but significantly. MANNA thought of itself as a paying client; it felt no hesitation about seeking speedy service or giving the kinds of directives about desired outcomes and priorities that dollar-paying clients give.

Lesson 6. Reciprocity turns an isolated exchange transaction into an ongoing relationship.

The relationship established through a client retainer differs from most pro bono transactions. When a legal matter is concluded for a client with no money, the book is closed. The relationship ends, and the files are sent to archival purgatory. That is not the case in corporate practice. Lawyers do not consider a relationship closed once and for all when they finish a particular legal transaction for a major corporate client. To the contrary, maintaining and preserving that relationship is the key to a lucrative practice.

The Holland & Knight retainer with MANNA set up a continuing relationship, one in which the law firm felt itself committed to providing ongoing legal assistance on a variety of other community issues that affected the neighborhood. Lawyer behavior changed: lawyers started volunteering to go to the neighborhood school they had kept open, and to tutor there.

The seemingly simple, mechanical restructuring of a service transaction into a fee-for-service relationship altered the dynamic, giving the lawyers a new sense of rootedness in community. Washington, D.C., has more lawyers per square inch than any other place in the world. These lawyers are recognized and retained by corporations and nations around the world to engage in power lawyering, to shape the policies and practices of government. Yet the local community of Washington, D.C., its residents, remain powerless, lacking a vote and representation in Congress, possessing the most limited home rule. The Council of the District of Columbia, the elected legislature, lacks final authority to determine how the taxes paid by D.C. residents are to be spent. Congress has the last word. The District is one of the world's last remaining colonies, wrestling with major problems of education, health, housing, AIDS, drugs, crime, economic development and poverty. In the midst of that community, sits this vast concentration of power brokers for the world, many of whom genuinely desire to make a contribution to enhancing their community. But there is no connection, no bridge, no rootedness. A chasm separates the residents from this vast resource.

Holland & Knight has found a way, a very simple way, to bridge that chasm. Regular pro bono work would not if the relationship ends when the matter is closed. A Time Dollar fee vests the clients with a sense of access to power as paying clients, entitled to treatment and able to represent themselves vis–a–vis the rest of the world as having retained a powerful champion. If there is a "payback" then a single transaction can develop into an ongoing relationship that expands the scope of the service, the nature of the activity, the duration of the engagement and the role of the parties.

This last step begins to take reciprocity to another level. It shifts it from means to end, from strategic mechanism to core value. Reciprocity is first and foremost an ongoing relationship, not simply a one-time transaction.

It embodies a shift in perspective from "You, the client, need me" to the perspective of reciprocity, "We need each other." "What goes around comes around" affirms a causal connection between what we do for others and our own fate.

Lesson 7. Reciprocity structures the Co-Production relationship between market and non-market economies.

"We need each other" applies to individuals, groups and institutions. It pertains equally to the relationship between the market and non-market economies in the context of Co-Production. They need each other. The secret is devising a win-win strategy that maximizes the synergy.

Holland & Knight understood that. The payoff is not necessarily linear—but it is real. Why did Holland & Knight do this? They did not originally do it for the Time Dollars income earned. They did not expect it to affect their bottom line–though in fact it did. One major accounting firm, aware of the public relations value of this effort, accepted Time Dollars from Holland & Knight as payment for accounting work done on an unrelated pro bono activity. Time Dollars saved Holland & Knight upward of $8,000. But more important, Holland & Knight did not just give; it received real value in exchange through this transaction.

The real pay-off did not come in money; it came in other forms. First, there is firm morale. The legal profession lives uneasily with the gap between its idealism and much of its behavior. Lawyer turnover reflects that ambivalence: the bottom line is an oppressively pervasive reality. Many lawyers wonder whether they made the right choice. The thrill of being on a treadmill generating billable hours is not what draws most people into law. And some haven't forgotten that original impulse to try to save the world. If nothing else, at cocktail parties and when they go home to their children, they want to be able to talk about legal work that makes a social contribution.

Second, and closely related, is the recruitment value of distinctive pro bono work. All that a law firm has to offer is brains. Competing for top brains at top law schools is a life-and-death struggle. Holland & Knight understood that pioneering a new pro bono model that generated good will and roots in the community would help them recruit the best from Harvard and Yale.

Third, this initiative was partly spurred by Holland & Knight's desire for an appropriate entrée into Washington. Getting known in town as a major player was critical. High-visibility pro bono work achieves that objective.

Fourth, when law firms bid for municipal contracts, a reputation for civic virtue helps. Law firms that seek to become bond counsel to municipalities with large minority populations know how important image and profile are. There is no guarantee that pro bono work will generate business. But it did not seem a coincidence when Holland & Knight won the contract from the D.C. government to review, overhaul and streamline its entire administrative law system.

Fifth, receiving the American Bar Association's award for outstanding pro bono service doesn't hurt. It may be why the firm's Annual Pro Bono Report is prominently displayed among the reading matter made available to clients in the firm's lobby. It helps diffuse the mindset that typical lawyer jokes impart.

Lesson 8. Reciprocity supplies the funding rationale, strategy and imperative to underwrite the cost of Co-Production.

Co-Production as a theorem asserts that the market economy needs the participation of the non-market economy—of families, of recipients, of the client community. And it further asserts that the market needs that non-market world, not as passive consumers with purchasing power, but as active co-producers.

Yet Co-Production costs money. Using Time Dollars can radically reduce the cost of generating that Co-Production. But there are real costs: a coordinator, an office, a phone, supplies, refreshments, a computer, meetings, local travel, brochures.

Reciprocity is a core element of Co-Production. By definition, it entails mutuality. We need each other. That is not just true of us as individuals, as human beings. It is also true of organizations and institutions. Fully embraced, reciprocity gives rise to a commitment to provide the resources necessary to fund Co-Production.

Reciprocity is thus simultaneously a core value, a moral imperative, and a fiscal imperative. It supplies a compelling case, a grounded rationale, for ongoing financial support. There can be no Co-Production without reciprocity. And if Co-Production is essential to an organization's effectiveness, it follows that no human service organization should claim the ability to produce desired results if it cannot demonstrate that it has made adequate provision to generate Co-Production. That has implications—for structure, staffing, programs, and budget. The organization needing Co-Production must incorporate it as a cost of doing business.

Elderplan supplies a prime example.

We Need Each Other

> *At Elderplan, fixing a broken towel bar counts as health care. It was a broken hip waiting to happen. An amputee could have gone into a nursing home at $35,000 a year. Instead he became a telephone counselor. Research has shown that isolated older folks are less healthy and use more medical care than those who are socially engaged. Rescigno (an Elderplan Member) can attest to that. He hasn't had more than a cold since 1992. "The only reason I am as healthy as I am," he says, "is that I'm so busy helping other people."* — U.S. News & World Report, January 6, 1997.
>
> *The Co-Production model redefines health from something bought for money to something people do.*
>
> — Jonathan Rowe, "Money With Care Built In"[28]

Co-Production combines self-interest and altruism on an institutional and professional level, just as Time Dollars combine them for individuals, transaction by transaction. On all levels, reciprocity supplies the binding force, the link between present and future return, between giving and receiving.

When Mashi Blech meets with the CEO of Elderplan to find out whether the CEO will continue to commit major financial resources to continue the program, she goes with plenty of ammunition: stories, charts, exhibits, and long lists of awards, recognition, and media coverage—all of which translate into market share and enhanced financial viability for Elderplan.

Reciprocity Pays Off

First come the individual savings. Those are largely anecdotal. But the anecdotes pack a fiscal punch. If there is no adequate support system at home, hospital stays must be prolonged even if the patient no longer needs hospital level care. Each day that a stay can be shortened because of the Time Dollar program saves Elderplan $1,000. One avoided nursing home stay saves $35,000.

There are other forms of cost saving. If medication isn't taken, regularly or in the right doses, there are costs. If a chronic condition worsens, the earlier the intervention, the better and the less expensive. Emergency room trips cost; hospital stays cost. Monitoring the health status of members is expensive. Elderplan's Member-to-Member program has built-in monitoring. The stories abound.

Visiting Elderplan, I was told: "There's Vincent, helping out an older man who was severely depressed and talking about suicide. One day he went with the man to an auto repair shop and noticed that the man's mood improved greatly when he got out of his house. After that, instead of meeting at the house amidst the ghosts of the past, they met at a coffee shop. The man no longer talks of suicide."

Elderplan has blazed new paths in demonstrating the health-related contributions that even home-bound elderly can make. Two recent get-togethers drive the point home.

Reciprocity Promotes Health

The first was a face-to-face meeting of Time Dollar telephone pals. Many had been earning Time Dollars for years, checking in with each other—but they hadn't known what the other person looked like. It was an emotional coming together. You can't see eyes water over the phone. And the smile lines on each side of the mouth say something beyond words.

The second event entailed a major logistical effort. Several dozen home-bound older folks had undertaken a Time Dollar project to provide nursing home residents with two things they really needed: an embroidered lap robe to keep their legs warm when they stay in a wheel chair, and a special tote bag to fit over the arm or back of the chair to hold all the things they might need. Each home-bound person had received a photo and a biography of the nursing home resident with whom they had been paired.

It took a small cavalcade of busses, ambulances, nurses, and stand-by attendants to get everyone together. But the joy on the faces of those in the wheelchairs and those homebound elderly who this night were bestowing their handmade gifts was electric. The tonic was magic: a new friend for both. The homebound seniors had no time to feel sorry for themselves;

they were giving something needed and valued—and they were so much more fit than those they were helping. Mashi Blech, the loving dream-weaver who made all of this happen, is now determined to think up something that the folks in the nursing home can do for others as an affirmation of their own capacity to give love and to celebrate life.

There's Dorothy Gochal, one of the first Elderplan members to enroll as a peer counselor for other seniors. She explains "[People my age] don't want to talk to some young girl in her 30s about the death of their husband." Until Elderplan came along, Dorothy thought she had nothing to offer. Mashi Blech puts it differently: "You can't hire a new best friend. You can't buy somebody you can talk to over the phone when you're worried about surgery."

Studies are now documenting the presence of depression and related mental health problems as a major contributing factor in a significant percentage of physician visits. Practitioners, academicians, and researchers agree that there is a mental health component in one-third to one-half of physical ailment cases treated by physicians. Increasingly, hard data are emerging that demonstrate the positive corollary: that volunteering seems to promote wellness and even longevity. The November 1999 issue of *Harvard Men's Health Watch* summarized a series of studies linking depression to heart attacks, strokes and death. "Men with a recent depressive episode were 1.75 times more likely to die from heart disease than men who were not depressed." Other studies suggest that depression heightens the risk of stroke by 66 percent and the likelihood of developing hypertension by 80 percent.

Patients who want attention take time. And time is money. If nothing else, seniors have a choice as to how they get attention: they can be a hypochondriac, or they can join Member-to-Member and get anything from telephone bingo, phone quizzes, walking clubs, bereavement counseling and neighbors who know how to fix leaky faucets. When Elderplan received its presidential Points of Light Award, the accompanying citation noted that 400 members had contributed more than 4,000 hours of service to others.

Reciprocity Builds Market Share

Another benefit for the sponsoring organization is good publicity, which translates into market share. New York is a tough environment for an HMO. Elderplan is a relatively small fish, swimming in shark-infested waters. Yet, it was ranked number 1 in New York City against all competing health maintenance organizations. It has consistently garnered the most prestigious awards: from the Governor of New York State, United Way, American Association of Health Plans, American Public Health Association, American Society on Aging, the Points of Light Foundation, and the Corporation for National Service.

But what makes the Marketing Department the biggest fans and supporters of Time Dollars is the consistent stream of high-visibility media coverage that carries far more credibility than the fanciest, slickest advertising campaign. It would be hard to top the record of the past decade: "The Donahue Show," "Inside Edition," *The Christian Science Monitor, Parade Magazine, Modern Maturity,* "The Today Show," *U.S. News and World Report,* National Public Radio, PBS "Livelihood," *The Wall Street Journal, The New York Daily News, and The Washington Post.* That kind of PR is hard to beat. It is what has laid the foundation for a citywide expansion of Elderplan from Brooklyn to Manhattan, Queens, and Staten Island.

Finally, there is the issue of retention. Typically, HMOs have high member turnover. Within Elderplan, the Member-to-Member program boasts the highest retention rate. That has life-or-death implications for any HMO. Don Kasle, CEO of Elderplan, says, "We are looking at a very modest expenditure for all the plusses we get out of it. And if we have to buy a few bingo cards, big deal! We could run this organization only doing the things that gave us an economic return, but I dare say we would have gone out of business because nothing would have differentiated us from the giants in the industry and we really wouldn't have been able to compete." Elderplan understands the bottom line meaning of reciprocity: "We need each other."

What will it take for us all to understand that building reciprocity into transactions, into professional practice, into entitlements, into charity, into volunteering, is imperative? For those charged with providing the help, it may require nothing less than confronting the failure and futility of our best efforts.

Chapter 16

Reciprocity: A Social Justice Perspective

> ***The Story of the Drowning Babies***
> *The first woman who sees the babies floating down the river tries to pull out as many babies as possible, but she misses more than she helps. The second woman decides if she can teach the babies to swim, some will learn and save themselves. The third woman decides the only way to save all the babies is to find the bum who's throwing them in and stop it at the source."* (As told by Jennifer Gordon)

The following story is not about Time Dollars. It is about what happens when insisting on reciprocity makes clients central to the action. What happens is that they become unstoppable.

In relatively affluent neighborhoods on Long Island, large numbers of immigrant workers have long been subjected to injustices of all kinds. They are beaten, burdened and sexually assaulted in restaurants by their bosses, who threaten to have workers deported when they complain. They suffer incapacitating nausea, blinding headaches, and full-body rashes from working unprotected with toxic chemicals in factories that go out of existence overnight to avoid inspection. They work hauling trash and mowing lawns, only to end the season without being paid for weeks and even months of work. These abuses are not isolated incidents. They are part of the system of exploitation that characterizes the underground economy.

Then along came Jennifer Gordon, J.D., with a legal redress strategy built on reciprocity. Jennifer Gordon is not your typical Radcliffe-Harvard Law graduate. She knew, of course, that legal rights were involved and violations of law were rampant. But she also knew that simply providing legal services could not be *the* answer.

Learning one's rights buys help

Ultimately, for change to occur, Jennifer was convinced that people would have to know and assert their own rights. So from the outset, those who came seeking help as clients were required to give something of themselves. There was a modest fee—but the basic prerequisite to being accepted as a client meant taking a nine-week course in labor law, immigration law, and organizing. Every would-be client learns that employers cannot withhold paychecks, are required to pay overtime, cannot threaten bodily harm, cannot fire someone in retaliation for demanding pay owed them. They are taught how to represent themselves in hearings.

Jennifer Gordon does not talk about reciprocity, Co-Production, or Time Dollars. Instead, she tells her story of babies floating down a river and what it will take to save them. She knows the limits of individual representation, and she knows about credentials as barriers. And she takes action.

Jennifer is a lawyer. She can and does go into court. She sues, and she wins. But for her, that is perhaps the least important accomplishment of the Workplace Project. What the clients do and have done is more important. They are non-citizens, powerless persons. They are without the vote and without money. But by virtue of learning their rights and organizing and contributing time on picket lines, demonstrations and legislative hearings, they have actually secured passage of the nation's toughest legislation protecting the right of workers to be paid what is their due. That legislation was signed into law by Governor Pataki, who considers himself a conservative Republican. It raises penalties from 25 percent to 200 percent against employers who repeatedly do not pay their workers, and it makes repeat non-payment a felony rather than a misdemeanor.

Organizing beats case-by-case representation

The Workplace Project has enlisted clients as more than lobbyists. It also has worked with clients to establish the first worker-owned landscaping cooperative. And collectively, those same clients have carried out an organizing campaign on street corners that has increased wages by more than 30 percent. Reciprocity was a core functional principle for the organization Jennifer Gordon developed. This particular professional understood the message, "We need each other." She knows what too few professionals understand: that sometimes what clients can do is much more effective in making law work than anything lawyers can do by themselves. She has successfully put reciprocity to work.

Clients can get the bum who's throwing the babies into the water. That takes no credentials—and probably a lot less training than rescuing babies thrown into the water or teaching those babies to stay afloat.

Mutual support—the fee

One of Jennifer's protegés has now moved on to Miami. There she has combined the original Workplace strategy with Time Dollars to address patterns of sexual abuse and harassment to which women from the Caribbean and from Central and South America find themselves subjected at home and in the workplace. All clients pay in time. They commit to earning Time Dollars in a variety of ways: accompanying another woman to her injunction hearing, providing transportation to a meeting for another member, writing a letter to a government official, meeting with a government official, participating in a picket, and sharing personal experience with the legal process with another member.

Legal representation in the past has been the exclusive preserve of lawyers, paralegals, and legal technicians. It is the quintessential monopoly, exacting profit from the absence of competition, preserving scarcity by building it into the method of production. Reciprocity can advance the rule of law further—by enlisting and training clients to represent themselves, mobilizing group action, and triggering the use of formal legal representation as a last resort when all else fails.

The significance of paying back—except in money—seems to elude most helping professionals. They resist it in ways that defy rational discourse. Getting that lesson more broadly understood, accepted, and internalized will take a paradigm shift. We may have to learn it the hard way.

Changing the Professional Paradigm

Stephen Covey shares a wonderful story from *Proceedings*, the magazine of the Naval Institute, to illustrate what he means by a paradigm shift.[29] It is the story of a battleship, sent out with other ships, on a training mission. Several days out, the ship, commanded by a captain, encountered fog for an extended period. Suddenly, off to the starboard, a light appeared. It seemed to be coming toward the battleship on a collision course.

> *The captain then called to the signalman, "Signal that ship: We are on a collision course, advise you change course 20 degrees."*
>
> *Back came a signal: "Advisable for you to change course 20 degrees."*
>
> *The captain said, "Send, I'm a captain, change course 20 degrees."*
>
> *"I'm a seaman second class," came the reply. "You had better change course 20 degrees."*
>
> *By that time, the captain was furious. He spat out, "Send, I'm a battleship. Change course 20 degrees."*
>
> *Back came the flashing light, "I'm a lighthouse."*
>
> *We changed course.*

Covey says: That was a paradigm shift.

Co-Production redefines the relationship between the non-market world and the market economy, between professionals and clients. Think of Co-Production as a lighthouse, set up on *terra firma*, grounded in families, community, and civil society. Reciprocity is the message that the non-market world is beaming to effect a paradigm shift. If helping professionals, agencies, and funders get the message, they will halt the unilateral transactions, cease the assertion of hierarchy, and change course so that their respective journeys end at their intended destination. They may learn what the captain learned: that sometimes hierarchy, status, and even raw power may not determine outcome. The captain heard it and took action, only when he realized he didn't have any choice. Maybe, we don't either.

If we think of the non-market world as the base and Co-Production as the light house trying to steer social policy battleships, commercial trawlers, and non-profit boats to a safe harbor, then Reciprocity is the signal sent out by clients, by community, by civil society. It says: *Change course.* It says: *Without reciprocity, you will flounder and fail. You will run aground.*

Clients and community have seen it all before, a thousand times: the best-intentioned efforts steaming toward them, going aground, breaking up on the rocks. We all—policy makers, helping professionals, taxpayers, caring human beings—need to confront the limits of the ways in which we do things when we proceed, under full steam, to do our best and somehow, get nowhere. The message comes in many ways.

Message 1: Change course. Too often, the first response is to dismiss the message as showing ingratitude or irresponsibility.

Many dedicated, hardworking, underpaid professionals are used to encountering indifference, hostility, and ingratitude. Clients in need of help will say anything they have to in order to get the help. And then, something happens. The client doesn't show up. They don't do what they are supposed to do. They don't seem to value the work the professional is doing. That is particularly hard to stomach when you are a professional who can barely get by on the salary earned, when the workload keeps growing, the hours get longer, and your own private life is in a shambles. It is particularly galling when the service you are providing is free, when you are doing something which you think the client should value. But you pay that price. You tolerate what feels like a lack of appreciation or basic consideration because you are dedicated, and you begin to think, it just goes with the territory. The message is *Change course*. Generally speaking, professionals don't get the message.

Message 2: Change course. Once again, those in command dismiss the message, declaring, How dare you impugn our motives?

No matter what agencies and professionals do, the problem seems to get worse. The money available is never enough. Most people go into some human service profession or job hoping they can make a difference. It doesn't take long to come to the conclusion that the paperwork is drowning you, that the meetings are eating up all your time, and that you spend most of your time writing CYA memos.

The message, *Change course*, is getting more insistent. If you do charity work, you are accused of *noblesse oblige.* If you are a helping professional, you get accused of creating dependencies. If you manage an entitlement program, you are told you are rewarding people for having problems. You can't win.

What we ought to consider is that ineffectiveness may be a message, and maybe we ought to heed it. The sender may only be a second class seaman, or someone even lower on the pecking order—a client. But that does not mean we can afford to ignore the message: *Stop the one-way transactions.*

Sometimes the message even comes with an explanation. One way transactions are self-defeating; they focus on needs, not strengths. Sometimes the message comes as an infuriating question: "What have you done for me lately?"

We know the frustration. Why won't that other ship turn? Why won't it respond? We don't know it's a light house. We stomach our pride and keep on course. Reciprocity. What is that? We are doing our best. Keep going. Dead ahead.

Message 3: Change course or sink. Those in charge reply, heard that before.

If your job, or your agency's funding is really on the line, it tends to get your attention. You are really certain that you and your organization have been helping a lot of people, doing the best job you could. You feel you are out there all alone, with too few resources and no appreciation.

You are angry with the media. The only time you get their attention is when something goes wrong. Reporters don't show up and there are no TV cameras when you have good news to tell. And as the attacks on your agency mount, as funding gets cut, as good programs get eliminated, you wonder why there is no public support, no constituency for the valiant work you are doing.

If you have been through funding crises before, you are certain you can ignore the message. You have lived through crises before. You know this one will pass. So you go back to business as usual. But you do sometimes wonder: Where are the troops? Why aren't the people and the communities you've been helping willing to come out for you?

The last thing in the world you want to hear is the reciprocity message from the Co-Production lighthouse: *One way transactions are self-defeating; they subordinate others; they create dependencies. They invariably result in a combination of isolation, frustration and vulnerability.*

Failure to embrace reciprocity in agency practice effectively deprives that agency, its program, and its mission of the very constituency that can fight for it. The third message may be the last. *Change course.*

Some may be ready to hear the message. Unfortunately, in recent years, some have not.

A Near-Fatal Collision

From 1994 to 1997, I went on a campaign to bring the principle of reciprocity to the heart of the national legal services program. It was a failure.

It didn't take a crystal ball to know that the Legal Service program would be in trouble when power shifted to the right and the opponents of legal services took control of Congress in 1994. To be sure, the program had been in trouble—but previously, the American Bar Association had been able to rally sufficient congressional support to protect the program. With Newt Gingrich singling the program out for termination, the odds for survival didn't look good.

Key strategists and leaders of the equal-access-to-justice movement thought that the usual mobilization of bar support on the local and national level would do it. It would be tough, they said, but it was just a matter of digging in and working hard and the usual fight would end the usual way. My crystal ball read the picture differently. And I called for a strategy that would enlist the clients of legal service programs as co-producers.

The method was simple: use the same Time Dollar fee structure I had sold to Holland & Knight. When clients left, they would then go to their local client council to "pay" the fee by helping others. The result would be "politically correct" for conservatives: indigent clients would be paying back; poor people would be engaged in self-help. But there would be one other not-so-obvious result: A vibrant client council or alternative community-based organization would exist in every state with a powerful membership base and a reason for defending a program that was busy generating a steady stream of new client-members functioning as Time Dollar workers.

The community groups that I spoke to were overwhelmingly enthusiastic. "Yes", they said, "we would like to be charged a fee in Time Dollars. That would give us a real say on priorities and use of resources." And when it came to final recommendations and resolutions, reciprocity topped the list. Paying for legal services with Time Dollars was more than just okay with the client groups; they wanted it.

But there was no support from the lawyers and the heads of programs, with the sole exception of the California Rural Legal Assistance program. I wrote to the head of the National Legal Aid and Defender Association; no answer. I tried to arrange a workshop or panel at the annual conference; nothing doing. I published a major piece called "Reinventing Poverty Law" in the prestigious Yale Law Journal, laying out the entire strategy; deafening silence.

The fight I had foreseen came—and went. Last-minute heroic efforts by the organized bar and by a legal service organization funded to lobby for the program barely averted its demise. Funding was cut by more than one-third. Lawyers in the program were hog-tied by a bunch of restrictions that no lawyer representing corporations or the wealthy would ever accept. The restrictions virtually gutted the program, specifying what cases lawyers could not take, what forums they could use, what appeals they could take, and what tactics they could employ.

One stark fact stands out in my mind. This program had helped more than 3 million people a year for 33 years. That's approximately 100 million households. Yet, on the national level, not a single client appeared to defend the program. The client voice was simply not heard.

Failure to build in reciprocity meant failure to do business in a way that would create a constituency for Justice. It was appalling. Those were the same days when the Corporation for Public Broadcasting fought and won a brilliant campaign for its own survival. Unlike the Legal Services Corporation, it was able to fend off an equally vitriolic congressional assault by mobilizing a listener constituency with whom it maintained an ongoing relationship.

On the merits, the legal services program had at least as compelling a reason to survive. For decades it had successfully restrained official lawlessness, checked child abuse and spousal abuse, and halted arbitrary cutbacks in such critical life support programs as Medicaid, food stamps, welfare, and disability.

The Preamble to the Constitution cites "To establish justice" as a primary reason for the founding of this nation. Newt Gingrich's Contract with America sought to wipe out that clause from the earlier contract. He nearly succeeded. Many would say he did.

No one can say for sure whether a relationship based on reciprocity with clients and client groups would have resulted in a better outcome. Reciprocity was never given a chance to show what impact it might have. It is possible that nothing would have turned the tide—or that it would have provoked even greater and less tractable opposition. But that same year, I did have the opportunity to test the power of reciprocity to create a constituency for justice, albeit on a smaller scale and in a different arena.

When Reciprocity Worked

The issue was life or death for the law school where I teach, the University of the District of Columbia School of Law. It is the successor to Antioch Law School, the law school I was trying to save when I had my heart attack. The community took possession of that law school and chartered it as a public law school, the law school of this nation's capital.

It had been based on a medical model. Medical schools have "teaching hospitals"; this law school had a teaching law firm that provided legal services to thousands in some of the District's poorest neighborhoods. It was expressly committed to equal justice and to opening up the profession to previously unrepresented groups.

Earlier that year, in anticipation of a survival battle, I sought an assignment to the legal clinic, and had that year instituted a new community development clinic that did outreach to community groups. As part of that clinic, we started up Time Dollar programs at Reverend Walter Fauntroy's New Bethel Baptist Church, at Kimi Gray's Kenilworth-Parkside housing complex, and in various public housing developments for seniors.

In 1995-96, the District of Columbia fell upon spectacularly hard times financially. *The Washington Post* and some prominent members of Congress targeted the law school for zero funding. The mayor was making no promises. The odds were heavily against the law school surviving at a time when money was being cut for programs for the homeless, job training programs, Medicaid, foster care, and housing. Every department and every budget was being cut.

Funding a public law school in a city with five other law schools (Howard, Catholic University, George Washington University, Georgetown and American University) looked like an indefensible luxury. *The Washington Post* ran news stories and editorials calling for the demise of the law school as a throwback to the days of deficit spending and bloated budgets that had brought the entire D.C. government into disrepute. We were accused of jeopardizing the little self-government that home rule advocates had secured.

Plenty of people said there was no way this one could be won. Pundits were already pronouncing the school dead. *The Washington Post* churned out obituaries for the law school. Commentators on the local public radio stations were busy rationalizing a painful but inevitable outcome.

The D.C. Council scheduled hearings on the law school's future. The usual suspects testified: the Dean, leaders of the bar, judges, students, public interest law groups. But what turned the tide were voices from the community.

One came from Reverend Fauntroy, who had originally helped mobilize the entire community to create the School of Law:

> *I think I know how tight the fiscal pressures are and how critical every dollar is. But I am tired of being told I must choose between bread and justice when I know, through the work of D.C. law students, that we can gain bread through justice. If we choose bread and not justice, then we know from long experience that soon, the bread will be withdrawn and we will have neither bread nor justice.*

Later came Kimi Gray, a former welfare recipient who single-handedly had turned Kenilworth Parkside from an open drug fair to a nationally heralded model of resident ownership and resident management. She started off declaring that law was the major industry of the nation's capital. Her children needed access to it. Then, she blasted the notion that there were ample law schools in the District:

> *I know we have five other law schools.... We know where we are welcome. We know where we are not welcome. So don't tell me about those other law schools. They don't want our children, except as tokens. D.C. School of Law is different.*

Then she spoke about Time Dollars and what that signaled in her community:

> *We are about building community, about creating a place where neighbors help neighbors, where we take responsibility for our kids, where we give back as much as we get. The students from the law school are part of that effort. And they are helping us to strengthen this community by helping to institute a program called Time Dollars. We have a lot of volunteering going on—but we don't begin to tap the full pool of talent and energy we have out here. We don't reward it. And we don't find ways of spreading the work around as much as we need to. So we are working now to use Time Dollars to reward people who are helping out, to have an information system that keeps track of the incredible volume of help that people give to each other, and that sends a message to our young people that there is more to life than money.*

Finally, she talked about the special relation that the law school had to the community:

> *I certainly know, better than most, how tight the resources are and how much each cut is hurting. But I have to say: when you start cutting, don't come after our law school. Because when you do, you are doing more than attacking a law school. You are attacking a special resource. You are attacking an ideal of hope and justice and service. You are saying money counts more than justice, more than equality, more than opportunity. I'm speaking out to say, "Don't even think about doing it."*

When Kimi Gray speaks, when Rev. Fauntroy speaks for Black church leaders, when other residents such as spokespersons for senior developments speak, D.C. Council members listen, because they know how to count votes. So they voted to keep the law school open and to give it the funding needed to get accreditation. That victory supplied a momentum and created an aura that continues to envelop the school in each succeeding year. Reciprocity has survival value. When we really need each other, we need to be able to say so—and mean it. We need to walk the talk.

ONE LEGAL SERVICE PROGRAM GOT THE MESSAGE

In California, one legal services program broke lock step with all other legal service programs and embraced reciprocity. A new immigration law in 1998 coupled with Draconian enforcement of old regulations posed a devastating threat to the client community. Roundups in the middle of the night, sweeps by immigration authorities, impossible deadlines for filing citizenship applications all made it critically important to get the word out to a rural, migrant population that spoke only Spanish and to create a massive system of filing for citizenship where minor inaccuracies, omissions, and ignorance of the law would prove catastrophic.

Citizenship protected one from deportation. But applying for citizenship carried all kinds of danger. One could be denied citizenship for a host of reasons: failure to register for the draft even if one believed one was exempt, failure to file income tax, any conviction resulting in 180 days in jail, gambling offenses, and any drug offense, no matter how far in the past. Often, a past criminal record was the result of an expedient plea bargain. But years later, there would be no way of re-opening that case, or challenging that arrest. Committing adultery, failing to pay child support, lying about a previous arrest have all been used as grounds for denial of the "Good Moral Character" verification required for naturalization. Merely applying for citizenship can now trigger a nationwide computerized record search of arrest records.

It is easy to see why many would feel it prudent to lie low rather than to risk all that. Moreover, with the exception of persons age 50 and over who had spent at least 15 years as permanent residents, everyone suddenly faced a citizenship examination in English.

Limited, but wholly inadequate, funding became available for immigration advocacy and public education campaigns. Just getting word out was important, but insufficient. People had to be urged to apply and simultaneously warned not to apply for citizenship if something in their past might trigger a denial or even, deportation. For those who spoke little or no English, language complicated any effort to convey the legal issues, and made preparation for a citizenship examination more difficult. Then, there was a larger issue: civic education. Citizenship ought to mean more than passing a test and avoiding the pitfalls. But how could it, under the circumstance? Basic values like democracy and community seemed inevitable casualties of the process.

For the first time, there was no escaping the reality: no quantity of lawyers, even with the aid of paralegals, could possibly move the process on the scale needed or in time to meet critical deadlines. Co-Production that enlisted the client community was the only answer. And reciprocity was the key to making Co-Production work.

So under the plan devised by California Rural Legal Assistance lawyers in collaboration with community leaders, priority was given on the basis of reciprocity: If you come and if you help, you get served first. If you come to the first background session, you go to the head of the line at the second session to get help filling out your forms. Then it's your turn to help coach, translate, explain, probe, and even fill out forms for others.

Time Dollars became a vehicle for earning preference—getting help by giving help. The only way in which an informed cadre of interviewers, translators, coaches, and reviewers could be created overnight was to accord them the status of co-workers. They earned Time Dollars that could be used to pay, first for the legal help received, then for the lengthier courses in citizenship needed to prepare them both for the test and for life in community. By using Time Dollars as a reward and as a management system, the use of reciprocity transformed scarce professional services into a collaborative undertaking—staffing and managing a triage system that can handle cases from the simplest to the most complex.

A series of mass workshops, handling two and three hundred cases a day, took place. Information that suggested a possible risk of deportation had to trigger red flag alerts. These then had to be probed more fully. Sometimes more facts would be needed; sometimes, documentation. The bottom line, particularly in high risk cases, is always informed consent by a client who really understands what is at stake. When many clients speak only Spanish and many lawyers only English, only the client community can supply the translators. Often, the source was those teenagers whom most professionals ignore. In immigrant communities, they are a special asset; they are the ones best able to bridge cultures and language barriers.

The world was no longer divided between professionals and clients; the world had become community. Those who could not translate could babysit. Those who could not understand English could serve food. Those who needed coaching and explaining and translation could commit to working at the next workshop. They would become the outreach workers needed to get frightened people to do what was necessary to secure control over their own lives and destinies. No one but clients could do that job. Interdependence was a central necessity if mission meant anything. "We really need each other" was literally true.

Means Become Ends

The attack on helping professionals is gaining momentum. The attack on all programs, public and non-profit, is growing in intensity. Issues of poverty, illiteracy, family cohesion, drug addiction, delinquency, congressional and electoral reform, educational opportunity, and equal rights have been downgraded as matters of national concern. The attacks come from all sides—those who share our values and those who don't. Anyone who even dares to earn a living engaged in dealing with social problems takes the risk of being blamed for failing, attacked for creating dependencies, and discredited as self-seeking and greedy.

In every field, there are experts in high places who will defend prevailing practice brilliantly and cogently. From the mountaintops, they will counsel sagely, *If it ain't broke, don't fix it.* Behind that advice is a veiled warning: Don't attract too much scrutiny. At least right now, there's room for a few caring people to make a decent living helping some people who need help.

We have stopped dreaming about righting wrongs, remedying injustice.

The Co-Production Lighthouse keeps beaming out the message of reciprocity. It says: *We need each other.* It says: *If we incorporate genuine reciprocity into all that we do, there can be enough for everyone.* And each of us will be there to come to each other's rescue so that good works, good people, and good organizations will not go down.

Reciprocity normally means giving back. I do for you. You do for me. That describes a course of action, a game plan, a way to get from here to there. From a strategic viewpoint, reciprocity is simply a means to an end. But in the context of Co-Production, reciprocity takes on other dimensions.

First, reciprocity redefines the relationship between the world of money and the world of community. It supplies the rationale and the moral imperative for restructuring that relationship. Each world says to the other, *We need each other.*

Second, reciprocity as a core element asserts: That need for mutuality is not optional. It is not peripheral. It is central to mission, to survival, and to credibility.

Third, reciprocity is not simply a way of characterizing an isolated transaction. It cannot be just a one-time thing. It establishes mutuality as an ongoing relationship between worlds. It declares that we need each other, and that we will be there for each other. We elect that.

The Bible says, "Choose life that you may live." We must choose reciprocity so that we may live and fulfill our dreams and our mission.

Fourth, reciprocity does not come free. Mutual obligation between the market and non-market economies comes with a price tag. It takes an infrastructure, a reward structure, an information system and staffing to generate and sustain reciprocity. The money is worth it if we really want to make a difference.

Otherwise, all of us who seek a more just society will consign ourselves to the fate of saving a few babies while the rest drown. We will never get to the cause. Our efforts will be dismissed more and more as futile. We will be maligned as merely serving our own self-interest. And in the end, we will be left alone, to fight the good fight without the allies we need, and indeed deserve.

Reciprocity means that we need each other. Not on a one time basis, not as window dressing, but as central and sustained—as a way of doing business. Viewed from the perspective of social justice, reciprocity means,

> *No more subordination of those we help as the price exacted for helping.*
>
> *No more ongoing dependency as the implicit price for receiving help.*

Chapter 17

Core Value Four: Social Capital

Social capital is the essential ingredient, we are told, for building or restoring civil society. Private goods and private transactions are not enough. Humans require a social infrastructure as much as they need roads, bridges, and utility lines. That requires an ongoing investment of something called social capital.

Robert Putnam, whose 1995 article "Bowling Alone"[30] put social capital on the agenda of the White House, foundations, and universities, tells us that social capital is composed of trust, reciprocity, and civic engagement. But he doesn't tell us how to produce it. In fact, his book, *Making Democracy Work*, ends with the challenge: "Building social capital will not be easy, but it is the key to making democracy work."[31]

Those involved with Time Dollars know exactly how to generate social capital. Trust, reciprocity, and civic engagement are Time Dollar staples. Putnam supplies a definition of reciprocity that captures some of what we have just been examining:

> *Each individual act in a system of reciprocity is* usually *charactered by a combination of what one might call short-term altruism and long-term self-interest: I help you out now in the (possibly vague, uncertain and uncalculating) expectation that you will help me out in the future. Reciprocity is made up of a series of acts each of which is short-run altruistic (benefitting others at a cost to the altruist) but which together* typically *make every participant better off.*[32]

Putnam then explains how networks of civic engagement strengthen trust and build social capital. Networks of civic engagement:

- increase the potential costs to a defection in any individual transaction
- foster robust norms of reciprocity reinforced by networks of relationships that depend on a reputation for keeping processes and accepting community norms
- facilitate communication and improve the flow of information about the trustworthiness of individuals
- embody past success at collaboration, which serves as a template for future collaboration

Ever since the first Time Dollar programs got underway in the late 1980s, we have seen ample proof of what such networks can do in terms of trust and trustworthiness. The inverse of the Golden Rule, "Do *not* do unto others what you would not have them do unto you," appears to have taken hold. In millions of transactions, there has not been a single mugging or "defection." We can say with certainty that not all members are saints; but none has been willing to jeopardize the support system to which Time Dollars gives them access.

The earliest studies of Time Dollar programs noted that "sites have tended to emphasize the establishment of relationships among participants—building a sense of community—over formal rules for banking or service exchange. As a result, programs have developed less as anonymous or mechanical exchanges than as community membership organizations."[33]

Social capital adds a future focus to Co-Production. It is about investment in the future that avoids a backward-looking fixation on fault-finding.

Culture, tradition, ritual, and custom are all forms of social capital created in the past in an effort to make the future manageable. They link members of a culture to each other, generate a sense of mutual obligation, and imbue each with collective responsibility for coming to each other's rescue. Social capital is the resource with which a culture equips its members to cope with the future.

There is a one requirement, however. To create new social capital, one must believe that one's actions have consequences, that there is a future, and that one can affect that future.

The Future as Possible: A Prerequisite of Social Capital

"How did you treat your substitute teacher?" When I ask that question, a smirk combined with a slightly demonic grin spreads across the faces of most people. Those days were like having a break. Even when the substitute teacher was really trying, no one listened. She could take down names and note behavior; she could threaten to contact the regular teacher. But none of that was real to us as children.

Those were days when we would try getting away with things we wouldn't dream of doing with the regular teacher. That's because it simply didn't count. No action had consequences because that substitute would simply be gone. You would never see her or him again. Memory didn't exist. I have yet to meet the person who can remember learning anything from a substitute teacher, or trying to do something special to make a good impression.

Now try to imagine living your whole school career with substitute teachers—or living your entire life in a world where nothing you did had consequences because you would never see today's people again. You could lie, and no one would find out. You could take something that belonged to someone else; no one would ever catch you or ask you to give it back. You could accidentally break something, and no one would ever know you did it.

At first, that might seem great. But if that were life, your whole life, if nothing you did mattered, why would you even try to do anything special? All that would matter would be what fun you could have, what goodies you could get, here and now. If life feels like a series of one-time encounters with substitute teachers, then why not treat every stranger as someone to take advantage of? Take the sucker for everything you can get. Why not?

That is the world we live in, many of us. Particularly children, and especially children growing up in poverty. That's 40 percent of the children in this country—and we are rich; maybe the richest country in the history of the world. Nearly half of our kids are growing up in a world where nothing they do matters. No one cares. No one will remember. For the most part, the chances of getting caught are pretty small—for taking advantage of someone, for lying or cheating or stealing or hurting someone. That's not exactly a safe world to live in. No trust, no honor, no restraint. That's the world that is now setting up commissions to study the disappearance of civil society. That's the world whose social infrastructure has crumbled.

When we reviewed videotape excerpts from live Youth Court hearings, this is what we heard:

> *Where do you think you'll be in five years?*
>
> *Dead or locked up.*
>
> A father speaking to his child: *You have to be your own man. Before it's too late.*
>
> Another father: *As a teenager, I didn't believe I'd live this long.*
>
> A juror cross-examining a respondent: *By the year 2000, if we are still alive, a high school degree won't be enough.*

How do you build social capital in an environment where distrust is pervasive and where self-interest translates into "Look out for yourself and only yourself"? How do you get people to help each other when you believe you are taking a risk by trusting anyone?

The Prisoner's Dilemma: Building Trust from Distrust

Long ago, this question was formulated as a puzzle called the Prisoner's Dilemma. There are lots of versions but they all boil down to the same set of choices.

- **You both win if you both help each other. But it is a small win.**
- **You win much more if the other guy tries to help you—and you betray him and turn him in. He loses big. You win big.**
- **You both lose (but only a little) if you both turn each other in. But it is a small loss.**

If you only get to play once, it doesn't pay to trust the other guy and try to help him. You stand to lose big if you take the risk of trusting your opponent and your opponent turns you in. And at best, if both trust, you will win a little—but so will the other player.

The choice is pretty clear. If you betray the other player, you might win big. You can only lose a little—and the other player will lose as much. Given those odds, there is no choice. In any single, isolated game, never trust the other person. Sell them down the river.

Banking on the Future

There is only one way out of this box. If the game is not an isolated one, if you are going to play against the same player in an open-ended tournament, it pays to start by trusting. It pays to help the other guy at least so long as he or she does the same. The first time they betray you, you do it right back. Tit-for-tat. Once you have shown them that you won't take a betrayal, then they will sooner or later figure out that it works best for both of you to keep trusting each other.

That's not just a fairy story. It's the conclusion reached by a political scientist at MIT named Robert Axelrod who was asking, *How does co-operation evolve when it pays more to take advantage of someone else?* He used the Prisoner's Dilemma, to test different strategies. He invited philosophers, computer programmers, logicians, and political scientists from all over the world to compete. And he took each strategy submitted and plugged it into a computer to see which strategy consistently generated the highest score.

He found that in a one-time encounter, the Prisoner's Dilemma game makes sure that no good deed goes unpunished. But more important, he found that when the game is part of a sequence in which you keep playing against the same player, cooperation and trust are the winning strategies. No bad deed goes unpunished. Tit-for-Tat socks it to the other player if that player tries betrayal. Likewise, no good deed goes unrewarded. Trust and cooperation become possible only if there is a future. Then, the shadow that the future casts on the present makes trust and cooperation in the present possible.

The Prisoner's Dilemma game sends two messages. The first is a message of despair. If present actions have no future consequences, then the only rational choice is "Screw the other guy." Trust doesn't pay. There is no future. There is only the present; you may as well enjoy it while you have it and go out in a blaze.

The second message is a message of hope, of possibility. If life can be seen as a sequence of transactions, if today's acts have future consequences, then reciprocity is a winning strategy. Cooperation and trust work. It doesn't mean you have to be a sucker. Using Tit-for-Tat, reciprocity becomes both sword and shield. You defect; you get it right back. You cooperate; you get cooperation.

The Prisoner's Dilemma says, If we link events in an open-ended chain, causation can be reinstated. We can build a world where "you reap what you sow." "What goes around, comes around" can both describe and shape reality.

Youth Court: Linking the present to the future

That is why the Time Dollar Youth Court seeks to establish a new causal relationship between present and future. Prior practice in the District of Columbia was almost uniformly to send a youth home at the first arrest. The prosecutor would "No Paper" the case. It wasn't worth taking it seriously. The message that sent was: You get three freebies before anyone takes you seriously. That meant three times getting caught—and who knows how many times not getting caught. By the time a youth came before a judge as a first offender, that youth was already well along a road that said: Acts don't have consequences. Nothing matters. Just try harder not to get caught. Guess where youngsters can turn for that kind of savvy? The streets.

These are the young people who have serious discussions about how they are to be dressed for their own funerals, what clothes they want on them, and what kind of coffin they want to be laid in. For them, there is no future. There is living now, going out in style and maybe, hopefully, leaving a baby or two behind.

Creating a Youth Jury is not just about processing cases. It means creating a peer culture where it is safe to say: Don't take that risk. It means getting youth to believe that acts have consequences and that they, as jurors, can help shape the future for themselves and for their peers. It represents an extraordinary leap of faith in a different possibility for a juror to press for a stiffer sentence of 30 hours of community service arguing: He knew what happens if you get into a stolen car. He knew that if you do something wrong, there are consequences.

Building social capital in the context of Co-Production depends on creating a different possibility. There must be a future that you can shape. If actions have consequences, if tomorrow can be determined by what you do today, trust is a winning strategy.

Peer culture is a form of social capital that the Youth Court generates when one youth can say to another, Don't do something stupid. When young people believe that they have the power themselves to alter their own life expectancy and each other's, we have created social capital.

Our Social Capital Legacy: Tradition and Culture

Some communities create social capital as a daily event. In Houston, one parent explained to me, "When we were growing up, that's how it was. If we had milk and the folks next door had cornflakes, then we all had breakfast."

Cultures survive by seizing the opportunity to create social capital at every turning point event: when newcomers move into the community, when a farmer is sick, when couples marry, when an elder dies.

In North Dakota, barn-raising for newcomers has not died out as a way of life. And neither has the practice of coming from all the surrounding farms with combines and tractors to harvest the crop if a farmer gets sick at harvest time. These are simple expressions of neighborliness that need no thanks and no special formality.

A Native American wedding

Native American cultures build extended families at turning point events: marriage and death. A Navajo wedding ceremony can go on for hours. My son's late wife, Ninebah Cahn, was a full-blooded Navajo, the daughter of a medicine man. The beginning of the wedding ceremony dealt with the couple. They washed each other's hands with holy water carried in a special vessel from a sacred mountain. They fed each other. They took vows in the Navajo way. But that was just the beginning.

Next the families had to tell their history, whence they had come, how they had survived and prospered, what they brought to this union. I told the story of my family, seven generations of rabbis and lawyers, a commitment to learning, to our religious tradition, and to justice. Ninebah's father told their story: how they had raised sheep, traded with the cavalry, made blankets and silver, educated their children, taught them trades, sent them to college. The bottom line was that this ceremony was the confluence of families, not simply the joining of two individuals. And that was just the beginning.

Because then, every guest at the wedding had to share stories about his or her marriage as a way of saying, You are now part of our family and we are part of yours. And as one guest put it, when you have a disagreement and she puts your saddle and blanket outside the hogan, you are welcome at all of our homes—because we are now family. And we know that marriages don't always go smoothly. So look around. Our doors will be open.

Grief and the creation of extended family

In 1999, the loss of a dear friend took me to Oklahoma for the funeral of Browning Pipestem, a great Native American, a lawyer who had devoted his life to his people's struggle for self-determination. It was a journey back in time to the homeland of the Otoe Indian nation. The ceremony began with a profound expression of gratitude to the family for entrusting the care, tending, and protection of this warrior's body to the tribe for those last hours before my friend would be returned to earth. Browning's wish and that of his family was that he be buried on tribal land, trust territory—land that can never be sold.

At the end of the ceremony, just before the burial, I was witness to something I had heard about but never understood. The family brought out a huge pile of Indian blankets, at least two hundred. One by one, the names of tribal members and friends were read out. One by one, each was embraced by each member of Browning's family. And the blanket or some other gift of value was formally bestowed. A Native American physician standing next to me commented, "In this tribe, dying can be quite expensive." I knew those blankets sold for between $100 and $150 dollars. And I was a bit shocked at a custom that would drain such resources from a family at a time of loss and bereavement. Then it all became clear.

The elder who presided over the ceremony then reminded all those who were present how much this family would need the support, the love, the care of all those present—now more than ever. He admonished: They must not think, "This is over. We can go about our business." Because above all, this would be the time when this family will need their prayers and their help.

His words were echoed by the religious leader who offered the final prayer before the body was lowered into the grave. And I suddenly understood what I had witnessed. In that tribe's way, the gift presented publicly, by name, coupled with an embrace—creates a debt that carries with it an implicit pledge. Before my eyes, the family and the hundreds who came to the funeral had been knit together—quite publicly, by name—in a web of reciprocal obligation. At its weakest moment, when it is most bereft, the family by giving to others had, by custom, been empowered to weave a vast fabric of support, of caring, of mutual help designed to carry it through the days and even years ahead. The loss, the emptiness, the great gap in their lives was to be filled by a ceremony that initiated healing, but that also conferred upon them a power over the future.

This was not just about grieving. It meant that at the very moment when mortality brings home the ultimate powerlessness of the human condition, an entire people was enabling that family to exercise collective power over the living to cope with the uncertainty and the vulnerability that death had brought.

Culture, custom, ritual, ways of doing things supply a form of social capital. They are the reserves one falls back on in crises or when the unexpected hits. They are the way we give life order, the way we make life manageable, the way we shape the future.

MAKING INTANGIBLES COUNT

New research is uncovering previously unidentified forms of social capital and new ways in which communities can co-produce the social capital they need to gain control over their destiny. The largest study ever undertaken of the causes of crime and delinquency recently yielded new data that help us understand Co-Production. Published in the August 1997 issue of *Science*, a multi-million dollar, multi-year study undertaken in Chicago by the Harvard School of Public Health concluded that poverty and joblessness could not account for the differences in crime they found in largely African American neighborhoods. [34]

The investigators classified 343 neighborhoods in Chicago in terms of the characteristics thought to be predictors of crime—poverty, unemployment, race, single-parent households—only to find that neighborhoods that looked alike in terms of these variables had very different levels of violent crime. Obviously, some other factor was involved. So they went looking. Eight thousand, eight hundred and seventy-two interviews later, they had an answer: *collective efficacy.*

What does that term mean? Behind the label, it was a willingness by residents "to intervene in the lives of children." That meant a willingness to step in to stop acts like truancy, graffiti painting, and street-corner "hanging" by teen-age gangs.

For once, the media covered some good news. *The New York Times* played up the extent to which this finding deviated from prevailing assumptions that low-income neighborhoods are powerless to cope: "Some neighborhoods in Chicago are largely black and poor, yet have low crime rates—so some other explanation is needed for the causes of crime.... The finding is considered significant by experts because it undercuts a prevalent theory that crime is mainly caused by factors like poverty, unemployment, single-parent households or racial discrimination."[35]

The chief researcher, Dr. Felton Earls, understood that this new finding had identified a long-overlooked asset, a form of social capital: "By far the greatest predictor of the violent crime was collective efficacy... a shared vision, a fusion of shared willingness of residents to intervene and social trust, a sense of engagement and ownership of public space. In particular we believe that collective expectations for intervening on behalf of neighborhood children is a crucial dimension of the public life of neighborhoods."

The critical factor was not "external actions" such as police crackdowns. What emerged was a finding of the "effectiveness of 'informal' mechanisms by which residents themselves achieve public order."

Collective Efficacy as Social Capital

There used to be a time when a neighbor, upon seeing someone's kid beating up a smaller kid, would step in, pull them apart and say, "Stop that, or I'll tell your mother." In some neighborhoods, people still do just that. In others they don't.

Social capital refers to that willingness to step in. Communities, paralyzed by fear, are themselves a victim of violence. Do nothing and your worst fears will be realized. Residents have to become co-producers of safety.

That alters traditional distinctions between providers and recipients, producers and consumers, professionals and clients. It creates a parity for individuals and for communities in their relationships with professional helpers.

Collective efficacy is real. Hard-headed, bottom-line policy makers want data, hard data—such as crime statistics or property values reflecting the prevalence of criminal activity. Now, suddenly, soft stuff takes on hard, statistical significance. Neighborhood interaction, networking, local custom, and just being nice can no longer be dismissed as fuzzy, irrelevant concepts. In this context, Time Dollars earned in neighborhood roles can be used as a measure of collective efficacy and as a reward to stimulate such conduct. Because numbers seem to count in public dialog, Time Dollars can function as a source of leverage. They supply evidence of the production of collective efficacy.

Ideally, such activity is spontaneous, the result of a tradition kept alive in the community. But when collective efficacy is not present, when the tradition has died or never had the chance to be born, it is important to find new ways to create it. It can be done: Organizing to "take back the streets" can do that. Grandma brigades are formidable.

Experiments with Time Dollars in a variety of settings are yielding new ways to produce that tradition, to generate that ethos by recording and rewarding that behavior. In Brooklyn, Miami, and Washington, D.C. when seniors earn Time Dollars helping other seniors, we do not hear about muggings. In the Chicago peer tutoring program, principals reported that when older kids earned Time Dollars tutoring younger students, the bullying after school in the playground stopped. Apparently one does not beat up one's tutee and equally important, one does not let other kids do that either.

The social capital we need to shape the future involves using whatever assets we have to enhance control over quality of life. There are some things individuals cannot buy. There are some things we cannot create for ourselves; sometimes that takes the culture speaking through its social, political, or economic institutions.

We acknowledge that it takes a village to raise a child. Now we are understanding that it takes collective efficacy to make that village a safe place to rear that child. Social capital is the asset that creates a sustainable habitat for our species. There is the potential to find it or create it in every community.

Building the village to raise the children

In Southeast Washington, D.C., five-year-old Natasha understands what it takes to create social capital. She lives in Benning Terrace, a housing complex where (until cleaned up by former gang members) graffiti warned visitors that they were entering a war zone. No grass grew—only hard-packed soil, littered with cans and broken glass. Simple City, as it was called by the media, was nationally notorious for the number of drive-by shootings. One year after a truce was negotiated by the Alliance of Concerned Men, former gang members were hired by the housing authority to dig up the soil, lay sod, and plant flowers.

I watched this five-year old, in her pigtails, go up to a six-foot hulk who towered over her, decorated with tattoos, gold tooth, and gold chains. She said to him pointedly, "We have trashcans here and we use them."

The teenager was completely taken aback. After staring at this little pipsqueak in amazement, he reached down, grabbed the litter he had just tossed on the ground, crumpled it up, stuck it in his pocket and walked away. Natasha didn't even know what raw courage her act took. She was just defending her sense of how her world should be kept. That was her Time Dollar job.

More precisely, it was one of her Time Dollar jobs, because she also serves on the graffiti patrol and earns Time Dollars attending storytelling sessions, listening to a senior who reads storybooks to five- and six-year-olds. Her pay is in Time Dollars, which makes her a breadwinner for her family. She earns two bags of groceries each month from the Benning Terrace Time Dollar food bank.

When residents first started the Time Dollar club at Benning Terrace, a lot of the hours were earned in preparing the food served after funerals for teenagers killed in drive-by shootings. Some neighbors earned Time Dollars as look-outs, using their phones to send coded warnings or all-clear messages to beepers that neighbors took whenever they left to go shopping.

For nearly a year now, the killings have dropped to zero. Much of the credit belongs to the Alliance of Concerned Men, who negotiated a truce between rival gangs. Then the housing authority provided some maintenance, gardening, and clean-up jobs for former gang members. Now the money is gone and the jobs have ended; but the sense of community remains, reinforced by the social network that the Time Dollars system has helped to generate and sustain. This past year, that translated into a total of 78,560 hours at different public housing complexes.

A new kind of village is emerging. If safety and security are forms of social capital, then that's what Natasha was producing.

Chapter 18

Social Capital: A Social Justice Perspective

Stop Strip-mining the Village

A social justice perspective says: stop the disinvestment in families and neighborhoods.

Our inner cities have been targets for disinvestment for as long as most of us can remember. First, it was urban renewal. That was called *Negro Removal*, as stable Black communities were leveled by bulldozers. Next came the highway program. A large number of inner city neighborhoods that were targeted for rebuilding through the model cities programs were simultaneously targeted for demolition by the national highway program. The combined effect was what Julius Williams has written about: the disappearance of work from the inner city.

Then came other programs. Those same neighborhoods became "targets" for various human service programs. Sometimes these were "outreach" programs where downtown agencies sent in professionals. Sometimes they were one-stop social service centers that brought multiple agencies right into the neighborhood. Sometimes, they were like Homebuilders, which brought social workers right into your kitchen. But the bottom line was that regardless of where the services were brought, the money exited on payday from the neighborhoods being served to the neighborhoods where the professionals lived. Multiple studies have confirmed that only about one third of the money spent to benefit the poor ever get into their hands.

Now comes the welfare program. We have exported the jobs. We have exported the money. Now we are going to export the people and require them, as the price of survival, to go hunt down the jobs. The only folks left during the day will be the children, the elderly, the homeless, the addicts, the gangs—and from 9 to 5 from Monday to Friday, the professionals engaged in outreach and "community development."

The welfare law is doing more than accelerating the exodus. We are overlooking the obvious: The faster we succeed in moving the most work-ready, upwardly mobile welfare mothers into jobs, the faster we disinvest in families and communities. Do we really want to drain fragile communities and disadvantaged neighborhoods of their most precious resource—indigenous leaders, community spokespersons, role models, caring parents, entrepreneurs, and norm setters?

A parallel "depopulation" has long been underway in rural areas. Small towns and villages are losing the young but retaining the old timers. The family farms that survived the Great Depression of the 1930s cannot survive head-on competition with automated agribusiness—ironically, in part because agribusiness is quick to gobble up the government subsidies enacted expressly to protect and preserve family farms.

We have been disinvesting in families for at least half a century. Much of it has been in the name of progress. As soon as grandparents got social security, the three-generation family started to evaporate. Grandparents were delighted to get some privacy, at long last. The women's movement has made major headway in freeing women from a status of subordination by opening up job opportunities. But progress has its costs. Increasingly the two-parent family became the one-parent family. Now, increasingly it is the no-parent-at-home family and the foster parent family. Or the no-family-at-all home: the shelter or half-way house. When the welfare reform law was signed into law, the word on the street summarized it as a new kind of transfer payment: Yes, they are taking the money from the mothers in order to build prisons for the fathers.

Forty percent of the homeless are former foster care children. All that remains is to criminalize homelessness and we can build some more prisons.

We are consuming our seed corn:

- The homicide rate for children 14–17 has risen 172 percent since 1985.
- Over 20 percent of children are growing up in poverty.
- The numbers of homeless children have tripled.
- The suicide rate among African American teenagers has tripled since 1980.
- Obesity among children 12–17 has doubled since 1970.
- Between 1960 and 1994, the suicide rate for teens nearly tripled.
- Between 1980 and 1995, the suicide rate for African American males aged 10–14 went up a staggering 240 percent.
- Forty-seven percent of African American children and 34 percent of Latino children are poor.
- Sixty-nine percent of poor children live in families where at least one adult is working.

The price tag we are paying nationally for foster care, casework, investigations, and adoption services now exceeds $11 billion a year.

How are we going to rebuild, reinvest, and repopulate the urban wasteland and the ghost towns we are creating? Where are the voices asking, Is this really what we want to do? Is this really where we want to go? Who will tend the home fires, mind the children, care for the elderly, maintain community life, rebuild our neighborhoods, and make our democracy work?

We are strip-mining our communities; we are depopulating our neighborhoods; we are atomizing families. The process keeps accelerating as every asset we can lay hands on gets sent to the market for sale at the prevailing price. That market is governed by a pricing system that devalues precisely those activities most critically needed in communities: caring, learning, rearing, neighboring, sharing, valuing, celebrating, participating, discussing, consoling, joining, visiting, worshiping, associating, socializing, and helping. The economy we need to rebuild is the one that we are cannibalizing.

The Rent We Pay

Marian Wright Edelman writes, "Service is the rent we pay for living." Time Dollars provides a way to convert that rent into a capital asset, a form of collective efficacy that enhances the life of the community.

Throughout the nation's public housing communities, a drama is underway to determine whether any of the social capital remaining in low-income communities is depleted or restored. In city after city, blowing up large, deteriorated public housing complexes has become a regular media event. It is convenient to say, Poor people cannot live in high-rise apartments. No one asks, How come rich people can, but poor people can't? Why are expensive high-rise apartments and condominiums possible in New York and Miami Beach? Was it the architecture or the way they were run and administered?

Housing officials thought they had successfully escaped that question by blaming it on the architecture. That supplied the rationale necessary to go to Congress for vast new programs, variously called Hope III, IV, V, VI, and so on. Blaming the architecture helped secure political support from politicians and developers who wanted to replace low-income developments with mixed-income populations.

Poor people occupy valuable urban real estate. Policy makers and cities need a compassionate rationale for reclaiming that property without appearing to be expropriating an asset from the poorest of the poor. Mixed income housing would improve the city's tax base, finance projects for developers, create a viable rental income stream. It would also solve another problem: It would get rid of thousands of poor families whose ability to pay any rent at all would soon be coming to an end as a result of the time limit imposed by the new welfare law.

That's what Baltimore was trying to do, until in the early nineties a court stopped them. The court said, *No. You have to let all the former residents get a first crack at the new housing.* Suddenly the ghost of Christmas Past returned: Those were the same families who couldn't live together before. Soon they would be losing their welfare checks. Just possibly, town house architecture might not be different enough to avoid a recurrence of the past. Would a change in aerial elevation and density do it? Or was it just possible that the fault was never in the structural engineering? Just maybe, it was in the human engineering. Was it just possible that the real issue was that only the consumers of housing can create community? That's the issue that Co-Production pinpoints.

When the court issued its ruling, Baltimore had already secured major multi-million-dollar funding from the federal government on a pledge to demonstrate that it was possible with new buildings and a mixed-income population to turn things around, to build new housing on an old site that would attract a mixed-income population. They called these spanking new buildings Pleasant View—and they laid it out as a new town within the town. It even has its own internal town square.

Intentional mobilization of residents as co-producers had not been part of the original game plan for rebuilding the neighborhood. The court's order suddenly made it imperative to find a way to prevent the new development from repeating the history of its predecessor.

Faced with this challenge, the housing authority has done what no other housing authority has attempted. It has sought to enlist tenants directly in building a community by including a Time Dollar component in the lease. It was explicit in both purpose and strategy: "[T]he Housing Authority of Baltimore City (HABC) seeks to make use of a local, tax-exempt currency known as Time Dollars to implement a uniquely innovative strategy to redefine the role of tenants in public housing as co-producers and partners in community building." As part of its monthly rent, every household would owe eight hours of community service each month, payable in Time Dollars.

The first big test was to find out how this would go down with the residents. Two years earlier, the Housing Authority had tried to impose a community service requirement on all public housing residents. They had to back off because of the huge outcry from public housing residents and advocates. They didn't want a repeat of that fiasco.

Time Dollars were introduced as a way to make that new requirement into an opportunity rather than a burden. When explained, residents understood that this worked for them. What they did for each other not only helped build community; it gave them purchasing power to get discounts, services, merchandise, and help they could not have otherwise obtained.

The Time Dollar program really took off with the appointment of coordinator Eva Riley in June, 1999. As a resident herself, Eva was in an excellent position to build good relations with tenants, homeowners, and local business. Already a range of local organizations have agreed to accept Time Dollars earned in the program for their goods or services. These include the local Mass Transit Administration, which (for one day only) allowed tenants to buy a monthly bus pass worth $50 using Time Dollars.

Others include:

- Entry for children to the Boys and Girls Club—and negotiations are under way so that they can pay with Time Dollars at the local snack kiosks there
- Shopping at Baltimore's Old Town Mall, for items that include clothing, shoes, books, coats, and hair accessories
- Shoe Express, which is giving participants a 10 percent discount if they show their Time Dollars ID card
- The St. Vincent de Paul furniture and clothing store
- The SHARE food program—on condition that the Time Bank program sends volunteers to help pack food in boxes and distribute it

Many of the residents earn more than the eight Time Dollars stipulated in their leases. They volunteer at the local elementary school, take part in security patrols, shop for seniors, along with providing ongoing neighbor-to-neighbor services for each other.

"My job has been to explain to them that they could decide what kinds of activities would be sanctioned for community service," said Rita Epps, the Time Dollar liaison working with the tenants and the Housing Authority. "The idea is popular now, because they know that this is their home and these are things we all need to be done, and this a good way of getting it done. The neighborhood council asked people what kind of things they wanted included. And of course new things can be added as time goes on."

Under a new HUD ruling, older people will be exempt from any community service requirement. But at Pleasant View Gardens, they are fully involved. "Doing community services doesn't necessarily mean walking or lifting," says Rita, "Telephone assurance is community service. We have to make sure they feel comfortable with this and they don't feel it is being imposed on them and/or that they have no freedom of choice. Taking part means they are involved."

On October 1, 1999, the eight-hour requirement went into effect nationwide for all public housing authorities. The law reads:

> *Notwithstanding any other provision of law, each adult resident of a public housing project shall (A) contribute 8 hours per month of*

> *community service (not including political activities) within the community in which that adult resides; or (B) participate in an economic self-sufficiency program for 8 hours per month.* 42 U.S.C.A. § 1437j

It remains to be seen how this provision will be enforced. Many will ignore it; some will try to enforce it as a way to get cheap labor. But if Baltimore sets the example, it can be a new way for residents to take control over their living space—not just the four walls of their housing units, but their living space, their village, their habitat.

Social Capital and Civil Obligation

There remains a profoundly disturbing question embedded in the Baltimore Housing Authority's experiment utilizing Time Dollars as an obligatory portion of the rent. Compulsion is repugnant to many of us involved with Time Dollars. The core values that constitute the essential elements of Co-Production surely are designed to enhance freedom and opportunity, to empower people, to expand their range of choice—not subject them to new forms of coercion. How, then, is it permissible to allow Time Dollars to be used in a compulsory scheme?

Each element of Co-Production would appear to militate against requiring the earning of Time Dollars. There would seem to be an internal contradiction between affirming the assets of each individual and coercing them to use those assets. Redefining work seeks to expand freedom of choice by conferring the power to exact a return for otherwise uncompensated contribution. Reciprocity operates as a catalyst by sending the message, "We need each other." How does one reconcile that with a coercive command, "You must contribute, or else!"? At first glance, a Time Dollar rent requirement does not look like an exemplary way to generate social capital. How do we respect people's basic participatory rights, how do we honor our commitment to democracy, if we permit the earning of Time Dollars to be exacted as an element of the rent?

The easy path for caring professionals is to back away from the implications, to avoid the possible unpleasantness, to say, "We can't proceed until we get fully informed consent. The issue has caused me a lot of soul-searching moments. As a law professor, my first recourse was to turn to the law books. Did this form of coercion violate some fundamental right? Was it off-limits as a new form of involuntary servitude?

Obligation That Enfranchises

The answer given by the U.S. Supreme Court was both definitive and somewhat unsatisfying. The Court declared that ever since the Middle Ages—indeed, going back to Roman days—service was an obligation that defined the meaning of being a citizen. For slaves and serfs, peonage and involuntary servitude defined their status. But for citizens and freeholders, an obligation to perform community service defined a different status:

> *In view of ancient usage and the unanimity of judicial opinion, it must be taken as settled that, unless restrained by some constitutional limitation, a state has inherent power to require every able-bodied man within its jurisdiction to labor for a reasonable time on public roads near his residence without direct compensation. This is a part of the duty which he owes to the public. The law of England is thus declared in Blackstone's Commentaries, 'as in the Roman law, with respect to the construction and repairing of ways and bridges no class of men of whatever rank or dignity should be exempted.' From this burthen no man was exempt by our ancient laws, whatever other immunities he might enjoy.* Butler v. Perry, 240 U.S. 328 (1916)

Around the nation, different school systems are experimenting with a community service requirement for graduation. Some folks didn't like having it shoved down their throat. So they sued, claiming this was slavery and thus outlawed by the Thirteenth Amendment. They didn't get very far. Court after court told them: This is not a badge of slavery. This is an obligation of citizenship. It's even a privilege, a badge of honor. There is nothing wrong with requiring you to perform service. It is a part of your education, your preparation for life.

That did not resolve the dilemma for Time Dollars. Saying it is "legal" does not mean it is "right." Saying it is not illegal or unconstitutional does not address the higher moral issue raised—or the equally distressing practical issue.

Any parent knows what grudging obedience is like. It's at least as painful to the parent as it is to the child. There are usually a lot better ways to get something done than compelling them to be done. Even if coercion is legally permissible as an option, that does not mean that this course of action is either wise or workable. Should we as a matter of principle take a stand opposing the use of Time Dollars if it is not entirely voluntary?

Whence Does Not Equal What

The originating act that causes one to do something does not determine what the act itself means. The two must be distinguished. There is a fallacy in the logic that says, the only way to get to democratic participation is via democratic participation. The reasoning traps one in an infinite regress. It is always possible to point to an earlier point in the process that was not participatory and to charge that the entire undertaking is therefore tainted with a participatory version of Original Sin.

The accident of origin does not necessarily define the nature of the object. A program or activity is what it is. It deserves to be judged on the merits, not by its origins. The call for a Constitutional Convention in 1787 was viewed by many as highhanded, aristocratic, dictatorial, and undemocratic. That leaves open the questions whether the Convention was democratic, and whether the Constitution it produced was democratic. Even if we acknowledge it was imperfect, we may still wish to conclude that the historical process it set in motion has fostered the evolution of a democracy and that the process is an unending one.

To use another example, all of us know of relationships, of marriages, that have sprung from unhealthy needs, immature impulses, acute insecurities. The issue is not the origin of those relationships. What matters is where they are headed. The real question is, Can that quest for a partner (however immature) grow into an ongoing relationship that fosters mutual growth and fulfillment?

We will not resolve the appropriateness of a Time Dollar rental charge if we fixate on the origin of the requirement. Participation on a jury is compulsory. But the debate within the jury is democratic. And the institution itself plays a critical role in making the system of law as fair as fallible human beings can make it.

When we had the military draft, a lot of people complained because it was compulsory. But many people now say that doing away with the draft meant doing away with a kind of universal experience that strengthened our respect for diversity and that enabled us to know more about our own country and our own world than anything else.

We have all seen people hate doing things they chose to do—and love doing things they were made to do. Democratic decision-making is not a necessary prerequisite to the introduction of a Time Dollar program. The initiative is what it is what it is. Either it has internal integrity based on mutual respect or it does not. Either it values people who would otherwise be discarded or it does not. It empowers them or it does not.

Nonetheless, as a general rule, shoving things down people's throat doesn't work. And if it doesn't work, then why endorse any form of compulsory participation in Time Dollars?

Freedom and Unfreedom

When Time Dollars are implemented as a way of discharging a community service obligation, the issue, whether to require it or not, is framed as if it were a choice between doing hard, distasteful work involuntarily and being a conventional tenant with no obligations other than to pay the rent. That's not the choice. Several choices, several issues have been bundled together. They need to be broken out as individual questions.

- Do the residents have any say over the particular task they are obliged to do? Can one choose how one will discharge that obligation? Are there limits on that choice? How does one deal with tasks that are distasteful, demeaning, or even dangerous?

- Do the residents collectively have any say or exercise any control over how the total volume of hours will be used, apportioned, and allocated.

Given a monthly "revenue" of X thousand hours of labor being available, it is critical to know how it will be used. Will those hours of labor be spent making their community safer and their schools better, providing after-school activities for their children, and beautifying the complex or maintaining it better? Or will the hours be spent in ways that enable management to cut corners on maintenance, upkeep, security, and repair, or to pocket money that was appropriated for mandatory services that the residents are performing. Who decides how those hours are budgeted? The residents or someone over whom the residents have no control and who is not accountable to them?

The ultimate issue is whether the obligation enhances or contracts resident control over the quality of life that residents will enjoy. In the past, they have not been offered that choice. Now Congress has provided a way for them to make that choice. It can be taken away from them, imposed in a punitive fashion, shaped in a way that does not give them any control over how it is implemented or what is done with the labor. Or it can be shaped in a way that empowers them to make a difference.

When Compulsion Creates Choice

Amartya Sen, winner of the Nobel Prize in Economics, uses the term "economic unfreedom" to define those situations where an individual is given the seeming choice of earning subsistence for family by risking life and limb or abandoning family. The choice is not choice, he says. Being poor and dependent upon public housing comes with a form of "unfreedom"—the necessity of surviving in an environment where human predators threaten one's physical well-being, where inadequate maintenance of the physical plant poses immediate threats to health and safety, where distrust (intensified and manipulated by authoritarian paternalism) sabotages attempts to create community and improve living conditions. If freedom means the choice between that kind of housing and homelessness, then it is certainly a form of "unfreedom."

Compulsion can be the prerequisite to expanded choice, to expanded freedom. Obligatory community service in fact confers a new choice and a new power: the choice to create and to live in the kind of community that was not conceivable in the kind of public housing that existed when these same tenants had "the choice" of whether or not to do community service.

Economists point out that there are some goods that by their very nature cannot be purchased privately. This is particularly true when it comes to environmental goods—whether they be a malaria-free environment or a neighborhood that is relatively safe and crime-free. Public goods cannot be purchased by individuals—and by the same token, others who may not have paid cannot be prevented from enjoying the benefits as "free riders."

Before we assume that freedom means the absence of all obligation other than that which we elect, ask yourself whence came all the wonders that we take for granted, from free speech to indoor plumbing. We depend on others to keep the air clean, the water drinkable, the streets safe. We depend upon our children to help pay for the health care we will need and the interest on the national debt accumulated in our life time and the social security benefits we may need to collect one day.

Government provides some public goods. But social capital is something that government cannot provide. We have to create it ourselves. It exists and grows in communities where people are willing to intervene on behalf of children, where bullies are stopped, where graffiti is prevented or cleaned up, where drug dealers are not welcome, where kids feel safe, and where seniors feel supported and valued. That does not happen behind closed doors. That happens in the space that we all share, in social settings that we create. That is why service is the rent we pay for living.

Collective Power to Rebuild Community

Floating around Washington, D.C., Hamden, Virginia, and Chicago is a proposal from the Time Dollar Institute to give neighborhood groups the opportunity to revive a tradition of civic obligation by creating Neighborhood Improvement Districts. The idea builds upon a new kind of zoning used by the business community. City after city has enacted laws creating Business Improvement Districts (BIDs). This is not like other zoning laws that establish a district. The merchants and property owners have to get together and set the boundaries for the BID. The law simply provides that when they do so, they can become a BID if 51 percent of them vote for it. Then, they can levy a tax on themselves and everyone in the District has to pay that tax. The good thing is that they then control how that tax is spent: for police, landscaping, social events and street fairs, better lighting, a shoppers' mini-bus, or pothole repair.

People are now asking: Why not use the same idea in neighborhoods—particularly neighborhoods that need more services, more improvements, more protection than the city budget will provide? The answer has been, *People in those neighborhoods don't have money*. Don't even think about giving them the power to tax themselves. It won't work. But the answer to that is now becoming, What about Time Dollars? Why couldn't people have a choice of whether they paid in dollars or Time Dollars? The absentee owners, the non-residents might have to pay in dollars, but the residents could pay in Time.

Most of us suspect that regardless of whether we pay more taxes, potholes won't get fixed faster and schools won't become instantaneously better. But we also know that if we had to serve on those pot hole crews or if we had to take a turn tutoring or helping oversee an after-school program, we just might see some changes we really liked.

If we ask ourselves, What will it take to build the kind of village we need? Just maybe, it will take our own sweat. Maybe it's not something we can buy. Maybe it's a form of investment we can make with the social capital generated by collective effort.

If we are serious when we say, *No more throw-away people*, then we will have to listen to other voices than those of the market. For that to happen, we will have to find a compelling answer to those who counsel that salvation lies with the market, only the market, and nothing but the market.

Maybe if we embrace Co-Production as an Imperative we will find we can create all the social capital we need to build a future worthy of our children and our children's children.

Chapter 19

The Future is Now

There is nothing as powerful as an idea whose time has come. As this book goes to press, developments are taking place and transactions occurring that give promise of unleashing Co-Production as a force for fundamental change on a global level.

Already, the stirrings are so widespread, the concepts so contagious, that new possibilities emerge daily. Hope is epidemic. Time banking has now reached Curacao, Dominican Republic, England, France, Japan, Mexico, and Shanghai. Once I could know of every new Time Dollar occurrence and trace each one back to a single conversation, phone-call, e-mail or presentation. Already, that is no longer possible. It has long been my dream to see such unfolding potential seriously out of control.

Here is what I know about possibilities taking shape and form here at the Time Dollar Institute:

- **A Masters in Social Justice program emerging as a first offering from a new Academy utilizing distance learning technologies to impart Co-Production to widely dispersed change agents.**
- **Transformation of the Time Dollar Institute into a web-based learning organization linking community-based Co-Production initiatives in a collective, conscious inquiry to brainstorm, share, and synthesize in a process of intentional evolution.**
- **Development of a Co-Production Audit for systematic assessment of organizational performance—for use internally as an organizational development tool or externally to enhance accountability measured against Co-Production standards.**
- **A global newsletter produced in partnership with the New**

Economics Foundation, and available for downloading by local communities for hard copy distribution

- **A web-based version of Time Keeper software enabling local programs to contract out the bookkeeping and information management tasks associated with time banking**
- **A web-based Time Dollar store utilizing e-commerce technology in tandem with tax-exempt charitable contributions to accelerate the development of attractive redemption options for the work entailed in Co-Production**

By the time this book sees the light of day, the Second International Time Dollar Congress will have taken place in St. Louis, Missouri, home of one of the largest, most diverse, deeply rooted time banking programs. The event will bring pioneers in time banking from England, Japan, Mexico and Curacao to meet, network, brainstorm and collaborate with their counterparts in the United States. The United Nations Education, Science and Culture Organization (UNESCO) has already posted a concept paper on approaches to utilization of time banking in developing nations prepared by the Institute. A major global conference in Rio De Janeiro will showcase Time Banking as a central concept in sustainable development and as a strategy to enable urban centers to address issues of identity and cohesion. Teams have been already been assembled to translate this book into Japanese, Spanish, French. (Eventually, perhaps, there may even be a translation into English.)

Yet, when all is said and done, the future is already taking on new shape and form based on events that are happening as I write.

Immigration and the Co-Production of Community

For many in Miami, Y2K still has a doomsday quality that has nothing to do with computers. A special window of opportunity is closing for immigrants who have been in the United States continuously for at least five years to obtain legal resident status. When New Year's day arrived, the law provided a means by which the dreaded knock on the door from the Immigration and Natural Service might be forever avoided — but only a few short months remained to gather the documentation. Legal help was critical. And then came the matter of fees for the application, fingerprints, a medical examination and vaccinations and photos. Even if legal help were available without charge, for a family of 4-5 persons the cost would be $2,000 or more.

The Annie E. Casey Foundation acted to make funds available to cover those costs for several hundred families. But the availability of "free" money was guaranteed to attract every hustler who knew how to plead poverty and weave a sad story. And when it comes to immigration, professional vultures are always circling to scavenge every available dollar from the vulnerable, the gullible and the desperate. Two organizations teamed up to try to develop a joint approach: Abriendo Puertas, the family resource center would provide a place where families could come; FIAC, the Florida Immigration Advocacy Center, would provide the lawyers and paralegals. But how should the money be dished out? How should the legal services be accessed? And where would the people power come from to help assemble, copy and organize the documents needed for each case?

On March 15, 2000, with two weeks remaining before all applications had to be filed, there was a kind of summit meeting to decide how families could "earn" the $2000 needed. The starting point was a proposal that would have assigned an arbitrary value of $20 for each Time Dollar earned. A family of four could earn the entire $2,000 needed if each member earned 25 Time Dollars. The proposal was pronounced DOA, Dead On Arrival because assigning any fixed monetary value to Time Dollars would jeopardize their tax-exempt status.

Interestingly, discussion focused on a different concern. Everyone at the table, the Foundation team, the representatives from Abriendo Puertas and FIAC all wanted to make sure that the provision of help — legal help and financial assistance — was not just a form of one-time emergency aid. The real agenda was Co-Production — of community, of strong families, of networks that would continue to provide mutual support.

The agreement hammered out created a new kind of Time Dollar club membership with a new kind of Time Dollar fee-for-service. Just as Frequent Flyer clubs have different levels, Bronze Gold and Silver, so the Time Dollar Club would establish a special membership category where a higher Time Dollar payment would qualify one for additional benefits. For a more elite class of membership, an initial 180 day enrollment would be expected. Additional Time Dollar activity fees would be charged for special programs such as computer instruction and arts and crafts. To reward those who stayed engaged, across the board benefits would be available to families that maintained a minimum balance of 100 Time Dollars.

The "rules" at least embodied the objective: to enable families to access needed services and funds without covertly adopting some new form of hourly wage. Somehow, the rules seem less important when one hears the actual cases.

From the Front Lines

When you are an immigrant, uncertain of your status, trying desperately for a new life, you avoid notice; you leave as few tracks as you can. Then comes a law that says you have to prove continuous residence for years and years. Yet, survival has meant staying out of sight, avoiding paper records. What do you do? You come to FIAC.

What happens when you gather what papers you have but you can't read or write and after waiting and waiting weeks or months for an appointment, the immigration officer at INS demands you sign some piece of paper—but you have a hard time fashioning the letters the way you remember you are supposed to. So he takes your card, tears it up and says, come back when you have everything together and are ready to sign forms you can't even read.

What happens when your boyfriend has a past arrest record and you don't know whether it counts because he was a juvenile. Now, you have two children and he is doing his best to support the family and be a good father. Should he even apply because that might trigger immediate deportation?

What happens when you have several children and grandchildren and their case depends on your case? How do you deal with a claim by the INS that leaving the scene of a traffic accident after waiting and waiting constitutes an aggravated felony that makes you subject to immediate deportation without possibility of a waiver.

One nineteen year old with 2 children, comes to FIAC every day, helping out by making copies, putting documents together, helping other clients get their documents. A homebound disabled mother with an adult daughter and grand daughter babysits for others so that she and they can get legal help. Others go to the food bank and earn Time Dollars to get food for the pot luck and for the small Abriendo Puerto food bank that everyone taps in an emergency. Some sew or embroider beautiful baby clothes. Others help with shopping or gardening. One can even fix a VCR. Still others help the receptionist, answer the phone, help serve as receptionists, just calm down a new family coming into the reception area for the first time, escort a senior to her car at night or just put a coin in a parking meter for someone in the middle of an appointment.

This is not work in the market economy. But it is what it takes to build the village. If all we have is money and market, then human beings are chattel, surging across national boundaries in any way they can in search of a better life. If money is the sole measure of one's worth, then those who do not have money are essentially worthless. Issues of immigration and work permits and residency are variations on the question: what does it mean to be a human being? What does it mean to be a member of the human family. Abriendo Puertas says we are all family. Together with FIAC, it is giving a new meaning to "Open Door."

Human beings are either assets or liabilities. That is the ultimate issue posed by a global economy. Immigration law simply provides the crucible in which our humanity will be tested.

Suddenly, the core values take on a different meaning.

EPILOGUE

The Stranger has Arrived

When the Stranger says: "What is the meaning of
this city?"
Do you huddle close together because you love
each other?"
What will you answer? "We all dwell together
to make money from each other"? or
"This is a community"?
And the Stranger will depart and return to the
desert.
O my soul, be prepared for the coming of the
Stranger,
Be prepared for him who knows how to ask
questions.
(T.S. Eliot, Choruses from the Rock)

"We did not inherit the world from our ancestors;
we borrowed it from our descendants."

Just recently, two biologists isolated the gene in earthworms that determines sociability, whether they eat alone or eat in clusters. Somewhere in our genetic make-up are genes that gave us a competitive edge to survive—genes that in some as yet unknown way, support the way in which we care for our young and our old, our weakest and our most vulnerable. Co-Production says: Now more than ever, that genetic heritage is precious.

Seven years ago, I flew down to Florida when my first grandchild was born. As I held him for the very first time, I remember thinking: "This species was not designed to survive." He was so frail, so helpless. All he had going for him was the ability to cry, to grimace and to grasp with those tiny little fingers. The ability to bellow and suck are the only native tools he had to try to subdue the vast, outside world into which he had been involuntarily expelled. And, oh yes. The eyes, large pleading eyes, expressive eyes, eyes that seem to fix directly on you and only you, eyes that said: Love me, I need you. They come as original equipment—direct from the Maker.

Unlike wolves or cats, our young are not able to crawl or ambulate, escape predatory animals, hide or arch their back or pretend ferocity. They are just small and helpless. It takes days before the eyes really focus or those tiny fingers squeeze, let go and then squeeze again. Gestation is slow; birth is slow; maturation is slow. Vulnerability, helplessness, fragility, innocence last for years—in a world that remains a jungle. Yet, somehow, we of all species have survived, adapted, dominated. Largely because of mother love.

To me, human beings are a miracle. I don't know how many trillion gigabytes it would take to produce an organism that can walk and talk, communicate and love. Yet, we make life and death judgments based on whether one of those miracles can master the rules contained in programs measured in mere kilobytes like Grammatik and Spell Check, can score a few decimal points higher on an SAT or LSAT or GRA or MCAT. We ignore, we deny and we discard the miracle. The Co-Production Imperative says that is no longer acceptable. No More Throw-away People.

Human beings inhabit an ecological niche on this planet. None of us "pay" full fare. We all draw upon a common stock: the cumulative knowledge and discoveries of our ancestors, the genetic pool that has demonstrated superior survival capacity and the ecosystems that provide us with a vast array of essential goods and services. Our ability to survive this next millennium will depend upon whether we function to exploit and deplete or, as trustees, to conserve, develop, and enhance that legacy.

Years ago, I was privileged to watch as a medicine man proceeded methodically to create a magnificent sand painting on the floor of a hogan. Atop a deerskin, he first spread a solid background with sand gathered from a local cornfield. Then, with meticulous care, using thumb and forefinger, he pushed thin streams of different color materials—sandstone, pyrite, pollen, charcoal—to create intricate Yei Be Chei figures, holy spirits on this floorbound canvas, preparatory to a healing ceremony that would last many hours. In that tradition, illness signified being out of harmony with nature; restoring health meant restoring harmony.

The patient sat crosslegged on that sandpainting—and then, at the end, to my horror, the medicine man proceeded to destroy the singular sand painting masterpiece, rolling it up in a way that commingled all the ingredients as he bundled up the skin and proceeded to leave the hogan. I asked my host where he was going—and he explained to me: it was custom to return that sand, together with those precious minerals to the cornfield from which the pollen had been gathered—because one must always restore to the earth that which had been taken. In the Navajo way, one takes only what one needs—and one restores to the Earth, that which one takes.

The challenge our species now faces is to create a healthy ecological niche: communities that nurture, space that is non-toxic, exchanges that do not deplete, relationships based on love and caring, transactions powered by the renewable energy of compassion and empathy and reciprocity. We have it within us to do so. Human ecology and global ecology are converging. We must build the village it takes to raise the child that can be each of us—at our very best. To do so, we must honor the economy of that village: we must elevate it at least to co-equal status.

My tradition taught me:

> *Just to be is a blessing.*
> *Just to live is holy.*
> *How should I live the life that I am?*

Perhaps the only answer to the Stranger's question is a question:

> *How should I live the life that I am?*

Co-Production provides a way to try to make that possible. It is, at least, a beginning.

Postscript from the United States 2004

Since 2000, there have been major advances in our understanding of Time Banks – what they do, how they work, and why they function. The many developments (technological, organizational, programmatic, and global) reflect the emergence of a movement that is gathering momentum and is poised to enter a new phase.

Time Banking 2004

The Core Economy

The first edition used the term "non-market economy" to describe the world of family, neighborhood, community and civil society. We now reject use of the term "non-market economy" for two reasons. First, it is imprecise because "non-market" also includes illicit conduct and tax-avoidance transactions. Second, and more important, "non-market" represents a negative formulation of the vast and positive economic contribution made by family, neighborhood, community and civil society.

Thanks to a critique by internationally renowned environmental economist, Neva Goodwin, we now understand that the economy we are seeking to build should really be called the Core Economy. It supplies the foundation, the substratum that underpins the private sector, the public sector and the independent, non-profit and philanthropic sector. That Core

Economy – of family, of neighborhood, of community, of civil society – has been hit hard. It has been called upon to handle more and more problems with less and less time and resources. And it has lost much of its capacity to produce what it used to produce: healthy children, maturing youth, functioning families, safe neighborhoods, viable communities, a robust civil society and open-minded, vibrant democratic governance of, by and for the people.

Use of that term has helped us gain increased clarity about the Core Economy as an economic system we are attempting to rebuild and about the nature of the challenge that confronts these efforts. First, it has heightened our awareness of similarities and relationships between the environment and the Core Economy as economic systems that engage in cycles of production and consumption. It took decades for environmental economists to get us to appreciate that natural ecosystems provide critical life support services that even a multi-million dollar biosphere was unable to duplicate.[1] In the past, we have ignored the economic significance of those systems, taking them for granted as infinitely renewable — until we had sufficiently damaged them that our own lives and well-being were imperiled.

In much the same way, we have ignored, overlooked, and undervalued the Core Economy as if we could always count on family, neighborhood, community, and civil society to be infinitely resilient and capable of renewing itself. Having inflicted sufficient permanent damage to the environment, economists began to find ways to measure the monetary productivity of natural ecosystems and activists made use of the legal system to require environmental impact statements as a vehicle to halt further environmental degradation. That awareness gave rise to new investments by both the public and private sector in the restoration and preservation of our planet's capacity to sustain life.

Much the same needs to happen with respect to the Core Economy. Home, neighborhood, and community are the ecological niche of our species. When materialism runs amuck, the toxicity and pollution of market value contaminates and fouls our habitat. Understood in this context, Time Banking programs are environmental preservation efforts, struggling to make our habitat viable, to make it possible to raise our young, to care for our elders. They seek to protect and restore the fragile biosphere that requires trust and decency and that nurtures healthy neighborhoods, preserves basic human rights and sustains democratic governance. The survival of our species depends upon the restoration of our habitat.

As a result, it has become necessary for us to restructure family, neighborhood, community, and civil society just as the Core Economy reframes the need for investment in that economy. Co-Production represents an attempt to clarify the purpose of that investment and the principles that should guide it. The Core Economy functions, like a hybrid car, on two fuels: psychic energy and money. The psychic energy takes many forms: love, duty, trust, empathy, compassion, moral authority, altruism – and in my tradition, guilt. But as emotional fuel, that energy drives much of the monetary economic activity that diverse economists agree[2] totals at least as much as 40% of the GDP. A partial catalog of that productivity would include: rearing children, preserving functioning families, creating safe, vibrant neighborhoods, caring for the frail and vulnerable, standing up for what's right, opposing what seems wrong or unfair, producing a work force (including corporate CEO's) that doesn't steal, holding officials accountable, and making democracy work.

Time Banking seeks to rebuild that economy by tapping the vast unused and under-used capacity of individuals and groups that the market rejects, undervalues or overlooks. We now understand (in retrospect) that it does so in very different ways. Understanding how that works represents the second major learning that has emerged since the first edition in 2000.

Beyond Neighbor-to-Neighbor:

Time Banking, Co-Production and System Change commentators often describe Time Banking as a local barter system, but it is actually much more than that. "What goes around comes around" is the slogan adopted by Time Banks UK. That translates into the explanation: A helps B who helps C who helps D who helps A. The name given to that kind of Time Banking is "Neighbor-to-Neighbor."

The phrase "Neighbor-to-Neighbor" is both descriptive and misleading. It captures the trust, the reciprocity, the warmth and the sense of community that comes when neighbors cease to be strangers and become friends that one can turn to for support, encouragement, and help.[3]

What the phrase Neighbor-to-Neighbor fails to capture is the real power that Time Banking has when it is utilized by a non-profit organization or government agency. If all the sponsoring agency understands is that Time Banking is about people helping people, the Time Bank will be regarded as "nice" but trivial or, worse still, irrelevant to mission. And that can be fatal when it comes to maintaining financial support.

If Time Banking does not directly advance an agency's mission, it becomes a luxury to maintain. It is dismissed as a form of volunteering that has no particular relation to program, to professional obligation, to funding, or to mission. It has thus become critical for Time Banking programs to adapt to and align themselves with the sponsoring agency's mission.

In the past four years, we have developed a radically different way of utilizing Neighbor-to-Neighbor that changes Time Banking from a program that is expendable to an embedded process that is central to mission. This re-definition of Neighbor-to-Neighbor is more than verbal packaging. It allows agencies to shape priorities within a Neighbor-to-Neighbor program so that the exchanges can be based on a specific outcome-related context. Case studies and record keeping then can document how that outcome is aligned to mission in ways that directly enhance effectiveness.

This new learning – that Neighbor-to-Neighbor works differently in different contexts – has major implications for the sustainability of Time Dollars and Time Banking. Full exploitation of this flexibility will make it possible for agencies to mold Neighbor-to-Neighbor Time Banks to fulfill agency mission. That is why agency directors, grant officers, and officials interested in system change and system reform are looking at Time Banking in a new way.

This enlarged understanding of the implications of Time Banking is driving a separate growth track. The benefits fall into five categories:

1. supplying a critically important missing element needed for a program to succeed
2. transforming the relationship between client and helping professional from one of subordination and dependency to one of contribution, mutuality and parity
3. securing critical resources for financially strapped programs
4. effecting system change
5. advancing social justice. (See Appendix A for enumeration of specific outcomes.)

Over the past four years, the Time Dollar Institute, in partnership with community – based organizations, has demonstrated different ways to use Time Banking to advance agency mission or address social problems. Some methods involve a use of Time Banking that restricts participants to a narrow range of activities (like tutoring or sitting on a Youth Court jury). In more and more situations, however, members of Time Banks exchange a wide range of services as in the Neighbor-to-Neighbor model – but in a context that directly advances agency mission. The more we mold Time Bank activities to address special needs and to realize agency mission, the more likely it is that agencies will find ways to provide the fiscal and personnel support needed to assure sustainability. Consider the following examples of Time Banking in specialized contexts:

- Problem students become co-producers of academic achievement
- Juvenile delinquents become co-producers of crime prevention and the rule of law
- Women returning from prison and undergoing recovery from drugs share their experience and wisdom with young women at risk of AIDS and unintended pregnancy
- Elderly patients function as co-producers of health maintenance and community-based care
- Families with children in need of wrap-around services become

the contributors and creators of an extended after-care support system for each other

The line between Neighbor-to-Neighbor and specialized program blurs because specialized agencies need the informal support systems, peer supports, and networks that Time Banking can provide.

Bridging Economic Systems: Time Banking Earns Access to Goods, Services and Educational Opportunity

As Time Banks begin to merge with agencies and generate solutions to social problems, considerable experimentation has had to be undertaken in order to meet a major challenge: how to build access through Time Dollars and Time Banking to the goods, services and opportunities provided by the public and private sectors. From the outset, is has been important to find ways to confer purchasing value on Time Credits without accepting a conversion rate that incorporates market pricing and without jeopardizing the exempt status accorded by both the Internal Revenue Service (US) and the Inland Revenue Service (UK). So long as one remains within the Core Economy, one hour for one hour operates essentially as a tax-exempt exchange system for services that neighbors and peers provide for each other. But in many contexts, the question arises: How can Time Banking provide budget relief or purchasing power to get access to good and services that require an outlay in dollars, pounds, yen or the prevailing market currency?

Several approaches have emerged:

- Some Time Banking programs have secured monetary discounts of 10%, 15% or 25% from the private sector of the kind accorded to members of organizations like AAA or AARP.

- Other programs have conferred a monetary value on Time Credits by arrangements that permit Time Credits to be redeemed for awards just as one does with frequent flyer miles. Sometimes, the Credits are actually "cashed in" or subtracted from one's account

- In other programs, the credits earned simply entitle one to a choice of awards as a form of recognition – but no credits are actually redeemed or subtracted.

- Still other communities are trying to define a graduated purchasing power by setting different purchasing or redemption privileges based upon Bronze, Silver, or Gold membership (where one's status can depend upon different variables: level of dues paid per month, total credits earned, length of time participating, or a combination).

- Elderplan has developed a catalog "Credit Shop" which enables members to exchange 75 credits or 150 credits for different categories of health-related devices (blood pressure, pulse meters, bath spa machines), taxi vouchers, social events for oneself and a companion, and home delivered meals for other elderly persons.
- In the UK, where any kind of purchase with Time Credits would breach Inland Revenue rules, Time Bank programs simply give awards based on rules adopted by each program. One university has agreed to credit Time Dollars toward tuition payments.
- Another approach to incentives builds upon reinforcing altruism. Thus, Elderplan permits its credits to be used to secure Meals on Wheels for seniors who are not included or might not be eligible. One suggestion that has generated enthusiasm among HMO members: use of their credits to secure medical coverage for women in a battered women's shelter. African-American churches found another way to reinforce altruism. Members could contribute their Time Credits to a church fund to be used for members in need. Their slogan: with one hour, you serve twice – first the person whom you help, the second, the church and those it needs to help.
- Bernard Lietaer has developed a brilliant scheme for Brazil to enable Time Credits earned in high school to be used to pay a portion of the tuition for higher education based upon computing the number of "empty seats" now available in universities and the far vaster number of "empty seats" potentially available with the implementation of distance learning technology. His thesis is that some income from underutilized capacity is better than no income so that universities will profit from any return on unused capacity. That principle has widespread applicability, once core costs are met and as technology drops the marginal costs of delivering education via the Internet.

We will need creativity to keep expanding the examples. Concern over incentives has primarily been to enable members to spend their credits for something they need. But newer thinking now is focusing on incentives for organizations to invest in Time Banking in ways that either advance their mission or enable them to address costs such as printing or publicity or long distance phone calls or even, staff vacations. As the movement gains momentum, we are likely to see more organizational incentives emerge. But the bottom line will also be: avoid any conversion that equates Time Credits with the market value of the labor.

Co-Production: A Concept Re-Born

In no small part owing to events flowing from this book and its dissemination, the term Co-Production has re-surfaced as a new framework for social policy and social programs. A more limited version of co-production had been briefly in vogue among political scientists in the 1980's.[4] It was then relegated to obscurity – perhaps because government agencies wanted to make the case for larger budgets, not for citizen participation. NO MORE THROW AWAY PEOPLE reframed Co-Production from an emphasis on how citizen engagement provided a cost effective way to improve government services to a more dynamic process of system change and empowerment. Co-Production now emerges as the missing piece necessary to make social programs effective and as a way to restore confidence and build support for critical investments in addressing social ills. Major policy papers[5], a widely read article in the *New Statesman*[6], a major foundation research grant[7], strategy seminars at the highest levels of government, workshops, presentations and keynote addresses at major professional conferences[8] all signal an awakening to Co-Production and a new willingness to explore and test expanded applications of the concept. The journey of discovery has just begun.

APPENDIX A

Aligning Neighbor-to-Neighbor Exchanges to Agency Mission

1. *Supply a critically important missing element needed for a program to succeed*

   Examples would include:

   - Providing an informal support system for fragile families or in case of disability or illness
   - Generating an informal social group with social events to reduce loneliness and isolation
   - Creating a peer group that provides support and supplies critical motivation for doing "the right thing" when one fears disapproval or rejection by one's peers
   - Anticipating the need for (and building a informal support system that can deliver) aftercare — the process must begin before paid services have to terminate
   - Accelerating hospital discharge and monitoring post-discharge appointments to reduce risk of re-injury or recidivism
   - Enlisting clients to spread the word, raise awareness, impart critical knowledge

- Rewarding prevention and changes in behavior that reduce risk or risk factors

2. *Transforming the relationship between client and helping professional from one of subordination and dependency to one of contribution, mutuality and parity*

   This happens in different ways; each yields a distinctive dynamic:

   - Ending or preventing dependency is possible only if clients, by using their abilities, can get respect, attention and help more effectively than by having problems and needs that foster dependency
   - Rewarding strengths and contribution makes it safe to show capacity and reduces fear of abandonment if one improves
   - Professional intervention alone is never enough to address chronic conditions associated with diabetes, obesity, depression, AIDS, high blood pressure or mental health
   - Payment or co-payment in Time Dollars turns the client into a "paying customer"
   - Enlisting clients as "co-producers" reduces no-shows for appointments, volunteer "burn-out," and failure to follow through on treatment or rehabilitation
   - Enhancing self-esteem by enabling a client to assert "I have really important work to do."
   - Client engagement can supply cultural competence and help overcome barriers of class and race that reduce effectiveness
   - Time Banking related incentives create a transparent system for conferring rewards untainted by favoritism

3. *Securing Critical Resources for Financially Strapped Programs*
   - Time Banking documentation provides the verification required by a funding source or the in-kind support promised in a grant application
   - Time Credits earned provided an objective measure of Return On Investment for funders
   - Enlisting clients who "earn" services can generate contribution by law firms, doctors, and businesses that feel their contribution generates reciprocal contribution in the community
   - Enlisting clients can help provide back-up and support for professionals coping with multiple simultaneous demands
   - Enlisting clients as "co-producers" creates a constituency that will speak up on behalf of programs

- Allocating organizational resources for meaningful rewards can counter criticism that funding for the disadvantaged merely supports middle class professionals and contributes to the establishment of a "welfare class"

- Enlisting clients as "co-producers" provides an answer to those who would "blame the victim." The victim's engagement becomes a central asset in finding remedies.

4. Effecting System Change

Time Banking can be used to create feedback loops, enhance accountability, document unmet needs, and transform clients from objects of pity to co-workers remedying social problems in the following ways:

- Professionals can fail because they have no way of knowing whether their intervention is working and formal data systems do not necessarily capture critical knowledge

- An assessment of the extent to which an agency actually engages clients as co-producers can be a major catalyst for system change and can help enhance performance and job satisfaction

- Neighbor-to-Neighbor client groups can function as an early warning system when a treatment isn't working, when a case "falls between the cracks," or when a new complication calls for additional intervention

- System change catalysts will emerge that provide important feedback on issues and problems that might otherwise have gone undetected

5. Advancing Social Justice

- Involvement by clients who frequently are disproportionately non-white can empower disenfranchised and vulnerable groups. Time Credits earned by civic work and civic engagement can counter apathy, reduce alienation and generate empowerment

- Occupational, employment and income ladders can be developed using Time Banking as an avenue into paid employment. Bank statement provides a verifiable work record and references for those seeking entry to the job market

- Stabilizing initial employment by providing back-up systems to reduce absenteeism (e.g. providing back-up support when transportation or child care breaks down)

- Enlisting clients as "co-producers" can educate them as to causal conditions and generate activism to remedy environmental and social causes

- Valuing efforts by the impaired, handicapped, bed-ridden,

underage and overage redefines the work force for social justice in ways that can impact public policy

Postscript from England 2004

By David Boyle, Author of *Funny Money: In Search of Alternative Cash*

The development of Time Dollars, as set out by Edgar Cahn in this book, is an overwhelmingly American success story. It is an idea, along with Co-Production, that arose naturally out of the civil rights movement and the failure of the ambitions of the visionaries behind President Johnson's War on Poverty. So how come it has spread to so many other parts of the world?

For one thing, the basic intellectual work was carried out by Edgar in 1986 at the London School of Economics – though the opportunity was not grasped at the time by the successors of the founders of the LSE, the Fabian pioneers Sidney and Beatrice Webb. For another, although the social crises in the USA are peculiar to US cities and often more extreme than other parts of the world, the basic problems remain the same. The breakdown of social ties, the corrosion of what Edgar calls the 'core economy', is a phenomenon that can be found all over the world – although the symptoms may be different everywhere.

Often the reciprocal use of time turned up unexpectedly in different countries by coincidence – it was an idea whose time had come. In China, it was the crisis of a burgeoning elderly population. In Japan, it was the national awakening of community consciousness in the wake of the disastrous Kobe earthquake in 1994. In Spain, it was the need for women to support each other. In Italy, it was the breakdown of local economic ties. In all those places, Time Dollars or Time Banks or *bancos de tiempo* began to emerge as a means of tackling their most urgent social need. Often the original inspiration began with Edgar's work, but the local movement had put down roots of its own.

In the case of Japan, Edgar's influence has also formed a parallel Time Dollar movement that is inspired more directly by his work. Time Dollars and Co-Production have emerged more immediately from the influence of the Time Dollar Institute in Latin America, parts of the Caribbean, in some of the countries in the former communist Eastern Europe, and there have been experiments in the Netherlands, New Zealand, France and other places.

But most of all the idea has taken root in Britain, thanks largely to a visit Edgar made to London and Newcastle in the fall of 1997, which reintroduced the idea effectively over the airwaves of the BBC. His one appearance on the radio chat show Midweek brought hundreds of letters from people around the country wanting to know more. The interview went out at the equivalent of 4am in Washington, but the Time Dollar Institute website over there registered a flurry of hits as Edgar came off the air.

Edgar's message – that the so-called 'problem' people have assets that the professionals need – has been warmly received on that visit and during subsequent visits he has made since, the first few of them made with the support of the healthcare foundation the King's Fund. In 1998, he was invited for a meeting in 10 Downing Street, as the new government under Tony Blair began scouting for ideas to tackle the collapsing social infrastructure. When the British government announced a new social programme called Better Government for Older People in March 1999, it was Watford Council's 'time bank' idea – Time Dollars became 'Time Banks' in the UK – that the minister chose to describe in the House of Commons.

As Edgar was making his first appearances in the UK, Martin Simon was resigning from his job at the Gloucestershire County Council social services department to set up the first Time Banks on this side of the Atlantic. His Fair Shares program, the first of its kind in the UK, opened its doors in the small Gloucestershire town of Stonehouse in November 1998. The defining characteristic of Stonehouse in Gloucestershire is that it is flat. Because of this accident of geology, it tends to attract retired people who are reluctant to trawl up the hills and valleys of nearby Stroud. After a fortnight, it had 20 people – aged between 14 and 90 – who between them were offering up to 52 different services, ranging from bereavement visiting to driving a van.

The Stonehouse Time Bank began after the local neighbourhood project got a call from an elderly lady who needed someone to walk her dog while she was confined to bed. They helped, and her friends started calling too. The second Time Bank, under the auspices of Fair Shares in the nearby town of Newent, worked on similar principles.

The third was launched by the think tank the New Economics Foundation in London and in a doctor's surgery. It was the brainchild of

Richard Byng, one of the doctors based there in the south London neighbourhood of Catford. Thanks to the Time Bank launched there in 2000, patients can now be prescribed if appropriate – not just with the usual pharmacological armoury – but with a friendly visit once a week, or a lift to the shops, or small repairs at home. They can also be referred to the Time Bank, for example in the case of long-term depression, if doctors feel that engagement of some kind would be useful.

The evidence is that this works. Early research at the surgery, Rushey Green, showed that 70 per cent of participants suffering from a combination of physical and mental problems reported some remission of their condition within six months of joining the time bank. There is confirmation of this in research by the Socio-Medical Research Group at King's College London, which shows that those participants who are most actively involved in the time bank experience the most improvements in both their mental and physical health.

The idea was catching on. Soon there was the HourBank in the south London downtown neighbourhood of Peckham, a run-down suburb with a long tradition of innovation, with a well-attended Wednesday café attracting local refugees from many countries, and – unusually for conventional volunteer systems – accepting that they had something to offer too. Then there was the time bank in Benwell, in Newcastle-upon-Tyne, set up by the New Economics Foundation (NEF) with support from the National Lottery. When NEF launched their 'Time Banks' website, developed by Sarah Burns – the organiser behind the development at Rushey Green, now co-ordinator of the London Time Bank – as many as 200 people joined the UK time bank network within six weeks.

Tony Blair's political inspiration, sociologist Professor Anthony Giddens, was at that time proposing a network of Time Banks based on the original American Time Dollars idea. Soon the new Time Banks network, Time Banks UK – a joint venture between NEF and Fair Shares, and later the Gorbals Initiative in Scotland and Valley Kids in Wales – was getting start-up funding from central government.

My own contribution to the idea was writing a book about it all – Funny Money: In Search of Alternative Cash, which introduced Edgar to and his ideas, I hope, to a wider market. "Let us give generously," said Blair in 2000, "in the two currencies of time and money." Well, maybe he didn't quite mean what we do by that phrase, but we certainly made use of it.

It is now nearly seven years since Edgar first brought his message to the UK. There are almost 130 Time Banks around the UK, though not all of them actually active yet. Nearly 40 of those are in the London Time Bank network run by NEF. We have experimented with Co-Production in schools, in mental health, housing and other areas. Three of the boroughs in London employ time bank development officers, and two major institutions – Hexagon Housing and the South London and Maudsley Mental Health Trust – are rolling out Time Banks.

They have been pretty thrilling years for me too. I even married Sarah

Burns whose original creation, the Rushey Green Time Bank, is increasingly attracting attention from researchers and politicians.

Of course, none of this has been easy. Certainly there have been mistakes and failures along the way. It has proved particularly difficult to persuade government officials and professional bodies that this is more than a neat idea – that Co-Production is a potentially revolutionary project that can actually make public services and welfare work, when the truth is that it hasn't before. But there have been small victories along the way, and a few committed individuals in each profession have run with the idea in their own organisations and carved out new ways forward. And there are signs that the message is getting through.

Over the past year, both NEF and Fair Shares have published major reports on Co-Production and health which, between them, have had an important impact. One is now being reprinted as a textbook by the Open University; phrases from both have been turning up in speeches by leading health professionals. The sheer intractability of modern government, the size of the task, the increasing inability of professionals to make things happen by authority alone, are all combining to create an important opportunity – to provide that missing ingredient in human endeavour at neighbourhood level that can make change happen.

This book is the key text that lies behind that opportunity and that new world that lies beyond.

David Boyle is an associate at the New Economics Foundation, and the author of The Money Changers and The Sum of our Discontent. More information about Time Banks and Co-Production in the UK is available at www.timebanks.co.uk (Time Banks UK), www.fairshares.org.uk (Fair Shares), www.londontimebank.org.uk (London Time Bank) and www.neweconomics.org (the New Economics Foundation).

Endnotes

Chapter 1

1. Judith Feder, Julia Howard and William Scanlon, "Helping Oneself by Helping Others: Evaluation of a Service Credit Banking Demonstration." Report prepared for the Center for Health Policy Studies. Georgetown University, Washington, D.C., 1991, p.2.

Chapter 4

2. This "primer" simplifies key elements of work begun at the London School of Economics. Its purpose is to convey the basic outlines of an economic framework that differs in pivotal respects from prevailing orthodoxy. In endeavoring to impart a fundamental shift in perspective, I have necessarily oversimplified market theory and scholarship. This book supplies the essential components of an alternative—a theoretical framework coupled with evidence demonstrating actual feasibility.
3. Although academic economists recognize the family as an economic unit, the theoretical implications have been inadequately pursued. In any case, they appear to jettison that knowledge when they assume positions of power.

Chapter 5

4. Gary S. Becker, *A Treatise on the Family*, 1981, p. 198.

Chapter 7

5. Of every dollar the federal government spends on Indian reservations to reduce poverty and build self-sufficiency, an estimated seventy-five cents flows out to border towns and beyond within 48 hours. A dollar put in a

poor community can exit in hours to a cigarette manufacturer or a multinational chain that has eliminated locally-owned business and reduced employment opportunities—or to a drug baron in Colombia.

Considerable spending power flows into low-income neighborhoods. It just doesn't stay there. A 1975 study of one McDonald's in Washington, D.C., found that two-thirds ($500,000) of the $750,000 gross revenue promptly left the community. A 1990 study of McDonald's in other communities concluded that three-quarters of consumers expenditures are exported.

Within 3-4 years of a Wal-Mart arrival, retail sales within a 20-mile radius go down by 25 percent; 20-50 miles away, sales go down 10 percent. In Iowa, the average Wal-Mart grosses $13 million a year and increases total area sales by $4 million. That means that it takes roughly $9 million worth of business away from existing stores. A typical Wal-Mart adds 140 jobs and destroys 230 higher paying jobs. Despite public investments in restoring downtown business districts, vacancies increase. Rents drop. Remaining enterprises pay lower wages and taxes. Competing chains in existing malls leave and are not replaced.

6. "It is all transaction and no goods. Without the need to plant, sow, harvest, ship, manufacture, or change the goods in any way, the currency market faces no delays; its transactions are instantaneous. With the speed of light, electronic impulses race around the globe, and dollars rush from Singapore to Sao Paulo, yen flood into the central bank of Zaire, Turkish pounds flee to Germany, and South African rands become Canadian dollars." Jack Weatherford, *The History of Money*, 1997, p. 256.
7. In 1996, *The Washington Post* carried a story about a hospital in Fairfax, Virginia, that had transmitted a digital recording of a physician's patient report to a typist for a quick-turnaround transcript to save another night's hospital stay. It shipped the recording at 7 a.m. and had a corrected copy back from a proofreader by 11:00 a.m. The typist to whom they sent the recording was in Bangalore, India. This specially trained transcriber earned approximately $2,500 a year, less than one-tenth the comparable wage in the United States. Mike Mills, *Global Trends 2005: An Owner's Manual for the Next Decade*, p. 169, citing "In the Modern World, White Collar Jobs Go Overseas," *Washington Post*, September 17, 1996, p. A1.
8. There is a new "global demographic mix (of professionals and cognitive elites), buoyed and supported with revolutionary technologies, such as the Internet, that vastly reduce the hiring barriers once posed by distance. These two developments are just on the verge of creating a truly international labor market, featuring head-on competition for wages and skills, even for cognitive elites." William Wilman & Anne Colamosca, *The Judas Economy: The Triumph of Capital and the Betrayal of Work*, 1997, p. 38.
9. *Ibid*, p. 37.
10. "We don't think of ourselves as an American company," says a top Hewlett-Packard executive. "We don't have a corporate policy of moving in or out

of the United States. We consider each business situation separately." 40 percent of Hewlett-Packard's workforce and 54 percent of its sales are outside the United States. *Ibid*, p. 36.

An Intel executive points out, "I see the same level of skills in Malaysia as in the U.S., even up to Ph.D.'s. And if you can get a job done cheaper elsewhere, you're at a disadvantage if you don't." A nine-year-old California company, Conner Peripherals, a manufacturer of disk drives listed on the New York Stock Exchange and considered a leader among the newer high-tech companies, has almost completely leapfrogged U.S. employment during its quick growth. It opened a plant in Singapore, then later a lower-cost one in Malaysia—now the company's largest—and most recently one in China. Currently, 90 percent of Conner's production and 75 percent of its 11,400 employees are located outside the United States. Aluminum Co. Of America, or Alcoa, has remade itself into a globally integrated giant over the last ten years. "We're not geographically bound, and that includes the Americans," says sixty-one-year-old Paul O'Neill, chairman and chief executive officer, responsible for the overhaul. Ibid, p. 32.

11. George Soros, *The Crisis of Global Capitalism*, 1998.
12. Robert H. Frank and Philip J. Cook, *The Winner-Take-All-Society*, 1995. Their thesis is spelled out in the book's subtitle: "How More and More Americans Compete for Ever Fewer and Bigger Prizes, Encouraging Economic Waste, Income Inequality, and an Impoverished Cultural Life."
13. Between 1980 and 1993, Fortune 500 industrial firms shed nearly 4.4 million jobs, more than one out of four. Sales increased by 1.4 times and assets by 2.3 times. Average CEO compensation increased by 6.1 times to $3.8 million. (David Korten, *When Corporations Rule the World*, 1995, p. 218.) GE over 11 years shed 100,000 employees bringing total employment down to 268,000 in 1992. During the same period, sales rose from $27 billion to 62 billion and net income from $1.5 billion to 4.7 billion.
14. Possibly, 80 percent is too conservative an estimate of how money is made. According to the Federal Reserve Bank, the Bank of England and the International Monetary Fund, global exports now constitute only 1.7 percent of all foreign exchange trading.
15. David Korten, *Op. Cit.*, p. 187.
16. Joel Kurtzman, *The Death of Money*, p. 149
17. Available from the Time Dollar web site: www.timedollar.org

Chapter 11

18. Sara Rimer, "Older People Want to Work in Retirement, Survey Finds," *New York Times*, September 2 1999, p. A10.
19. Peter S. Arno, Carol Levine, and Margaret M. Memmott, "The Economic Value of Informal Caregiving," *Health Affairs*, Vol. 18, no. 2., 1999, pp. 182-188.

Chapter 12

20. Jerome G. Miller, "From Social Safety Net to Dragnet: African American Males in the Criminal Justice System," *Washington and Lee Law Review*, Spring 1994 (pp. 479-490). See, generally, research conducted by The National Center on Institutions and Alternatives. www.igc.org/ncia.

Chapter 13

21. Nancy Folbre, 'Children as Public Goods', American Economics Review, 84 (2), May 86-90, 1994. Reprinted in *The Economics of Family* (International Library of Critical Writings in Economics, No 64) Nancy Folbre, Editor, p. 675.
22. Jonathan Swift, *A Modest Proposal*, 1729.
23. Mark E. Courtney, "The Costs of Child Protection in The Context of Welfare Reform: The Future of Children," *Protecting Children From Abuse and Neglect* Vol. 8, No. 1 Spring 1998, pp. 93-94.
24. Sylvia Ann Hewett and Cornel West, *The War Against Parents*, 1998, p. 118.
25. Barbara Vobejda, "At 18, It's Sink or Swim; For Ex-Foster Children, Transition is Difficult," *Washington Post*, July 21, 1998, p. A1, summarizing study by Mark Courtney and Irving Piliavin, School of Social Work, University of Wisconsin.
26. *Ibid.*

Chapter 15

27. John McKnight, *The Careless Society: Community and Its Counterfeits*, 1995, p. 46.
28. Jonathan Rowe, "Money With Care Built In," *YES! A Journal of Positive Futures*, Spring 1997, pp. 20-25.

Chapter 16

29. Stephen R. Covey, *The 7 Habits of Highly Effective People*, 1989, p. 33.

Chapter 17

30. Robert Putnam, "Bowling Alone," *Journal of Democracy* 6, 1995, pp. 65-78.
31. Robert Putnam, *Making Democracy Work: Civic Traditions in Modern Italy*, 1993, p. 185.
32. Robert Putnam, "Bowling Alone," p. 75 (emphasis in original).
33. Feder, Judith, Julia Howard, & and William Scanlon, *Op.cit.*
34. R. Sampson, S. Raudenbush & F. Earls, Neighborhoods and Violent Crime: A Multilevel Study of Collective Efficacy, *Science Magazine* Vol. 277, 15 August 1997, pp. 873-1004.
35. Fox Butterfield, "Study Links Violence Rate To Cohesion In Community," *New York Times*, August 17, 1997, Section 1 p. 27.